ILLUSTRATING BBC-BASIC

Donald Alcock

The right of the
University of Cambridge
to print and sell
all manner of books
was granted by
Henry VIII in 1534.
The University has printed
and published continuously
since 1584.

CAMBRIDGE UNIVERSITY PRESS

CAMBRIDGE
LONDON NEW YORK NEW ROCHELLE
MELBOURNE SYDNEY

CAMBRIDGE UNIVERSITY PRESS
Cambridge, New York, Melbourne, Madrid, Cape Town, Singapore, São Paulo

Cambridge University Press
The Edinburgh Building, Cambridge CB2 8RU, UK

Published in the United States of America by Cambridge University Press, New York

www.cambridge.org
Information on this title: www.cambridge.org/9780521314954

First published 1986
Re-issued in this digitally printed version 2008

A catalogue record for this publication is available from the British Library

ISBN 978-0-521-31495-4 paperback

To the men of the Surrey Fire Brigade
who quenched the fire in the Old
Georgian House before it could consume
the draft of this book. Had they
arrived a little later ...

CONTENTS

PREFACE

BBC-BASIC is the main language of the BBC Microcomputer, widely used in schools in Britain and some countries abroad. To make the computer *do* something it must be given instructions encoded in BBC-BASIC, a full set of such instructions being called a *program*. Programs written in BBC-BASIC can make the computer do mathematical calculations, display animated pictures in colour on the screen, play tunes in harmony, maintain records of names and addresses, and do many other things besides. This book explains how to write such programs in BBC-BASIC and run them on the BBC Microcomputer.

This book should be found directly applicable by users of BBC Master Series Microcomputers which offer BBC-BASIC (BASIC IV) as a programming language. BASIC IV has several new facilities ≈ such as plotting stipple patterns, ellipses, circles, rectangles ≈ which are not described here. But the rest of the language should be compatible. The many example programs in this book were developed on the BBC Model B Microcomputer using BASIC III.

Although this book is concerned with programming in a particular language on particular ranges of computer it will be found useful by those who have to write in other dialects of BASIC on other computers. The programs in this book are short and explained in fine detail, so will be found readily translatable.

BBC-BASIC features some "structured" statements which make it possible to write more intelligibly than could be achieved in the original BASIC of 1964. In particular it is often (though not always) possible to avoid the GOTO statement ≈ an instruction distasteful to many teachers of computer science. In this book, those programs which have no need of GOTO are presented without the distraction of line numbers.

The book is organized as a programming language manual. After an introductory example in chapter 1 (analysed in some depth for the benefit of the complete beginner) there is a quick canter through the rudiments of programming in chapter 2. Here are introduced such basic concepts as variables, expressions, strings, decisions, loops and functions; easy going for the reader who can already write programs.

Chapter 3 is short but important; it explains the notation used throughout the remainder of the book for defining the syntax of BBC-BASIC. But if this notation appears self explanatory the reader may prefer to skip chapter 3, using it only for occasional reference.

From chapter 4 onwards the book introduces each facility of BBC-BASIC in turn and provides examples of its use. *Nothing is introduced without example*. The longer examples serve a double purpose: to illustrate a facility of BBC-BASIC and explain a fundamental technique of programming.

How do you make a computer sort names into alphabetical order? Not as obvious as it might seem. Three different sorting techniques are explained by example in this book: bubble sort, monkey puzzle (more formally the "binary tree") and Quicksort. Quicksort relies on recursion ≈ an important programming concept which is explained and demonstrated. Making coloured objects rebound around the walls of a squash court is another technique demonstrated; so is making voices sing in harmony; so is computerizing a humble address book.

Because of the wide scope of BBC-BASIC, and the many "back door" facilities dealt with in chapter 14, there was not enough room to introduce more tricks of the programmer's trade. Sadly missing are such techniques as stacks and queues, linked lists, parsing expressions and so on. Several of these techniques are explained among my other books published by Cambridge University Press: *Illustrating BASIC* (1977), *Illustrating Fortran* (1982), *Illustrating Super-BASIC* (1985).

This book may be used as a self-contained manual for BBC-BASIC. Information is tabulated in a form handy for reference. Page 163, for example, tabulates all characters in the ASCII range; pages 124-5 summarize all information needed when composing screens of MODE 7 graphics. A quick reference for all operators and functions is given on page 179; the syntax of every statement and command of BBC-BASIC is summarized on pages 180-1.

I have retained the hand-written format of my earlier books because this medium best permits *pictorial* explanation of concepts, reducing verbiage to a minimum.

Reigate
Surrey, U.K.

Donald Alcock
January 1986

1

INTRODUCTORY EXAMPLE

A PROBLEM

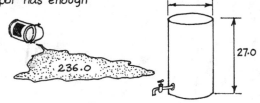

All my introductory books start with this problem: how many pots of paint are needed to paint this water tank? The paint manufacturer claims that every pot has enough paint to cover an area of 236.

Recall that the area of a circle is given by πr^2 ⟨ where r is its radius ⟩ or $\pi d^2/4$ ⟨where d is its diameter⟩. The value of π is about 3.14:

$$\text{AREA OF LID} = 3.14 \times 6.5^2 \div 4 \quad = \quad 33.17$$

Recall that the circumference of a circle is given by πd ⟨ where d is its diameter as before⟩. Therefore:

$$\text{AREA OF WALL} = \text{CIRCUMFERENCE} \times \text{HEIGHT}$$
$$= 3.14 \times 6.5 \times 27.0 \quad = \quad 551.07$$

The area to be painted is the sum of the two areas computed above:

$$\text{TOTAL AREA} = 33.17 + 551.07 \quad = \quad 584.24$$

Into this must be divided the coverage of a pot of paint so as to give the number of pots needed:

$$\text{POTS} = 584.24 \div 236.0 \quad = \quad 2.48$$

But you can't buy a fraction of a pot of paint, so the number calculated above must be rounded up to the next whole number. Look at it another way; take the *integral part* of 2.47558 ⟨ which is 2 ⟩ and add 1 ⟨which makes 3 ⟩.

$$\text{NUMBER OF POTS} = 2 + 1 \quad = \quad 3$$

Of course, if the number of pots had worked out at 3.0000 then this approach would yield 3 + 1 = 4 which would be wrong mathematically but nevertheless a more practical answer than 3.

NOW suppose the painter wanted to set down this method of calculation so as to be able to calculate the number of pots of paint ⟨ having perhaps a different coverage ⟩ for a tank of any specified diameter and any specified height.

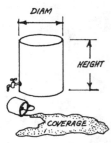

A possible list of instructions is set out on the opposite page.

SOLUTION IN ENGLISH

Instruction 1. "Input" three numbers representing the diameter and height of a particular tank and the coverage of a pot of paint. To "input" a number, draw a box for it and give each box a name thus:

d [   ]   h [   ]   coverage [   ]

then "put" the number "in" the box.

≈ example ≈   d [6·5]   h [27·0]   coverage [236·0]

Instruction 2. Work out the area of the lid of the tank by the formula $\pi d^2 \div 4$ where d is the number to be found in the box named d. Draw a little box; name it *lid*; write the answer inside the box

lid [33·17] ⟵ $\pi \times 6·5^2 \div 4$ ≈ example ≈

Instruction 3. Work out the area of the vertical wall of the tank by the formula $\pi \times d \times h$ where d is the number in the box named d; h is the number in the box named h. Draw a new little box; name it *wall*; write the answer inside the box.

≈ example ≈   wall [551.07] ⟵ $\pi \times 6·5 \times 27·0$

Instruction 4. Add the areas found in the boxes named *lid* and *wall*; divide this sum by the number found in the box named *coverage*. Draw a new little box; name it *paint*; write the answer inside this box.

≈ example ≈   (33.17 + 551.07) ÷ 236.0 ⟹   paint [2.48]

Instruction 5. Take the integral part of the number found in the box named *paint* and add 1. Draw a new little box and name it *pots%* (the % in this context does not mean *per cent*; when appended to the name of a box it is a signal to say that the box is for storing whole numbers ≈ *integers*). Write the answer inside this box.

≈ example ≈   2)·48 + 1 ⟹ pots% [3]
(integral part) (fractional part)

Instruction 6. Print the value found in the box named *pots%* between the phrases "You need" and "pots of paint".

≈ example ≈   [You need 3 pots of paint]

In computer jargon a set of instructions like this is called a *program*. This program is in English; on the next page it is translated into BBC-BASIC.

3

SOLUTION IN BBC~BASIC
GOOD FOR ANY
SIZE OF TANK

Here is the water-tank program in BBC-BASIC:

```
1  INPUT   d, h, coverage
2  LET  lid = PI * d ^ 2 / 4
3  LET  wall = PI * d * h
4  LET  paint = (lid + wall)/coverage
5  LET  pots% = INT(paint) + 1
6  PRINT "You need "; pots%; " pots of paint"
```

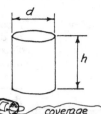

coverage

The English instructions on the previous page have a one-to-one correspondence with the statements above ((*statement* is computer jargon for *instruction*)). But before typing the program ⁓ and making the computer obey it ⁓ it is worth looking at some of the niceties.

| 1   INPUT d, h, coverage |

Every statement in this example begins with a number ⁓ a *line number* ⁓ followed by a *keyword*. In statement 1 the keyword is "INPUT". Keywords make up the vocabulary of BBC-BASIC; all are defined in this book. The keyword after the line number tells the computer what sort of thing to do. "INPUT" tells the computer to draw some little boxes and give them the names listed ((in this case the names d, h and *coverage*)). The computer jargon for "little box" is "variable", so d, h and *coverage* are names of *variables*. The keyword "INPUT" also tells the computer to display a question mark on the screen, wait for the operator to type a number, then *PUT* that number *INto* the next variable. The computer must do this for each nominated variable of the list in turn.

| 2   LET lid = PI*d^2/4 |

Statement 2 begins with the keyword LET. When LET is the keyword there is always an equals sign as well. On the left of the equals sign is the name of a variable ((in this case *lid*)); on the right is an *expression* ((in this case PI*d^2/4)). The computer is told to evaluate the expression and assign the resulting value to the nominated variable. So this kind of statement is called an *assignment* statement.

The expression PI*d^2/4 needs clarification:

PI   could be replaced by 3·14159265 without altering the
          effect of this program. PI ((denoting π)) when
          written as part of an expression simply implies
          3·14159265 ((more accurate than 3.14 as used earlier))

*   says *multiply by*

^   says *raise to the power of* ((thus ^2 says "squared"))

/   says *divide by*

d   implies the number to be found in the variable
          named d ⁓ this is a fundamental concept.

```
3  LET wall = PI * d * h
```
Statement 3 is another assignment statement. The computer is told to multiply 3.14159265 by the number found in the variable named d, then multiply the product by the number found in the variable named h, then assign the result to a variable which the computer is to create and give the name wall.

```
4  LET paint = (lid + wall) / coverage
```
Statement 4 is another assignment statement. The computer is told to add the numbers found in the variables named lid and wall, then divide this sum by the number found in the variable named coverage, then assign the result to a new variable to be named paint. Notice the effect of the brackets; they tell the computer to do the addition before the division. Without the brackets the division would be done first because it has higher precedence. The precedence of operators is:

∧   is applied first. In statement 2 the $d \wedge 2$ is done before the multiplication or division as one would expect ((πd^2 means $\pi \times (d^2)$ not $(\pi d)^2$))

/ *   are applied next, from left to right unless brackets signify otherwise. In statement 2 the * is applied before the /

− +   are applied last, from left to right unless brackets signify otherwise.

```
5  LET pots% = INT(paint) + 1
```
Statement 5 is another assignment statement. The expression involves INT( ) which is a *function*; it tells the computer to take the integral part of what is inside the brackets. ((There are many other useful functions provided by BBC-BASIC; they are all explained in this book.)) The value in the brackets is, in this example, simply the number to be found in the variable named paint. The computer is told to add 1 to the resulting integer and assign the result to a new variable to be named pots%. The % says this new variable is to be a variable for storing integers ((you cannot store 2·4 in a variable whose name ends in %)).

Although all the above assignments begin with the keyword LET, it is allowable in BBC-BASIC ((as in most other BASICs)) to omit the word LET.

items separated by semicolons

```
6  PRINT "You need "; pots%; " pots of paint"
```
Statement 6 begins with the keyword PRINT which tells the computer to display something on the screen ((the word PRINT having been adopted as a keyword in BASIC in the days of clattering typewriter terminals)). The computer is told to copy anything in quotes exactly as quoted, but to replace the *names* of variables outside the quotes with the *contents* of those variables. So in this example the computer would make the screen display:

```
You need 3 pots of paint
```

TYPE THE PROGRAM

The keyboard is arranged like this:

The screen should now show > which is a prompt saying "Type something."

The middle light (caps lock) should be on; if not press [CAPS LOCK] and the light should glow ≈ this is a "push on, push off" switch.

Now type this program. Some freedom is allowed with spacing, but for the time being put spaces where shown. (To type a space press the space bar as on an ordinary typewriter.) After typing each line press [RETURN] to get the > prompt at the start of the next line.

```
>1  INPUT  D, H, COVERAGE
>2  LET  LID = PI * D^2 / 4
>3  LET  WALL = PI * D * H
>4  LET  PAINT = ( LID + WALL) / COVERAGE
>5  LET  POTS% = INT( PAINT) + 1
>6  PRINT "YOU NEED "; POTS%; "  POTS OF PAINT"
>
```

This is the same as the program on previous pages except that everything is in capitals to make typing easier. However, names of variables *may* be typed in lower-case letters. To do this press [CAPS LOCK] which makes the middle light go out; then type the name (it appears in small letters); then press [CAPS LOCK] again. But be consistent; don't type "WALL" on line 3, for example, and "wall" on line 4 because "WALL" and "wall" and "Wall" are all distinct names. Also, don't type "LET" as "let" because *all keywords must always be in capitals*.

In the rest of this book capital letters are used except for remarks and texts; I adopted this policy because I found it impractical to press [CAPS LOCK] twice for every name, and would always forget whether the light was on or off with infuriating results.

To type % hold down [SHIFT] and press [% 5], or press [SHIFT LOCK] and then [% 5]. When [SHIFT LOCK] is pressed the third light comes on and the middle light, if on, goes out. On pressing [SHIFT LOCK] again, the third light, if on, goes out. To touch typists these lights are inconveniently placed, being always shielded by the left hand.

There are three ways of correcting a typing mistake. If the mistake is noticed straight away, press DELETE which erases the character to the left of the cursor. The whole line may be deleted by holding this key down and letting it repeat. If a mistake is seen on a previous line then simply type that line again, but correctly, making sure that it has the same line number as before. (A line may be erased completely ≈ line number and all ≈ by typing just the line number and pressing RETURN.) The third method involves the arrow keys and is explained below.

Pressing an arrow key ← → ↑ ↓ causes an extra cursor to appear. It is called the *copy* cursor. Whereas the usual cursor is a flashing underscore the copy cursor is a stationary rectangle. The flashing cursor may be moved about the screen by the arrow keys; the copy cursor stays put whilst the flashing cursor is moved.

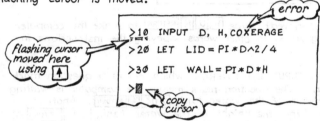

Pressing COPY makes the character above the flashing cursor reappear under the copy cursor. The copy cursor then moves one position to the right.

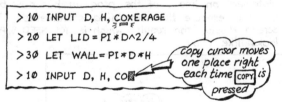

By pressing COPY again and again the erroneous line may be copied until the flashing cursor reaches the error. Then the correct character (or characters) may be typed at the keyboard. Then the erroneous characters may be skipped by pressing →.

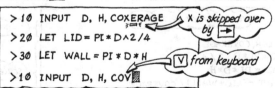

Finally the rest of the line may be copied by pressing COPY as before.

When RETURN is pressed, the copied (and corrected) line 10 replaces the erroneous line 10 in the computer's memory. With a little practice this "screen editor" becomes automatic to the fingers.

LIST, RUN, RENUMBER COMMANDS OF BBC-BASIC (SEE ALSO CHAPTER 13)

Having typed the program opposite, type `C` `L` `S` `RETURN`. CLS is an abbreviation of "CLear the Screen". Its effect is to make the screen turn black. But a clear screen does not imply a vacant memory; type `L` `I` `S` `T` followed by `RETURN` to prove the program is still there.

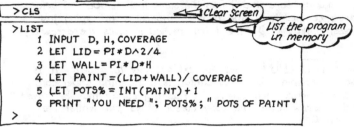

```
>CLS                              ◄— CLear Screen
```

```
>LIST                                      LIST the program
   1 INPUT D, H, COVERAGE                   in memory
   2 LET LID = PI * D∧2/4
   3 LET WALL = PI * D*H
   4 LET PAINT = (LID+WALL)/ COVERAGE
   5 LET POTS% = INT(PAINT) + 1
   6 PRINT "YOU NEED "; POTS% ; " POTS OF PAINT"
>
```

Now the big moment has arrived; type `R` `U` `N` `RETURN` to make the computer begin *executing* the program ⇌ in other words obeying the instructions in sequence.

The first statement is `1 INPUT D, H, COVERAGE` which causes a question mark to appear on the screen. The question mark means the computer is waiting for data. Type the diameter of the water tank: `6` `·` `5` `RETURN`. Another question mark appears. Type the height of the water tank: `2` `7` `RETURN`. Yet another question mark appears. This time type the coverage of a pot of paint: `2` `3` `6` `RETURN`.

The INPUT statement on line 1 of the program has now been satisfied; the computer goes on to execute the remaining statements. The final statement makes the screen display the result. which is YOU NEED 3 POTS OF PAINT. The screen now looks like this:

```
>RUN
?6.5
?27
?236
YOU NEED 3 POTS OF PAINT  ◄— the result
>
```

Now type `R` `E` `N` `U` `M` `B` `E` `R` `RETURN` then `L` `I` `S` `T` `RETURN`. The result:

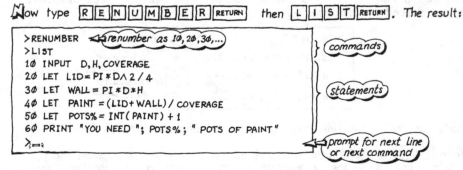

```
>RENUMBER  ◄— renumber as 10, 20, 30, ...        }  commands
>LIST
10 INPUT D, H, COVERAGE
20 LET LID = PI * D∧2 / 4
30 LET WALL = PI * D*H                            }  statements
40 LET PAINT = (LID+WALL) / COVERAGE
50 LET POTS% = INT(PAINT) + 1
60 PRINT "YOU NEED "; POTS% ; " POTS OF PAINT"
>                                          ◄— prompt for next line
                                              or next command
```

Now save the program on cassette or disk as explained opposite.

8

AUTO — MAKE THE COMPUTER PROVIDE LINE NUMBERS AUTOMATICALLY

When typing a program it is not necessary to type line numbers, the computer may be made to provide them automatically. All that is necessary is to type the command AUTO and press RETURN.

```
>AUTO          cursor
  10 ;
```

Unless instructed otherwise the computer offers 10, 20, 30,... as the line numbers.

To make the computer *stop* offering line numbers, press ESCAPE :

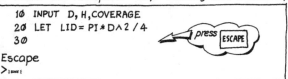

```
10 INPUT D, H, COVERAGE
20 LET LID= PI * D∧2 / 4          press ESCAPE
30

Escape
>;
```

Automatic line numbering can be restarted at any line number :

```
>AUTO 30          cursor
     30 ;
```

SAVE AND LOAD — JUST THE ESSENTIALS : SEE CHAPTER 13 ALSO THE USER GUIDE, CHAPTER 5

If the computer is fitted with a disk, to save the program type the command SAVE followed by a name in quotes. Then type the command *CAT ((short for catalogue)) to ensure the program has been properly saved:

```
>SAVE  "TANK1"
>*CAT
```
        list of programs saved on disk; should now include a program named TANK1

To save a program on cassette, rewind the tape and set the counter to 0000. Type SAVE "TANK1" and press RETURN. The message "RECORD then RETURN" should now appear. Fast forward the tape to the place where the program is to go, preferably with a multiple of 100 on the counter. Then press the RECORD button(s) on the cassette recorder, then the RETURN key on the computer. Press ESCAPE and start again should anything go wrong.

To bring a program back into the computer's memory, use LOAD :

```
>LOAD  "TANK1"
```

If using cassette tape, locate the tape just before the start of TANK1 and so avoid a long delay whilst the tape is being searched for the program with this name.

EXERCISES

1. Use AUTO and type the example program. Try the program with data provided in this book; try with other data too.

2. Practise with the screen editor

3. Practise with SAVE and LOAD

2

RUDIMENTS

COMMANDS VERSUS STATEMENTS

In the introductory example notice the difference between:

> RUN ⟵ *command*

and

10 INPUT D, H, COVERAGE ⟵ *statement*

The "RUN" is obeyed as soon as you press RETURN. The same applies to RENUMBER and LIST as illustrated on page 8. These are called *commands* or *direct commands*.

The "10 INPUT D, H, COVERAGE" is *not* obeyed straight after typing and pressing RETURN. It is simply stored with other numbered lines. Numbered lines contain *instructions* to be obeyed. Instructions are usually called *statements*.

In general a keyword (e.g. PRINT) may be used *either* as a command *or* as a statement; the distinction is made by the absence or presence of a *line number*.

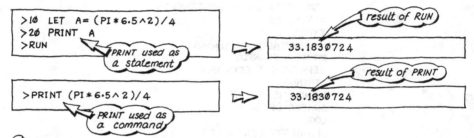

```
>10 LET A=(PI*6.5^2)/4
>20 PRINT A
>RUN
```
PRINT used as a statement

result of RUN ⟶ `33.1830724`

```
>PRINT (PI*6.5^2)/4
```
PRINT used as a command

result of PRINT ⟶ `33.1830724`

Statements may be *typed* in any order; they get *stored* in line-number order. The line numbers may be typed individually but are better generated automatically:

```
> AUTO
10 ;
```
cursor ready for typing statement

Enter the command AUTO. This causes the first line to be numbered 10, the second 20, the third 30 and so on. Stop the action of AUTO by pressing ESCAPE.

There may be several statements on a numbered line; they should be separated by colons. A numbered line may occupy several rows of the screen. The cursor jumps automatically when each row is full; *don't* press RETURN until ready to begin a new numbered line. Here is a complete program comprising several statements on a single numbered line spread over several rows of the screen.

```
>10 PRINT "Type a diame
ter": INPUT D: LET A=(PI
*D^2)/4: PRINT "The area
is ";A: PRINT "Type RUN a
nd press the RETURN key fo
r another try": STOP
```

If you want to stop a program which is currently running, press ESCAPE. However, it is possible to make this key do other things than stop a program from running. In desperation press BREAK which not only stops a program running but also makes the computer forget what it was doing. Chapter 13 describes operation.

VARIABLES

The little boxes described in the introductory example are called *variables*.
A variable is a conceptual box having a
name and a *content*. To say " PAINT *is*

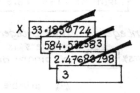

PAINT 2.47683298

2.47683298 " demands an unnecessary level of abstraction because PAINT is
not 2.47683298; PAINT is the *name of a variable which currently contains* 2·47683298.

A variable is created inside the computer ≈ and given its name ≈ simply
by referring to it.

> 10 INPUT D, H, COVERAGE

> D 6.5   H 27.0   COVERAGE 236

This statement, when obeyed, causes three
variables to be created and the numbers
subsequently typed on the keyboard to be
put into them.

The LET statement causes the expression
to be evaluated and the result to be
assigned to the nominated variable. If
no such variable exists then one is
created automatically and given the
quoted name.

> 30 LET WALL = PI * D * H

> WALL 551.349511

In the introductory example the contents of the variables do not change;
each has a number put into it and there the number stays. But the program
could be modified to use fewer variables. In the following version variable
X is used over and over again.

use AUTO to provide the line numbers

```
PRINT  "Please give the diameter of the tank"
INPUT  D
PRINT  "Now give the height"
INPUT  H
PRINT  "Now the coverage of a pot"
INPUT  COVERAGE
X = (PI * D^2)/4
X = X + PI * D * H
X = X / COVERAGE
X = INT(X) + 1
PRINT "Please supply "; X; " pots of paint"
```

X 33.1950724
584.532583
2.47683298
3

At the line X = (PI * D^2)/4 , X is created and named. From the next line
onwards all references to X are references to an *existing* variable.

The variables discussed above are for storing *numbers*. However, there are
three types of variable in BBC-BASIC and the distinctions among them are
explained on the next page.

No variable should be referred to without having been assigned a value
(for example by LET or by INPUT). An error message is printed if an
unassigned variable is included in a PRINT statement.

> NEW
> 10 PRINT A
> RUN

wipes out any existing program & its variables

No such variable at line 10

13

TYPES

TYPES OF VALUE AND VARIABLE: REAL, INTEGER, STRING

Values in BBC-BASIC come in three types: *real*, *integer*, *string*.

Variables which store such values come in three corresponding types: *real variable*, *integer variable*, *string variable*.

• *real*

D [6.5]

A *real* is a number which may have a fractional part. In BBC-BASIC reals may be huge or miniscule:

- about the biggest positive real is 1.7×10^{38} (170 ⟶ *36 more noughts*)
- about the biggest negative real is -1.7×10^{38}
- about the smallest positive real is $1.7/10^{38}$ (0. ⟵ *37 noughts* ⟶ 17)
- about the smallest negative real is $-1.7/10^{38}$

precision about 9 significant digits

A real is held to a precision of about nine significant decimal digits: 1.234567899 would be held approximately as 1.23456790 (precision cannot be stated precisely in decimal arithmetic; numbers are stored in binary).

A real may be written in exponent form. For example $1.23456790 \times 10^{26}$ may be expressed 1.2345679E26 and $1.2345679/10^{26}$ as 1.2345679E-26. The E says "times ten to the power of..."

Reals may be put into real variables as illustrated below:

```
INPUT X:  LET Y = 3.5 :  LET TINY = 1.23E-30
```

• *integer*

POTS% [3]

An *integer* is a whole number. In BBC-BASIC the range of integers is −2147483648 to +2147483647. (The pattern of binary digits in an integer is explained on page 44.)

A variable is signified as an *integer* variable by writing % after the last character of its name.

Integer variables may be made to store integers as illustrated below:

```
INPUT I%:  LET J%=-6 :  LET K% = 3000000000
```

(Too big!)

• *string*

Q$ [Yes or No]

A *string* is a sequence of characters. In BBC-BASIC a string may be as long as 255 characters. An empty (null) string has no characters at all.

A variable is signified as a *string* variable by writing $ after the last character of its name.

Strings may be put into string variables as illustrated below:

```
INPUT NAM$ :  LET CURRENCY$ = "£" :  LET ME$ = "Error"
```

There is more about strings and string variables in chapter 5.

NUMERICAL EXPRESSIONS

The introductory example illustrates numerical expressions in LET statements. Here is one of them:

```
20  LET  TOP = PI * D ∧ 2 / 4
```

The PI signifies 3.14159265. Like INT( ), PI is a *function*. Functions supplied by BBC-BASIC are defined in chapter 4, but the means of defining one's own special functions are introduced on page 23 and fully covered in chapter 8.

The variable named D 《above》 contains 6.5. So the expression to be evaluated is:

$$3.14159265 * 6.5 ∧ 2 \ / 4$$

The * and ∧ and / are called *operators*. Operators have *precedence*. The precedence of ∧ is higher than that of * or / so 6.5 ∧ 2 is evaluated first. 《This is what one would expect: πd^2 means π times the square of d, not the square of πd.》

The precedence of * is the same as that of / unless brackets intervene. Brackets may be added to the above expression thus: (PI * D ∧ 2) / 4 to ensure that the multiplication is done before the division but are not necessary. In the absence of brackets, operators of equal precedence are applied from left to right.

The precedence of every operator is defined in chapter 3. Application of precedence is like the successive application of conceptual brackets, working outwards from operators with the highest precedence:

```
        3 * 2 +     4 ∧ 2 ∧ 3     *    -5
        3 * 2 +     4 ∧ 2 ∧ 3     *    (-5) ... unary minus 《highest》
        3 * 2 +   ( 4 ∧ 2 ) ∧ 3   *    (-5) ... leftmost ∧
        3 * 2 +  (( 4 ∧ 2 ) ∧ 3 )  *   (-5) ... next ∧
      ( 3 * 2 ) + ((( 4 ∧ 2 ) ∧ 3 ) *  (-5)) ... * and * again
     (( 3 * 2 ) + ((( 4 ∧ 2 ) ∧ 3 ) *  (-5))) ... finally +   《lowest》
```

Rather than *assume* the automatic application of conceptual brackets would correctly resolve an expression 《correct according to one's intention》 it is safer to add brackets, so forcing the computer to do the arithmetic in a desired order:

```
20  LET  LID = ( PI * ( D ∧ 2 )) / 4
```

It may seem strange, but > and < are operators too; 1 > 2 is *false*, and *false* in BBC-BASIC is represented by zero. Conversely, 1 < 2 is *true* which is represented by −1. So it is possible to have:

```
LET  Q = X > Y
```

which assigns either 0 or −1 to the variable Q according to the relative sizes of the values stored in variables X and Y. There is more about this subject on page 42.

 **PRINT** AND **INPUT**

The introductory example showed:

```
60   PRINT "You need "; POTS% ; " pots of paint"
```
space *space*

The PRINT statement makes the quoted messages and specified numbers appear on the screen. The "You need" does not necessarily start on a fresh line; the output simply follows whatever was previously printed. But the screen could first be cleared as follows:

```
59 CLS
```
⟵ *clear the screen; start again at top left corner*

Punctuation in the PRINT statement is complicated, and fully described on pages 90 and 91. But for the time being:

● a semicolon between items says the items are to be abutted (notice the spaces incorporated in the above messages to compensate for this)

● a comma between items says the items are to be tabulated in columns, each column being 10 characters wide (the 10 may be altered as later described).

When there is a punctuation mark at the *end* of a list of items it means the list is to be continued in the next PRINT statement. The three statements here are equivalent to the single statement illustrated above.

```
60   PRINT "You need ";  ⟵ more to come
61   PRINT POTS%; ⟵ more to come
62   PRINT " pots of paint"  (line complete)
```

When a PRINT statement ends without a punctuation mark it says the output from the next PRINT statement to be obeyed is to start at the left of a fresh line.

The introductory example showed:

```
10   INPUT D, H, COVERAGE
```

and when this statement is obeyed a question mark appears on the screen. The program then waits for the user of the program to type three numbers and press [RETURN] (the numbers may be separated by commas or [RETURN] pressed after each one). Only then is the INPUT statement concluded; the numbers are received and put into the nominated variables ≈ or refused if wrongly typed. So it is usual for the programmer to make the screen display a helpful prompt:

```
5   PRINT "diameter, height, coverage "
10  INPUT D, H, COVERAGE
```

Page 98 explains how prompts may be *combined* with the INPUT statement:

```
10   INPUT "Give diameter, height & coverage" D, H, COVERAGE
```

REPAYMENTS

The monthly repayment, M, on a mortgage loan of S pounds at P percent compound interest over N years is given by ⟹

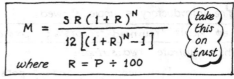

$$M = \frac{SR(1+R)^N}{12\left[(1+R)^N - 1\right]}$$

where $R = P \div 100$

take this on trust

Here is a program which asks its user for details of a proposed loan, works out the monthly repayment, sets out the implications on the screen.

use AUTO to supply line numbers

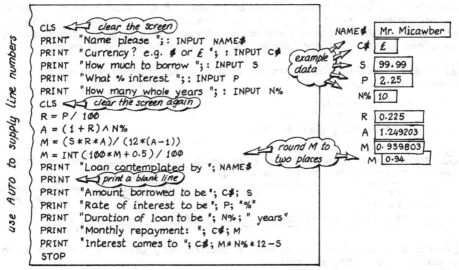

```
CLS              ← clear the screen
PRINT "Name please ";: INPUT NAME$
PRINT "Currency? e.g. $ or £ "; : INPUT C$
PRINT "How much to borrow ";: INPUT S
PRINT "What % interest ";: INPUT P
PRINT "How many whole years "; : INPUT N%
CLS              ← clear the screen again
R = P / 100
A = (1 + R) ∧ N%
M = (S * R * A)/(12 * (A-1))
M = INT(100 * M + 0.5)/100      ← round M to two places
PRINT "Loan contemplated by "; NAME$
PRINT            ← print a blank line
PRINT "Amount borrowed to be"; C$; S
PRINT "Rate of interest to be"; P; "%"
PRINT "Duration of loan to be "; N%; " years"
PRINT "Monthly repayment: "; C$; M
PRINT "Interest comes to "; C$; M * N% * 12 - S
STOP
```

example data

NAME$	Mr. Micawber
C$	£
S	99.99
P	2.25
N%	10
R	0.225
A	1.249203
M	0.939803
M	0.94

On typing RUN, and pressing [RETURN], the first prompt appears at the top of the screen as illustrated below:

Name please ? ← question mark supplied by the computer

and the cursor flashes in anticipation on the same line. Type a person's name and press [RETURN]. The next prompt appears:

Name please ?Mr. Micawber
Currency? e.g. $ or £ ?

press [SHIFT] and [£] then [RETURN], and so on. After responding to the final prompt the screen clears and displays the awful details:

```
Loan contemplated by Mr. Micawber

Amount borrowed to be £99.99
Rate of interest to be 2.25%
Duration to be 10 years
Monthly repayment: £0.94
Interest comes to £12.81

STOP at line 190
>
```

17

The introductory example showed:

```
60 PRINT "You need "; POTS% ; " pots of paint"
```

which illustrates two *strings*:

"You need " and " pots of paint"
_{space} _{space}

A string in BBC-BASIC may contain as many as 255 characters where each character may be letter, digit, space or symbol. A quotation mark is excluded because quotation marks are used to mark the beginning and end of a string in the manner illustrated above. (However, a quotation mark *may* be included in a string by writing two of them: for example "X""Y" to signify X"Y. A bit confusing.)

Here are more examples of strings, each enclosed in quotation marks to show where it begins and ends:

"Words only"
"Digits 1234"
"Anything goes! */ = 99#"

A string may be assigned to a *string variable* which is automatically made as long as necessary to contain the string:

```
LET N$ = ""
LET A$ = "*"
LET B$ = "First of April 1987"
```

Strings may be joined end to end (concatenated) using the plus sign as an operator in a string expression:

```
PRINT "Date" + A$ + A$ + B$ + A$ + A$
```
⇨ `Date**First of April 1987**`

String expressions may be assigned to string variables:

```
LET D$ = "Date" + A$ + A$ + B$ + "##"
PRINT D$
```
⇨ `Date**First of April 1987##`

Strings may also be put into string variables by the INPUT statement:

```
INPUT D$
REM
REM
PRINT D$ + "!"
```
⇦ `? Date**First of April 1987`
text typed in response to '?'
⇨ `Date**First of April 1987!`

Strings may be compared for equivalence and relative ordering. The comparison of strings is explained on page 49 and the IF is introduced opposite.

```
IF Q$ = "NO" THEN STOP
IF A$ >= B$ THEN PRINT "error"
```

Strings may be broken into substrings, converted to numerical values, and generally manipulated using the string functions ASC( ), CHR$( ), VAL( ), STR$( ), LEN( ), INSTR(,), STRING$(,), LEFT$(,), RIGHT$(,), MID$(,,) which are defined in chapter 5.

DECISIONS

INTRODUCING CONDITIONS AND
TRANSFER OF CONTROL

A program may be made to do different things according to the outcome of a *condition*. For example:

```
IF STOCK < 12 THEN PRINT "Order more maglets"
```

where STOCK < 12 is a *condition* or *logical expression*. Its value is either *true* or *false*. If the value currently held in variable STOCK is less than 12 then the condition is *true* and the message "Order more maglets" gets printed; otherwise control simply passes to the next numbered line without the message being printed.

Here is another example:

```
IF PROFIT > LOSS THEN PRINT "Hooray" ELSE PRINT "Oh dear"
```

where one or other message gets printed according to the condition, PROFIT > LOSS, being *true* or *false*. In either case control then passes to the first statement on the next numbered line.

There may be more than one statement following THEN; also more than one statement following ELSE. The only limitation ❨ a serious one ❩ is that the entire IF statement must be contained on a single numbered line.

```
100  IF PROFIT > LOSS THEN LET A = 0 : LET B = 0 : LET C
 = 0 : LET D = 0 ELSE LET A = 1 : LET B = 100 : LET C = 100
 0 : LET D = 10000
```

the IF statement all on one numbered line

So when there are many statements to follow THEN or ELSE it is usual to "go to" somewhere else in the program using a GOTO statement.

GOTO is one word

```
150  IF PROFIT <= LOSS THEN GOTO 220
160  PRINT "Hooray"
```

lines 170 to 210 here

```
220  PRINT "Oh dear"
```

Use of GOTO demands backwards thinking; notice the proximity of "Hooray" to PROFIT <= LOSS which, if *true*, gives no cause for cheer. GOTO also demands that line numbers become part of the *logic* of the program ❨which is a silly association when one thinks about it ❩.

The *conditions* in the above examples are simple comparisons, but conditions may be more complicated:

```
IF PROFIT > LOSS AND BORROWING = 0 AND A$=B$ THEN
```

or as simple as a single term:

```
IF OK% THEN
```

If variable OK% contained a value of *zero* the condition would be treated as *false*, whereas if OK% contained *any non-zero value* the condition would be treated as *true*.

19

SHAPES

Here is the flow chart of a program designed to compute the area of a geometrical shape: rectangle, triangle or circle.

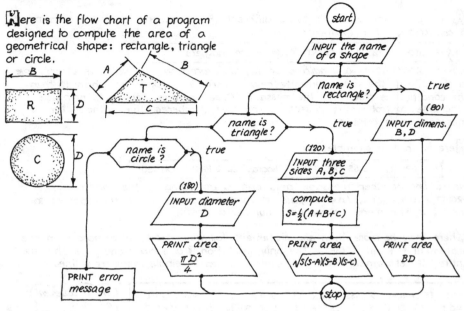

Here is a program to reflect the flow chart:

```
10  CLS:  PRINT  "Area calculator"
20  PRINT  "Rectangle, Triangle or Circle?  R,T or C"
30  INPUT  C$
40  IF  C$ = "R"  THEN  GOTO  80
50  IF  C$ = "T"  THEN  GOTO  120
60  IF  C$ = "C"  THEN  GOTO  180
70  PRINT  "Error: run afresh": STOP
80  REM  Deal with rectangles
90  PRINT  "Give length"; : INPUT B
100 PRINT  "Give breadth"; : INPUT D
110 PRINT  "Area is "; B*D:  STOP
120 REM  Deal with triangles
130 PRINT  "Give side A";: INPUT A
140 PRINT  "Give side B";: INPUT B
150 PRINT  "Give side C";: INPUT C
160 S = 0.5 * (A+B+C)
170 PRINT  "Area is "; SQR(S*(S-A)*(S-B)*(S-C)): STOP
180 REM  Deal with circles
190 PRINT  "Give diameter"; : INPUT D
200 PRINT  "Area is "; PI*D*D/4 : STOP
```

Notice the line numbers 80, 120, 180 following GOTO. These have become part of the logic of the program; in composing line 60 how did the programmer know where line 180 would be? However, if RENUMBER is used the integrity of line numbers and GOTOs is automatically preserved.

A program may be made to go back and obey a sequence of instructions
several times over:

```
FOR HUMBUG = 1 TO 3
   PRINT "We wish you a merry Christmas"
NEXT HUMBUG
PRINT "And a happy new year"
```

More usefully:

```
PRINT "Which times table";: INPUT T
FOR N = 1 TO 10
   RESULT = N * T
   PRINT N; " times "; T; " equals "; RESULT
NEXT N
```

If the operation of the above programs is not immediately obvious they
should be tried on the computer before reading on; looping is fundamental
to programming.

The FOR... NEXT loop illustrated above is also called a "deterministic" loop
because the number of times the statements are executed is determined
beforehand. Not so with the REPEAT... UNTIL loop below:

```
PRINT "Which times table";: INPUT T
LET N = 1
REPEAT
   RESULT = N * T
   PRINT N; " times "; T ; " equals "; RESULT
   LET N = N + 1
UNTIL N > 10
```

The statement LET N=N+1 makes a change to the content of N in each
cycle, the content of N then being tested against a criterion for leaving the
loop. The above is a trivial example of a REPEAT... UNTIL loop intended to
illustrate its structure and compare this structure with that of the FOR...
NEXT loop. There is a realistic example of the REPEAT... UNTIL loop in the
game of MOOO at the end of this chapter.

In BBC-BASIC the loops described above have special characteristics; these
are fully explained later. Two important characteristics are worth
mentioning here:

- each loop is executed at least once, even if the
  condition is meaningless (FOR I = 2 TO 1)

- it is wrong to jump out of a loop by GOTO, or
  equivalent statement, unless you jump back in
  again. (Jumping out of a loop is common practice
  with some BASICs.)

 **OLD GLORY**

In 1912 "Old Glory", the American flag, had 48 stars (one per State of the Union) and 13 stripes (one per original Colony). The program below displays a rough approximation of Old Glory *circa* 1912. It is left as an exercise to add another two States to bring the flag up to date.

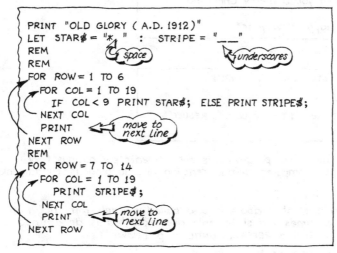

```
PRINT "OLD GLORY ( A.D. 1912 )"
LET STAR$ = "* " :  STRIPE = "___"
REM                    ← space          ← underscores
REM
FOR ROW = 1 TO 6
   FOR COL = 1 TO 19
      IF COL < 9 PRINT STAR$; ELSE PRINT STRIPE$;
   NEXT COL
   PRINT            ← move to next line
NEXT ROW
REM
FOR ROW = 7 TO 14
   FOR COL = 1 TO 19
      PRINT STRIPE$;
   NEXT COL
   PRINT            ← move to next line
NEXT ROW
```

Notice the "nesting" of the FOR...NEXT loops; one contained within another. It is a mistake to specify loops whose paths cross one another.

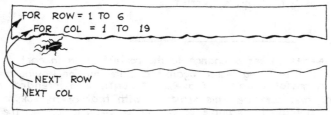

```
FOR  ROW = 1 TO 6
   FOR  COL = 1 TO 19
      ~~~~~~~~~~~~~~
   NEXT  ROW
NEXT COL
```

In the example above, *real* variables named ROW and COL are employed to control the FOR...NEXT loops. It would be more efficient to employ *integer* variables ≈ say ROW% and COL% ≈ but in a silly example like this one the improvement in speed of execution would be unnoticeable.

Here is a shorter version of the program:

```
LET STAR$ = "* ": STRIPE = "___"
FOR ROW = 1 TO 14
   FOR COL = 1 TO 19
      IF (COL<9)AND(ROW<7)PRINT STAR$; ELSE PRINT STRIPE$;
   NEXT COL
   PRINT
NEXT ROW
```

FUNCTIONS

There is no function in BASIC for computing the area of a circle given its diameter:

```
PRINT  AREA(6.5)
```

but you may *define* such a function yourself, then use it just as you would use SQR( ) or INT( ).   The only annoyance is that every function defined by the programmer in BBC-BASIC must have a name starting with the capital letters FN which makes the name difficult to pronounce.

```
PRINT  FNAREA(6.5)
```
o.k. as long as you define FNAREA( )

Here is how to define function FNAREA( ) :

```
DEF  FNAREA(X) = PI * X^2 / 4
```
short for DEFINE

All such definitions should be placed at the end of the program which is to use them ≈ typically after the END statement ≈ where control cannot run into them thinking they are collections of statements to be obeyed.

What is the X doing in the definition? Nothing really; it is a *dummy argument* saying " Do this with whatever the programmer puts in my place." So in the example below, the program would do with D whatever the definition says should be done with X.

```
PRINT  "What diameter"
INPUT  D
PRINT  "The area is "; FNAREA( D)
END
DEF  FNAREA(X) = PI * D^2 / 4
```
definition placed after the END statement where it cannot be "obeyed"

The name X could safely be used elsewhere to name a variable in the program; there is no interference by a variable with a dummy argument of the same name. A dummy argument is *not* the same thing as a variable.

A function may return a *string* rather than a number :

```
DEF  FNATICAL (W$) = "We want "; W$; " now! "
```
try PRINT FNATICAL("JUSTICE")

There may be more than one argument ≈ each of any type. The definition may have several statements, in which case the equals sign is displaced to make room for intermediate statements :

```
DEF  FNTH(F%, NTH%)
LET  A% = 10 ^ NTH%
= INT( 10 * ( F% − A% * INT(F% /A%))/ A%)
```
the equals sign removed
the equals sign marks end of definition

The function FNTH(,) returns the N^{TH} digit from the *right* of integer F. This function is needed for the game of MOOO which is described overleaf.

```
PRINT FNTH(7654,1), FNTH(7654,2), FNTH (7654,3),FNTH(7654,4)
```
⟹ | 4 | 5 | 6 | 7 |

23

PROCEDURES

DEFINE YOUR OWN KEYWORDS
(PROVIDED THAT THEY BEGIN PROC...)

When any piece of program is to be used more than once it should be parcelled up as a *procedure* and given a name by which to invoke it. The name must, unfortunately, start with the capital letters PROC... which renders all but a few names unpronounceable.

In the game of MOOO one player thinks of a four-digit number in which no two digits are alike; say:

$$9876$$

The other player keeps guessing at the above integer trying to score four bulls. For instance:

$$1979$$

for which the score is one *bull* ((the 7 is a direct hit)) and two *cows* ((both nines match a digit in the target but neither is a direct hit)).

To automate the game a piece of program is needed for computing the number of bulls, BULLS%, and the number of cows, COWS%, in a target, X%, with guess Y%. This piece of program may be defined as a *procedure* in a manner similar to that of defining a function but with a fundamental difference: a function returns a value; a procedure returns nothing. The procedure below delivers results by changing the values stored in BULLS% & COWS%

Here is a procedure for putting values in variables BULLS% and COWS% given values in variables X% and Y%:

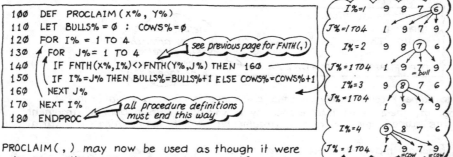

```
100   DEF  PROCLAIM (X%, Y%)
110   LET  BULLS% = Ø  :  COWS% = Ø
120   FOR I% = 1 TO 4
130     FOR J% = 1 TO 4
140       IF FNTH(X%,I%)<>FNTH(Y%,J%) THEN  160
150       IF I%=J% THEN BULLS%=BULLS%+1 ELSE COWS%=COWS%+1
160     NEXT J%
170   NEXT I%
180   ENDPROC
```

see previous page for FNTH(,)

all procedure definitions must end this way

PROCLAIM(,) may now be used as though it were a keyword like LET or FOR or PRINT. After the word itself should come the *arguments* separated by commas and inside brackets:

PROCLAIM (9876, 1979)

or:

PROCLAIM (TARGET% , GUESS%)

It does not matter which values, if any, were contained in the variables BULLS% and COWS% before invoking this procedure. After invoking this procedure these variables would contain the score of bulls and cows deduced from the arguments supplied.

A procedure in BBC-BASIC *cannot change values of its arguments*. This procedure changes values stored in "global" variables BULLS% and COWS%.

A GAME TO ILLUSTRATE FUNCTIONS, PROCEDURES, LOOPS AND DECISIONS

You play the game against the computer. The computer thinks of a target integer of four digits of which no two are alike. When the screen shows the word MOOO you type a guess at the target integer and press [RETURN]. The computer reports your score of bulls and cows deduced in the manner explained opposite. Try again and again until you score four bulls.

You score a bull for every digit which matches a digit in the target integer both in value and location. You score a cow for every digit which matches a digit in the target integer in value but has the wrong location. Thus if you guess 3333 for a target integer of 0123 you score one bull and three cows.

The computer uses RND(9999), a function defined on page 41, to generate a random target integer between 0001 and 9999. To avoid target integers with duplicated digits the random integer is first scored against itself. If this score shows one or more cows it means the target has duplicated digits and must be rejected. (Notice that 9999 scored against itself would yield 12 cows and would therefore be rejected; a refinement to exclude this and other unsuitable integers is suggested below.) Only when RND(9999) generates a number that scores no cows against itself does the game proceed.

Here is the game:

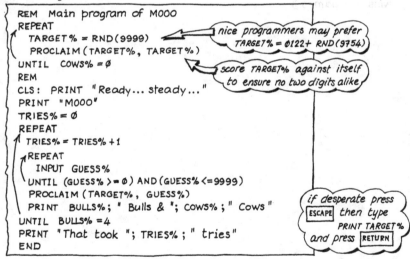

```
REM  Main program of MOOO
REPEAT
   TARGET% = RND(9999)
   PROCLAIM(TARGET%, TARGET%)
UNTIL  COWS% = Ø
REM
CLS:  PRINT "Ready... steady..."
PRINT "MOOO"
TRIES% = Ø
REPEAT
  TRIES% = TRIES% + 1
  REPEAT
    INPUT  GUESS%
  UNTIL (GUESS% >= Ø) AND (GUESS% <= 9999)
  PROCLAIM(TARGET%, GUESS%)
  PRINT  BULLS%; " Bulls & "; COWS%; " Cows"
UNTIL  BULLS% = 4
PRINT "That took "; TRIES%; " tries"
END
```

nice programmers may prefer TARGET% = 0122 + RND(9754)

score TARGET% against itself to ensure no two digits alike

if desperate press [ESCAPE] then type PRINT TARGET% and press [RETURN]

This program invokes the procedure named PROCLAIM(,) which, in turn, invokes the function named FNTH(,). This procedure and this function should be included with the MOOO program. They should be placed after the END statement so that the computer would not try to obey them directly.

I find the percentage sign terminating names of integer variables distracting; it is an unfortunate choice of symbol, bringing to mind ratios like 8.75% which is anything but integral in character. Because of this distraction, integer variables are not much used throughout the rest of this book.

EXERCISES

1. Implement the Repayment program. This version fails if 0% interest is specified; modify the program to cope with this eventuality.

2. Implement "Old Glory" — either version. Modify the program so that the wind blows the other way, showing the block of stars on the right.

3. Implement "MOO". Modify the program so that:

   - it offers six games

   - treats failure to guess the target number in ten tries as a win for the computer

   - after the sixth game, prints the score of games won and the average number of guesses per winning game (and watch out for division by zero if the player wins no games)

3

NOTATION

SYMBOLS
ELEMENTS
REM
SPACING
SYNTAX
{LET}
STATEMENT(S)

 **SYMBOLS**

To define the written form of any computer language properly it is essential to use a concise notation. The notation described below was devised to be helpful for reference as well as being concise. It combines features of existing notations such as BNF and railway diagrams.

Italics	Italic letters are used to name the entities being defined: *digit*, *symbol*, *expression* and so on
:: =	says " is defined to be..."
Romans & + (* 0 1 2 etc.	These stand for themselves; copy them from the definitions just as they are
{ }	Braces surround the definitions of items which are *optional*
[ ]	Square brackets offer a choice of precisely one item ❲ row ❳ from the brackets
	This offers a choice of one *or more* items from the brackets
	If there is a circle its content displays the separator to use when writing more than one item. No circle means no separator.
■	This symbol says "where" and is put in front of subsidiary definitions and explanations beyond the scope of this notation
▶	This symbol says " for example" and is put in front of illustrative examples.

28

ELEMENTS

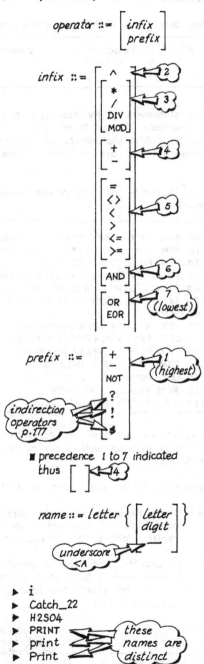

symbol ::= [
(space)
!
"
#
$
%
&
' (apostrophe)
(
)
*
+
,
−
.
/
:
;
<
=
>
?
@
[
\
]
^
_ (underscore)
£
]

■ symbols arranged in ascending order

▶ £ is greater than #

digit :: = [
Ø
1
2
3
4
5
6
7
8
9
]

character ::= [symbol / digit / letter]

▶ $
▶ 9
▶ A
▶ a
← distinct

letter ::= [
A B C D E F G H I J K L M N O P Q R S T U V W X Y Z
a b c d e f g h i j k l m n o p q r s t u v w x y z
]

■ letters arranged in ascending order

▶ u is greater than I

operator ::= [infix / prefix]

infix ::= [
^ ← 2
[* / DIV MOD] ← 3
[+ −] ← 4
[= <> < > <= >=] ← 5
[AND] ← 6
[OR EOR] ← 7 (lowest)
]

prefix ::= [
+ − NOT ? ! $
] ← 1 (highest)

(indirection operators p.177)

■ precedence 1 to 7 indicated thus [ ] ← 4

name :: = letter { [letter / digit] }

(underscore <A)

▶ i
▶ Catch_22
▶ H2SO4
▶ PRINT
▶ print
▶ Print
← these names are distinct

29

≈ *WHICH STANDS FOR REMARK* ≈ *A STATEMENT DEFINITION*
TO ILLUSTRATE THE NOTATION DESCRIBED SO FAR

The definition of the REM statement is:

```
REM { │ character │ }    ▪ terminated by │RETURN│
```

▶ REM
▶ REM EVALUATE
▶ REM *-*-*-*-

This statement is for making a program comprehensible to other programmers 《 and to one's self when returning to a program after a while 》. REM statements are ignored by the computer during execution of a program but are reproduced when that program is listed.

Here is the water tank program again, reorganized and annotated with remarks.

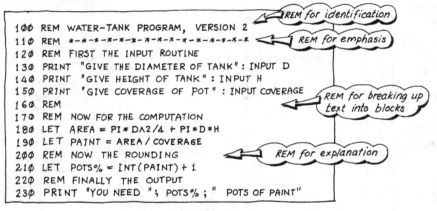

```
100 REM WATER-TANK PROGRAM, VERSION 2          REM for identification
110 REM *-*-*-*-*-*-*-*-*-*-*-*-*-*-*          REM for emphasis
120 REM FIRST THE INPUT ROUTINE
130 PRINT "GIVE THE DIAMETER OF TANK": INPUT D
140 PRINT "GIVE HEIGHT OF TANK": INPUT H
150 PRINT "GIVE COVERAGE OF POT": INPUT COVERAGE
160 REM                                         REM for breaking up
170 REM NOW FOR THE COMPUTATION                 text into blocks
180 LET AREA = PI*DA2/4 + PI*D*H
190 LET PAINT = AREA/COVERAGE
200 REM NOW THE ROUNDING                        REM for explanation
210 LET POTS% = INT(PAINT) + 1
220 REM FINALLY THE OUTPUT
230 PRINT "YOU NEED "; POTS%; " POTS OF PAINT"
```

Programs in this book are not annotated with REM statements; they are classified instead with little clouds and arrows so as to save space on the page.

Returning to the definition of REM:

- There need be no space after REM. If you typed REMARK or REMISS or REMount or anything beginning with the capital letters REM it would be treated as a REM statement

- │ character │ indicates an indefinite sequence of characters. A colon is a character. This implies that REM *makes* itself the last 《 or only 》 statement on a numbered line.

all part of the remark

```
REM WARNING :    PRINT "NEVER GETS PRINTED"
```

 A SPACE IS MADE BY PRESSING THE
SPACE BAR ONCE OR MORE TIMES

Spacing of words and other items is generally free. Careful spacing makes a program more comprehensible than one typed without regard for appearance. Here is a statement from the introductory example, first with wide spacing, then again with minimal spacing:

```
100  LET  LID = PI * D^2 / 4
```
↖ confusing
```
100LETLID=PI*D^2/4
```

Both the above statements are correct but the second looks like an assignment to a variable named LETLID. This example illustrates an important restriction in BBC-BASIC: the name of a variable may not begin with letters which spell a keyword. Thus names such as LENGTH (starts LEN) and POSITION (starts POS) cannot be used as names of variables unless written in lower case letters : length & position. LEN and POS are keywords.

Typing a space in a name (say L ID instead of LID) is a mistake because it creates two names: "L" and "ID". The result is certain to be an error message; probably "Mistake at line 100".

Similarly a space in a constant is a mistake: 1 000 000 does not signify a million, it signifies *unity* followed by two *zeros*. The result would probably be the message "Syntax error at line 120".

Some operators comprise two symbols: for example >= . A space between the two symbols would constitute a mistake.

General rules on spacing are:

- no space within a *name* or *constant* or *operator*: these are single entities and should be typed as single entities

- spaces are optional on either side or both sides of an operator or individual symbol such as = : + -) * # (LET X = - 3 is allowable for X=-3)

- spaces may be omitted altogether in some expressions and statements (FORI=1TO4) but not in others (LETX=AMODB should be LETX=A MOD B). The safest rule is to include a space wherever a variable's name would otherwise run into a keyword or vice versa.

- no space between a name and the character % or $ used to denote an integer or string variable (LET A$="A")

- spaces in between quotes count as characters in their own right (LET A$= " IN ")
  space   space

31

SYNTAX OF *expression* OF *string* OF *condition*

IN TERMS OF THE ELEMENTS PREVIOUSLY DEFINED

numerical-identifier ::= $\left[\begin{array}{c} name \\ name\% \end{array}\right]$ { ([expression]) }

▶ X
▶ SCORE%
▶ VEC(2*K)

numerical-function ::= name { ($\left[\begin{array}{c} expression \\ string \end{array}\right]$) }

digits ::= [digit]

▶ PI
▶ SQR(PI/3)
▶ FNM(A,B,C,D)
▶ OPENOUT("NUFILE")

constant ::= $\left[\begin{array}{c} digits \\ digits. \\ .digits \\ digits.digits \end{array}\right]$ { E $\left\{\begin{array}{c} + \\ - \end{array}\right\}$ digits }

▶ 13
▶ 13.
▶ .999
▶ 45.2
▶ 45.2E-2

expression ::= {prefix} $\left[\begin{array}{c} numerical\text{-}identifier \\ numerical\text{-}function \\ constant \\ string\text{-}comparison \\ (expression) \end{array}\right]$ infix

with due regard to precedence

▶ N%
▶ SQR(X/3)
▶ 45.2
▶ Q$ = "YES"
▶ N% + (SQR(X/3)-45.2)
▶ N% * (Q$="YES") ◀ o.k.

N% * Q$ = "YES" — type mismatch

string-identifier ::= name$ { ([expression]) }

▶ X$
▶ PER$
▶ LIST$(2*K)

string-function ::= $\left[\begin{array}{c} name\$ \\ FN\,name \end{array}\right]$ { ($\left[\begin{array}{c} expression \\ string \end{array}\right]$) }

▶ LEFT$(PER$,3)
▶ INKEY$(2*C%)
▶ FNATICAL(X$)

quotation ::= " [[character]] "   "" ""

▶ "T42 & 24T"   significant spaces
▶ "A""B"   PRINT "A""B" gives A"B

string ::= $\left[\begin{array}{c} string\text{-}identifier \\ string\text{-}function \\ quotation \\ (string) \end{array}\right]$ (+)

▶ LIST$(2*K)   ▶ A$
▶ INKEY$(5)   ▶ FNATICAL(F$)
▶ "YES"   ↙ space
▶ LIST$(2*K)+((INKEY$(5)+A$)+ " ")

string-comparison ::= string $\left[\begin{array}{c} = \\ <> \\ > \\ >= \\ < \\ <= \end{array}\right]$ string

▶ Q$ = "YES"
▶ A$ + B$ <> C$ ◀ o.k.

A$ + (B$ <> C$) — type mismatch

condition ::= expression ∎ reducing to zero for *false*, non-zero for *true*

{LET} ~ *THE ASSIGNMENT STATEMENT* ~ *ITS DEFINITION FURTHER ILLUSTRATES THE SPECIAL NOTATION*

The LET statement ~ the *assignment* statement ~ has already been demonstrated. Here is its definition:

$$\{LET\} \begin{bmatrix} numerical\text{-}identifier & = & expression \\ string\text{-}identifier & = & string \end{bmatrix}$$

▶ LET A = 6 * B%   ▶ LET Q$ = " PLEASE "   ▶ TABL(ROW, COL) = 12.5

The third example above illustrates an assignment to an *array element*, a subject not yet covered. Arrays are introduced in chapter 7.

The braces round the keyword LET signify that the keyword may be omitted as in the third example above. Throughout the rest of this book the LET is generally omitted but is included wherever its presence makes an example clearer.

Here is the water tank again but with the keyword LET omitted from assignment statements:

```
100 REM  WATER-TANK PROGRAM,  VERSION 3
110 REM  *-*-*-*-*-*-*-*-*-*-*- *-*-*-*-*-*
120 REM  FIRST THE INPUT ROUTINE
130 PRINT "GIVE DIAMETER OF TANK": INPUT D
140 PRINT "GIVE HEIGHT OF TANK" : INPUT H
150 PRINT "GIVE COVERAGE OF POT": INPUT COVERAGE
160 REM
170 REM   NOW FOR THE COMPUTATION
180 AREA = PI*D^2/4 + PI*D*H
190 PAINT = AREA / COVERAGE
200 REM  NOW THE ROUNDING
210 POTS% = INT( PAINT) + 1
220 PRINT "YOU NEED "; POTS%; " POTS OF PAINT"
```

Assignment of a real value to an integer variable causes *truncation* of the fractional part whether positive or negative:

LET A% = 456.789 : PRINT A%	456
LET B% = -456.789 : PRINT B%	-456

Real arithmetic is employed to resolve the / symbol:

A% = 14 : B% = 5	
LET X = A% / B% : PRINT X	2.8

STATEMENT(S)

A program, or piece of program, comprises statements on one or more numbered lines. In subsequent definitions a piece of program is denoted:

statements

A numbered line begins with a line number in the range 1 to 32767.

Each statement on a numbered line may be any of those defined in this book. For example the LET statement is defined earlier; according to that definition the following is a *statement*:

LET A = 6 * B

On each numbered line is one or more statements separated by colons:

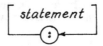

A limit to the number of statements on a numbered line is imposed by the REM statement which *makes* itself the last by treating everything following the keyword as part of the remark.

A numbered line is not limited by the width of screen; typescript fills the screen row by row automatically. A numbered line may be of any practical length. But because programs are edited by retrieving *complete* numbered lines from memory and displaying them on the screen, numbered lines should be kept manageably short.

A numbered line is terminated by pressing RETURN . Then it joins other numbered lines in memory. There it finds its place among other lines according to line number. When a new line is given the same line number as that of an existing line then the new line obliterates and replaces the original numbered line. Typing *just* the line number *deletes* the original line with that number: line and line number vanish.

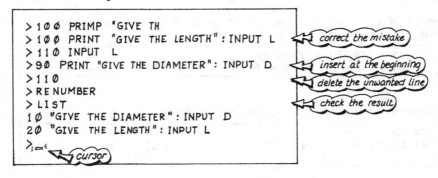

34

4

ARITHMETIC

ARITHMETIC OPERATORS $\wedge \; \underset{MOD}{\star} \; / \; \underset{DIV}{+} \; =$

Arithmetic operators bind together the terms of an expression. In the absence of brackets the operators are applied from left to right in order of precedence as though by successively adding brackets. Below is an example of brackets added successively.

(i) $3*2+4\wedge2\wedge3*-5$ | (iv) $3*2+((4\wedge2)\wedge3)*(-5)$
(ii) $3*2+4\wedge2\wedge3*(-5)$ | (v) $(3*2)+(((4\wedge2)\wedge3)*(-5))$
(iii) $3*2+(4\wedge2)\wedge3*(-5)$ | (vi) $((3*2)+(((4\wedge2)\wedge3)*(-5)))$

OP	OPERATION	PRECEDENCE
+	leave alone	1
−	negate	(high)
∧	raise to the power of	2
*	multiply by	3
/	divide by	
+	add to	4
−	subtract from	

AS PREFIX OPERATORS

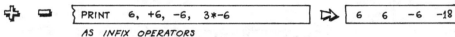

```
PRINT   6, +6, -6, 3*-6
```
➡ | 6   6   -6   -18 |

AS INFIX OPERATORS

```
PRINT   6+3,   3-6
```
➡ | 9   -3 |

```
PRINT   6*3,  6/3,   3/6,   3/-6
PRINT   6/0 🐛
```
➡ | 18   2   0.5   -0.5 |
    | Division by zero |

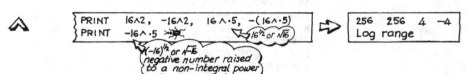

```
PRINT   16∧2,  -16∧2,  16∧.5, -(16∧.5)
PRINT   -16∧.5 🐛
```
$\sqrt{16^{1/2}}$ or $\sqrt{16}$
➡ | 256   256   4   -4 |
    | Log range |

(-16)^{1/2} or √-16 negative number raised to a non-integral power

---

The operators DIV and MOD work with whole numbers. If you write $14.6 \text{ DIV} -5.9$ the computer treats this as $14 \text{ DIV} -5$, each value being truncated to the nearest integer towards zero (not like INT( ): see later). Neither operand may be greater than 2147483648.

OP	OPERATION	PRECEDENCE
DIV	division to the nearest integer	3
MOD	remainder of above operation	

The DIV operator yields the result, to the nearest integer, when the first value is divided by the second. The MOD operator yields the remainder of that same operation. In BBC-BASIC the signs of the results are such that $(i \text{ DIV} j)*j + (i \text{ MOD} j) = i$

DIV

```
PRINT   9 DIV 35,   35 DIV 9
PRINT   5 DIV 3, 5 DIV -3, -5 DIV 3, -5 DIV -3
PRINT   1 DIV .99  (same as 1 DIV 0)
```
➡ | 0   3 |
  | 1   -1   -1   1 |
  | Division by zero |

MOD

```
PRINT   9 MOD 35,   35 MOD 9
PRINT   5 MOD 3, 5 MOD -3, -5 MOD3, -5MOD-3
PRINT   1 MOD .99 🐛
```
➡ | 9   8 |
  | 2   2   -2   -2 |
  | Division by zero |

There must be a space between the first operand and DIV or MOD if that operand is a name. Thus 6MOD4 is correct but XMODY is not; it should be written X MODY, or better still, X MOD Y.

ARITHMETIC FUNCTIONS

RETURN A SINGLE NUMERICAL VALUE

Some arithmetic functions of BBC-BASIC are defined below. Each returns a numerical value.

ABS(expression)
THE ABSOLUTE (i.e. POSITIVE) VALUE OF THE ARGUMENT

```
PRINT  ABS(·2),  ABS(Ø),  ABS(-·3)
PRINT  ABS(3E12)
```
⇒
```
Ø.2     Ø     Ø.3
3E12
```

INT(expression)
THE LARGEST INTEGER WHICH IS LESS THAN THE ARGUMENT

N.B.

```
PRINT  INT(23.9),  INT(Ø),   INT(-3·1)
PRINT  INT(2.147483648E9)
```
⇒
```
23      Ø     -4
Too big
```

SGN (expression)
IF ARGUMENT >0, RETURNS +1; IF ARGUMENT = 0, RETURNS 0; IF ARGUMENT <0, RETURNS -1

```
PRINT  SGN(7.3),   SGN(Ø),   SGN(-1·8)
```
⇒
```
1      Ø     -1
```

SQR(expression)
not negative

SQUARE ROOT OF A NON-NEGATIVE ARGUMENT

```
PRINT  SQR(16),   SQR(·64),   SQR(Ø)
PRINT  SQR(-16)
```
⇒
```
4     Ø.8     Ø
-ve root
```

LN(expression)
positive

NATURAL LOGARITHM (BASE e) OF A POSITIVE ARGUMENT

```
PRINT  LN(1.Ø), LN(2·718282), LN(2·718282∧1·234)
PRINT  LN(Ø),   LN(-1)
```
⇒
```
Ø       1      1.234
Log range
```

EXP(expression)
NATURAL ANTILOGARITHM (BASE e); IN OTHER WORDS EXP(x) IS e^x

e approx.

```
PRINT  EXP(Ø), EXP(1), EXP(1.234)
PRINT  EXP(-1), EXP(LN(1ØØ))
```
⇒
```
1   2.71828183  3.43494186
·367879441   100
```
$e^{-1} = \frac{1}{e}$

LOG (expression)
positive

COMMON LOGARITHM (BASE 10) OF A POSITIVE ARGUMENT

```
PRINT  LOG(1.Ø), LOG(1Ø.Ø),  LOG(1Ø∧1.234)
PRINT  LOG(Ø),   LOG(-1)
```
⇒
```
Ø      1      1.234
Log range
```

10∧1·234 is the antilog of 1·234

TRIGONOMETRICAL FUNCTIONS

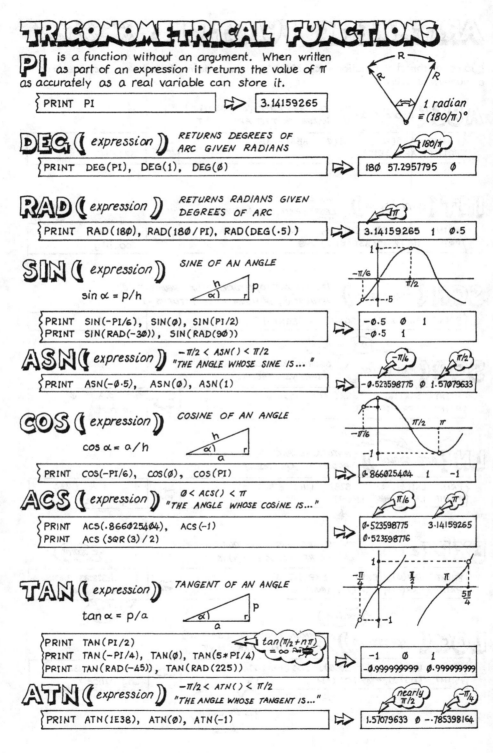

PI is a function without an argument. When written as part of an expression it returns the value of π as accurately as a real variable can store it.

{ PRINT PI ⟹ 3.14159265

1 radian ≡ (180/π)°

DEG (expression) RETURNS DEGREES OF ARC GIVEN RADIANS

{ PRINT DEG(PI), DEG(1), DEG(∅) ⟹ 18∅ 57.2957795 ∅

180/π

RAD (expression) RETURNS RADIANS GIVEN DEGREES OF ARC

{ PRINT RAD(18∅), RAD(180/PI), RAD(DEG(.5)) ⟹ 3.14159265 1 ∅.5

π

SIN (expression) SINE OF AN ANGLE

sin α = p/h

{ PRINT SIN(-PI/6), SIN(∅), SIN(PI/2)
{ PRINT SIN(RAD(-30)), SIN(RAD(90)) ⟹ -∅.5 ∅ 1
-∅.5 1

ASN (expression) -π/2 < ASN() < π/2
"THE ANGLE WHOSE SINE IS..."

{ PRINT ASN(-∅.5), ASN(∅), ASN(1) ⟹ -∅.523598775 ∅ 1.57079633

-π/6   π/2

COS (expression) COSINE OF AN ANGLE

cos α = a/h

{ PRINT COS(-PI/6), COS(∅), COS(PI) ⟹ ∅.866025404 1 -1

ACS (expression) 0 < ACS() < π
"THE ANGLE WHOSE COSINE IS..."

{ PRINT ACS(.866025404), ACS(-1)
{ PRINT ACS (SQR(3)/2) ⟹ ∅.523598775 3.14159265
∅.523598776

π/6   π

TAN (expression) TANGENT OF AN ANGLE

tan α = p/a

{ PRINT TAN(PI/2)
{ PRINT TAN(-PI/4), TAN(∅), TAN(5*PI/4)   tan(π/2+nπ) = ∞
{ PRINT TAN(RAD(-45)), TAN(RAD(225)) ⟹ -1 ∅ 1
-0.999999999 0.999999999

ATN (expression) -π/2 < ATN() < π/2
"THE ANGLE WHOSE TANGENT IS..."

nearly π/2   -π/4

{ PRINT ATN(1E38), ATN(∅), ATN(-1) ⟹ 1.57079633 ∅ --785398164

TRIANGLE

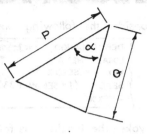

Given the length and two sides of a triangle, and the angle between them, it is possible to derive formulae for the area of the triangle, the other two angles, and the length of the third side. All formulae are given below in terms of P, Q and α.

- area $= \frac{1}{2} PQ \sin \alpha$

- angle $A = \tan^{-1}\left(\dfrac{Q \sin \alpha}{P - Q \cos \alpha}\right)$

- angle $B = \tan^{-1}\left(\dfrac{P \sin \alpha}{Q - P \cos \alpha}\right)$

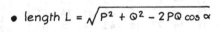

- length $L = \sqrt{P^2 + Q^2 - 2PQ \cos \alpha}$

Here is a program to evaluate the formulae:

```
CLS
PRINT "Give length P": INPUT P
PRINT "Give length Q": INPUT Q
PRINT "Give included angle (degrees)" : INPUT ANGL
ALPHA = RAD(ANGL)
AREA = 0.5 * P * Q * SIN(ALPHA)
A = DEG (ATN(Q * SIN(ALPHA) / (P-Q*COS(ALPHA))))
B = DEG (ATN(P * SIN(ALPHA) / (Q-P*COS(ALPHA))))
L = SQR(P*P + Q*Q - 2*P*Q * COS(ALPHA))
PRINT "Area is "; AREA
PRINT "Angle A is "; A; " degrees"
PRINT "Angle B is "; B; " degrees"
PRINT "Length of third side is "; L
```

Tried with sides of length 3.0 and 4.0, and included angle of 90°, the result should be AREA = 6, A ≈ 53°, B ≈ 37°, L = 5. If the data are such that a base angle is obtuse then the formula evaluates the 180° complement. For example:

A ≈ −64°

B ≈ 37°

RANDOM NUMBERS

Consider the following function:

```
DEF FNDANGO        ← no arguments
LOCAL NEX%
NEX% = SEED%
SEED% = (1 * SEED% + 33) MOD 100
= NEX%
```

> sequence of 100 integers from 0 to 99

Invoke the function as follows:

```
SEED% = 0    ← sow any seed from 0 to 99
FOR I% = 1 TO 100 : PRINT FNDANGO; " "; : NEXT I%
```

and it should produce:

0	33	66	99	32	65	98	31	64	97	30	63	96	29	62
95	28	61	94	27	60	93	26	59	92	25	58	91	24	57
90	23	56	89	22	55	88	21	54	87	20	53	86	19	52
85	18	51	84	17	50	83	16	49	82	15	48	81	14	47
80	13	46	79	12	45	78	11	44	77	10	43	76	9	42
75	8	41	74	7	40	73	6	39	72	5	38	71	4	37
70	3	36	69	2	35	68	1	34	67					

> note: if you run this program you will find that the screen displays far fewer numbers on each line

In the above sequence (not "random"; it exhibits patterns) each of the 100 integers in the range 0 to 99 appears precisely once. The sequence is a permutation of the integers 0 to 99. Let the program run FOR I% = 1 TO 600 and the identical permutation is repeated 6 times. The first item to be generated is the "seed" sown before the function is first invoked. There is nothing "random" about it.

Now change the last statement of the function; make it deliver a *fraction* when the function is invoked:

```
DEF FNEREAL
LOCAL NEX%
NEX% = SEED%
SEED% = (1 * SEED% + 33) MOD 100
= NEX% / 99        ← returns a real fraction
```

Don't use the above to generate random numbers ≈ the use of a proper generator is explained opposite ≈ the above functions are just to illustrate four characteristics of pseudo-random integers and fractions:

• the cycle of items generated is fixed; it repeats itself when exhausted

• every seed in a cycle of N items is unique and lies in the range 0 to N-1

• the random *fraction* lies in the range $0 \leqslant fraction \leqslant 1$

• it is possible, by sowing a seed, to start the cycle at any chosen item.

To generate a *practical* cycle of 65536 fractions, change the constants 1, 33, 100, 99 in function FNEREAL to 25173, 13849, 65536, 65535 respectively.

THE RND FUNCTION

The RND( ) function of BBC-BASIC may be used to generate integers or fractions as explained opposite. The argument of RND( ) determines the range and type of number delivered.

With no argument at all, RND returns a random integer in the range −2147483648 < RND < 2147483647 .

RND

```
PRINT   RND
PRINT   RND
SEED = RND : PRINT SEED
PRINT   RND
PRINT   RND
```

```
1.88641908 E9
1.06851935 E9
−1.6921604 E9
2.00429984 E9
1.22051703 E9
```

With a negative seed as the argument, the function first delivers the value of that negative seed. The generator then continues its fixed cycle from this point. Compare the examples above and below. This facility enables the random-number generator to deliver an identical sequence of numbers each time a program is run. When debugging a program, make LET X= RND(-1) the first statement; the random numbers would then be delivered in the same sequence each time the program was run.

RND (-seed)

```
PRINT   RND( SEED)
PRINT   RND
PRINT   RND
```

SEED holds −1.6921604E9 from example above

```
−1.6921604E9
2.00429984E9
1.22051703 E9
```

With a whole number, n, greater than 1, RND( ) returns a random integer in the range $1 \leqslant RND(n) \leqslant n$

RND (n)

```
PRINT   RND(6),   RND(6)
```

With an argument of unity, RND(1) returns a random *fraction* in the range $0 \leqslant RND(1) \leqslant 0.999999$

RND (1)

```
PRINT   INT(1 + RND(1) * 5) ,   INT(1 + RND(1) *5)
```

With a zero argument RND(0) returns the same fraction as was returned by the previous RND(1)

```
PRINT   INT(1+ RND(1)*5),  INT (1+ RND(0)*5)
```

1 Note!   *0 Note!*

always throws a double

41

LOGICAL OPERATORS *with* NUMERICAL OPERANDS

The operators tabulated here produce a result of −1 if the comparison is *true*; 0 if *false*. This representation is a convention of BBC-BASIC; see below.

Logical operators are typically used in the IF statement:

```
IF PROFIT > LOSS PRINT "Hooray!"
```

but may also be used in arithmetic expressions and assignments:

```
LET EXCESS = PROFIT > LOSS
IF EXCESS PRINT "Hooray!"
```

OPERATOR	COMPARISON	PRECEDENCE
=	equal to	5
>	greater than	
>=	greater than or equal to	
<	less than	
<=	less than or equal to	
<>	not equal to	

true false

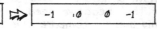
```
PRINT  10=5,  5=10,  10.0 = 10,  1E7=1E7+1
```
⇨ `0    0    -1   0`

```
PRINT  10>5,  5>10,  10>10,  0>-10
```
⇨ `-1   0    0   -1`

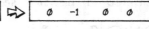
```
PRINT  10>=5,  5>=10,  10>=10,  0>=-10
```
⇨ `-1   0   -1  -1`

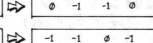
```
PRINT  10<5,  5<10,  10<10,  0<-10
```
⇨ `0   -1    0    0`

```
PRINT  10<=5,  5<=10,  10<=10,  0<=-10
```
⇨ `0   -1   -1   0`

```
PRINT  10<>5,  5<>10,  10<>10,  0<>-10
```
⇨ `-1  -1    0   -1`

LOGICAL OPERATORS *with* STRING OPERANDS

With string operands these operators behave as explained on page 49 and illustrated by examples below:

```
PRINT  "A" = "A",     "A" = "ABC"
PRINT  "B" > "A",     "9" > "1",   "9" > "100"
PRINT  "B" >= "A",
PRINT  "A" < "B",     "A" < "a",   "$" < "£"
PRINT  "A" <= "B"
PRINT  "A" <> "a",    "10" <> "10.0"
```
⇨
```
-1   0
-1   -1   -1
-1
-1   -1   -1
-1
-1   -1
```

TRUE (−1), FALSE (0) *LOGICAL CONSTANTS*

There are two logical constants (strictly speaking *functions*) which may be used in place of −1 and 0 to signify *true* and *false* respectively:

```
PRINT  TRUE
PRINT  FALSE
```
⇨
```
-1
0
```

LOGICAL OPERATORS *WITH* *LOGICAL OPERANDS*

The operators tabulated here produce a result of –1 (*true*) or 0 (*false*) as defined by the tables.

Notice that (X AND Y) would produce the same result as (Y AND X): in other words AND is commutative. The same applies to OR and to EOR.

These operators should be preceded and followed by a space so as not to join adjacent names. XANDY is a single name: if the intention is to be X AND Y then spaces, or brackets, are essential: X AND Y or (X) AND (Y).

Brackets are essential where the precedence defined on page 29 would otherwise be wrongly interpreted.

brackets needed

OPERATOR	COMPARISON		PRECEDENCE
NOT	only operand		1
	true	*false*	*highest*
	0	–1	
AND	2nd operand		6
	true	*false*	
1st operand true	–1	0	
1st operand false	0	0	
OR	2nd operand		7
	true	*false*	*lowest*
1st operand true	–1	–1	
1st operand false	–1	0	
EOR	2nd operand		
	true	*false*	
1st operand true	0	–1	
1st operand false	–1	0	

NOT
```
PRINT  NOT TRUE ,  NOT(2*2=4),  NOT FALSE
```
0   0   –1

AND
```
PRINT   TRUE AND TRUE ,   TRUE AND FALSE
PRINT   FALSE AND TRUE,   FALSE AND FALSE
```
–1   0
0   0

OR
```
PRINT   TRUE OR TRUE,    TRUE OR FALSE
PRINT   FALSE OR TRUE,   FALSE OR FALSE
```
–1   –1
–1   0

EOR
```
PRINT   TRUE EOR TRUE,    TRUE EOR FALSE
PRINT   FALSE EOR TRUE,   FALSE EOR FALSE
```
0   –1
–1   0

the EXCLUSIVE OR is called "exclusive" because TRUE EOR TRUE is excluded from truth

NOT and **<>** may be used to the same effect:
```
PRINT  A<>B ,   NOT(A=B)
```
same result

Logical operators are used most commonly in the IF statement defined in chapter 6. An example is:
```
100  IF STOCK < 12 AND  ORDERS > 0  THEN
PRINT  "Re-order now"  ELSE PRINT "No
 need to re-order"
```

The operators NOT, AND, OR, EOR may be used for *bitwise* operations as explained overleaf.

STORAGE OF INTEGERS

NOVICES MAY CARE TO SKIP THIS

An integer is stored as 32 consecutive binary digits (bits). There are 8 bits to a *byte*, so an integer may be thought of as a pattern of 4 consecutive bytes. The decimal value of a positive integer is given by the sum of the values found against bits which are set to 1.

Thus the value of the integer shown stored above is:

$$11010 \text{ (binary)} \quad \text{or} \quad 16 + 8 + 2 = 26 \text{ (decimal)}$$

The biggest possible integer stored in this manner is 0111111111111111111111111111111 (binary) or 1073741824 + 536870912 + 268635456 + 134217728 + 67108864 + 33554432 + 16777216 + 8388608 + 4194304 + 2097152 + 1048576 + 524288 + 262144 + 131072 + 65536 + 32768 + 16384 + 8192 + 4096 + 2048 + 1024 + 512 + 256 + 128 + 64 + 32 + 16 + 8 + 4 + 2 + 1 = 2,147,483,647 (decimal).

Zero is stored as 00000000000000000000000000000000

The bit marked ⇧ (the most significant bit) signifies a *negative* integer when set to 1.

To interpret this, reverse all the bits thus:

which looks like 26 (decimal) as depicted at the top of this page. But it does not represent −26; it represents −27.

Why the extra 1? Consider 11111111111111111111111111111111. Reversing all the bits gives 00000000000000000000000000000000. But this represents zero. So in a pure "twos complement" convention there would be two zeros; +0 and −0, and that is awkward. We say that 11111111111111111111111111111111 represents −1 instead. That means applying −1 to every negative number so as to preserve continuity. The computer does this automatically of course.

Knowing this convention, any pattern of bits can be set in an integer variable by assignment. For example, for the first two bit patterns above:

```
LET N% = 26 : M% = -27
```

Such bit patterns are used extensively when dealing with colour graphics.

The useful function FNXBAS (, ,) on page 80 converts numbers from one base to another; it may be used to convert numbers from binary to decimal and vice versa:

```
PRINT FNXBAS ( "1101", 2, 10 )
PRINT FNXBAS ( "26", 10, 2 )
PRINT FNXBAS ( "2147483647", 10, 2)
```

(from binary)
(to decimal)

```
26
11010
1111111111111111111111111111111
```
(31 ones)

44

BITWISE OPERATIONS *with* *INTEGER OPERANDS*

The operators NOT, AND, OR, EOR operate on individual bits in the integer operands. For each bit the result is as tabulated below:

NOT	-1	0
	0	-1

AND	-1	0
-1	-1	0
0	0	0

OR	-1	0
-1	-1	-1
0	-1	0

EOR	-1	0
-1	0	-1
0	-1	0

e.g. NOT -1 is 0
NOT 0 is -1

e.g. -1 AND -1 is -1
-1 AND 0 is 0

e.g. -1 OR 0 is -1
0 OR 0 is 0

e.g. -1 EOR -1 is 0
-1 EOR 0 is -1

Below is a set of examples of the use of bitwise operators. The first of these explains the BBC-BASIC convention of representing *true* by -1 and *false* by zero.

```
PRINT TRUE, FALSE
PRINT NOT TRUE, NOT FALSE
```
⇨
```
-1      0
 0     -1
```

TRUE `1111111111111111111111111111111`
FALSE `00000000000000000000000000000000`

NOT TRUE `00000000000000000000000000000000` NOT FALSE `11111111111111111111111111111111`

NOT TRUE ≡ FALSE   *NOT FALSE ≡ TRUE*

The internal representation of the following example is depicted opposite.

```
PRINT  26, -27
PRINT  NOT -27,  NOT 26
```
⇨
```
26     -27
-27     26
```

AND
```
PRINT 10 AND 12
```
⇨ `8`

10 `00000000000000000000000000001010`
12 `00000000000000000000000000001100`
10 AND 12 `00000000000000000000000000001000`

OR
```
PRINT 10 OR 12
```
⇨ `14`

10 `00000000000000000000000000001010`
12 `00000000000000000000000000001100`
10 OR 12 `00000000000000000000000000001110`

EOR
```
PRINT 10 EOR 12
```
⇨ `6`

10 `00000000000000000000000000001010`
12 `00000000000000000000000000001100`
10 EOR 12 `00000000000000000000000000000110`

EXERCISES

1. **T**ype the various examples in this chapter to verify the results given on the right of each page.

2. **I**mplement the triangle program. Modify the program so that it uses fewer trigonometrical functions (it was originally contrived to illustrate as many as possible).

3. **G**iven the base length and base angles of a triangle as shown, the area is:

$$\text{AREA} = \frac{a^2 \sin B \sin C}{2 \sin A}$$

where $A = 180° - B - C$

Write a program to compute the area of such triangles.

4. **W**rite a program to throw two dice. Each time you press RETURN the program should display:

Your throw is 2 & 5

(or whatever numbers turn up)

5

STRINGS

CHARACTER FUNCTIONS
LOGICAL OPERATORS
STRING FUNCTIONS
SEXISM (EXAMPLE)
STRING TO NUMERICAL (AND VICE VERSA)
EXPRESSIONS AS STRINGS

CHARACTER FUNCTIONS

The word ASCII ⟨ which rhymes with Spaski ⟩ stands for American Standard Code for Information Interchange. Every character has an ASCII code. For example the character Q has ASCII code 81; the character £ has code 96; the character 9 has code 57. Below is a table which shows the ASCII code for every visible character.

Unless the *mode* is changed ⟨ mode is explained on page 97 ⟩ the computer displays characters in Teletext code which differs from ASCII code in a few places. Where codes differ the Teletext code is shown in brackets: e.g. (←)

ASCII CODE	\	\	\	LAST	DIGIT	OF	CODE	\	\	\
	0	1	2	3	4	5	6	7	8	9
0										
1				new line		empty spaces are for "control codes" (shown on p.163)				
2										
3			space	!	"	#	$	%	&	'
4	(	)	*	+	,	−	.	/	0	1
5	2	3	4	5	6	7	8	9	:	;
6	<	=	>	?	@	A	B	C	D	E
7	F	G	H	I	J	K	L	M	N	O
8	P	Q	R	S	T	U	V	W	X	Y
9	Z	[(←)	\ ('½)	] (→)	∧	_	£	a	b	c
10	d	e	f	g	h	i	j	k	l	m
11	n	o	p	q	r	s	t	u	v	w
12	x	y	z	{ ('¼)	¦ (‖)	} (¾)	~ (÷)	backspace		

FIRST DIGIT(S) OF CODE

The following functions are for returning the ASCII code of a given character, and for returning the character which corresponds to a given ASCII code, respectively:

ASC(*string*)

RETURNS THE ASCII CODE OF THE FIRST CHARACTER OF THE NOMINATED STRING

```
PRINT ASC("Q"),  ASC("QUID"),  ASC("quid")
PRINT ASC("£9"),  ASC("9£")
```
⟹
```
81   81   113
96   57
```

CHR$(*expression*)

RETURNS THE CHARACTER CORRESPONDING TO THE GIVEN ASCII CODE

```
PRINT CHR$(81),  CHR$(9*9)
PRINT CHR$(96)+ CHR$(57)+ CHR$(57)
```
⟹
```
Q   Q
£99
```

When characters are compared ⟨ using =, >, <, >=, <=, <> ⟩ the ASCII code determines which is the "greater" character:

```
PRINT  "A" < "a"      equivalent
PRINT  ASC("A") < ASC("a")
```
⟹
```
−1   true
−1
```

LOGICAL OPERATORS *with* STRING OPERANDS

The logical operators are tabulated here ⇨

⊟	equal to	⟨⟩	not equal to
▷	greater than	⟨	less than
▷⊟	greater than or equal to	⟨⊟	less than or equal to

A single character is greater than another if its ASCII code is greater than that of the other:

```
PRINT  "B" > "A"
```
⇨ -1 *(true: see ASCII table)*

A string is equal to another when each contains identical characters in identical order:

```
PRINT  "Ab*/22"  =  "Ab*/22"
PRINT  "AB*/22"  =  "Ab*/22"
PRINT  "Ab*/22"  =  "Ab*/21"
```
⇨
-1 ⟵ *(true)*
0 ⟵ *("B"≠"b")*
0 ⟵ *("2"≠"1")*

A string is greater or less than another according to the ASCII code of the earliest character from the left which fails to match:

(earliest which differs)
```
PRINT "DIG"  >  "BIG"
PRINT "BIGGER"  >  "BIGGAR"
```
(earliest which differs)
⇨
-1 ⟵ *("D" > "B")*
-1 ⟵ *("E" > "A")*

When comparing strings of different length, imagine a *null* character appended to the shorter string as depicted below:

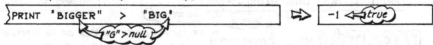
```
PRINT "BIGGER"  >  "BIG"  (null appended)
```

where the *null* character is assumed to have an ASCII code of *zero*. The rule for comparison may now be applied as before:

```
PRINT "BIGGER"  >  "BIG"
```
("G" > null)
⇨ -1 ⟵ *(true)*

Here are more examples arranged to yield -1 for *true*:

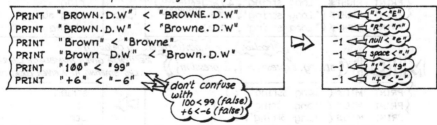
```
PRINT  "BROWN.D.W"  <  "BROWNE.D.W"
PRINT  "BROWN.D.W"  <  "Browne.D.W"
PRINT  "Brown"  <  "Browne"
PRINT  "Brown D.W"  <  "Brown.D.W"
PRINT  "100"  <  "99"
PRINT  "+6"  <  "-6"
```
don't confuse with 100 < 99 (false) +6 < -6 (false)
⇨
-1 ⟵ *("." < "E")*
-1 ⟵ *("R" < "r")*
-1 ⟵ *(null < "e")*
-1 ⟵ *(space < ".")*
-1 ⟵ *("1" < "9")*
-1 ⟵ *("+" < "-")*

STRING FUNCTIONS

The following functions are for manipulating strings. An example of their use is given opposite.

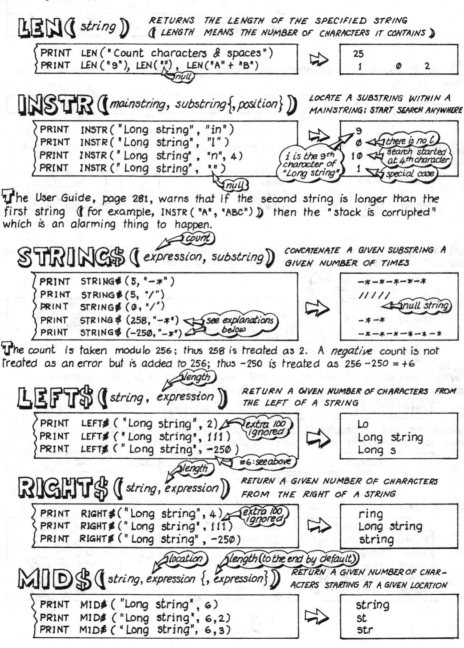

LEN (string)
RETURNS THE LENGTH OF THE SPECIFIED STRING
(LENGTH MEANS THE NUMBER OF CHARACTERS IT CONTAINS)

```
PRINT LEN ("Count characters & spaces")
PRINT LEN ("9"), LEN (""), LEN ("A" + "B")
```
⟵ null

```
25
 1    0    2
```

INSTR (mainstring, substring {, position })
LOCATE A SUBSTRING WITHIN A MAINSTRING: START SEARCH ANYWHERE

```
PRINT  INSTR ("Long string", "in")
PRINT  INSTR ("Long string", "l")
PRINT  INSTR ("Long string", "n", 4)
PRINT  INSTR ("Long string", "")
```
⟵ null

```
9      ⟵ i is the 9th character of "Long string"
0      ⟵ there is no l
10     ⟵ search started at 4th character
1      ⟵ special case
```

The User Guide, page 281, warns that if the second string is longer than the first string (for example, INSTR ("A", "ABC")) then the "stack is corrupted" which is an alarming thing to happen.

STRING$ (expression, substring)
⟵ count
CONCATENATE A GIVEN SUBSTRING A GIVEN NUMBER OF TIMES

```
PRINT  STRING$ (5, "-*")
PRINT  STRING$ (5, "/")
PRINT  STRING$ (0, "/")
PRINT  STRING$ (258, "-*")    ⟵ see explanations below
PRINT  STRING$ (-250, "-*")
```

```
-*-*-*-*-*
/////       ⟵ null string
-*-*
-*-*-*-*-*-*
```

The count is taken modulo 256; thus 258 is treated as 2. A negative count is not treated as an error but is added to 256; thus -250 is treated as 256 - 250 = +6

LEFT$ (string , expression)
⟵ length
RETURN A GIVEN NUMBER OF CHARACTERS FROM THE LEFT OF A STRING

```
PRINT  LEFT$ ("Long string", 2)     ⟵ extra 100 ignored
PRINT  LEFT$ ("Long string", 111)
PRINT  LEFT$ ("Long string", -250)  ≡ 6 : see above
```

```
Lo
Long string
Long s
```

RIGHT$ (string, expression)
⟵ length
RETURN A GIVEN NUMBER OF CHARACTERS FROM THE RIGHT OF A STRING

```
PRINT  RIGHT$ ("Long string", 4)    ⟵ extra 100 ignored
PRINT  RIGHT$ ("Long string", 111)
PRINT  RIGHT$ ("Long string", -250)
```

```
ring
Long string
string
```

MID$ (string, expression {, expression})
⟵ location   ⟵ length (to the end by default)
RETURN A GIVEN NUMBER OF CHARACTERS STARTING AT A GIVEN LOCATION

```
PRINT  MID$ ("Long string", 6)
PRINT  MID$ ("Long string", 6, 2)
PRINT  MID$ ("Long string", 6, 3)
```

```
string
st
str
```

SEXISM

AN EXAMPLE PROGRAM FOR EDITING SEXIST PROSE AND ILLUSTRATING STRING FUNCTIONS

The program below is designed to edit prose by replacing the personal pronoun HE with HE/SHE; replacing HIS with THAT PERSON'S; replacing HIM with HIM/HER.

To use the program, type RUN and press RETURN. When the question mark appears type the text to be edited and press RETURN. The edited text is then displayed below the errant text.

Use only capital letters in the text. Punctuation is allowed, but not immediately before or after the word HE or HIM or HIS. The reason for the restriction is that the program searches for ⌴HE⌴ etc. and would not recognize HE, or HIM? or ⌴HIS etc.

Here is the program:

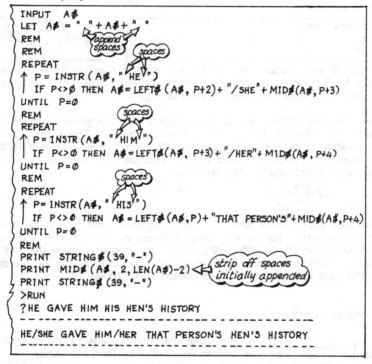

```
INPUT  A$
LET  A$ = " "+A$+" "
REM                        ← append spaces
REM                        ← spaces
REPEAT
↑  P = INSTR ( A$, " HE ")      ← spaces
│  IF P<>0 THEN A$= LEFT$ (A$, P+2)+ "/SHE"+ MID$(A$, P+3)
UNTIL  P=0
REM                        ← spaces
REPEAT
↑  P = INSTR (A$, " HIM ")
│  IF P<>0 THEN A$=LEFT$(A$, P+3) + "/HER"+ MID$(A$, P+4)
UNTIL  P=0
REM                        ← spaces
REPEAT
↑  P= INSTR (A$, " HIS ")
│  IF P<>0 THEN  A$ =LEFT$(A$,P)+ "THAT PERSON'S"+MID$(A$,P+4)
UNTIL  P= 0
REM
PRINT  STRING$ (39, "-")
PRINT  MID$ (A$, 2, LEN(A$)-2)   ← strip off spaces initially appended
PRINT  STRING$ (39, '-")
>RUN
?HE GAVE HIM HIS HEN'S HISTORY
- - - - - - - - - - - - - - - - - - - - - - - - - - - - - - - - - -

HE/SHE GAVE HIM/HER THAT PERSON'S HEN'S HISTORY
- - - - - - - - - - - - - - - - - - - - - - - - - - - - - - - - - -
```

Notice that HEN'S is not converted to HE/SHEN'S nor is HISTORY converted to THAT PERSON'STORY. This is because substrings in the INSTR(,) function (see above) all begin and end with a space.

Notice, also, that spaces are appended to the original text. Without the leading space the initial HE would be missed in the example above.

51

STRING TO NUMERICAL *AND VICE VERSA*

Sometimes a programmer needs to change a string such as "123" into a numerical value (in this case 123). At other times it is necessary to change a numerical value such as 123 into a string (in this case "123"). A function for each of these requirements is defined below.

STR$ (*expression*)   RETURNS A STRING CORRESPONDING TO THE GIVEN NUMERICAL VALUE

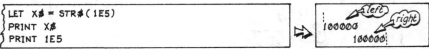

```
PRINT STR$(6)+ STR$(2*3),   STR$(2*3)+ "-shooter"
```
note comma

⇨   66   6-shooter
left justified *left*

Notice that both items are left justified in their respective fields because they are now strings, not numerical items.

Here is another example:

```
LET X$ = STR$ (1E5)
PRINT X$
PRINT 1E5
```

⇨   100000   *left* *right*
    100000

to show that the *format* chosen for 1E5 by the STR$( ) function is the same as that chosen by the PRINT statement to print the numerical value 1E5, but the *justification* is of opposite hand: left not right.

For the above example it is assumed that nobody has tampered with the special variable @% which is fully described on page 94. The content of this special variable is a code which defines the format of numbers to be printed (the number of decimal places etc.). This code is best analysed as a hex number with eight digits. For example:

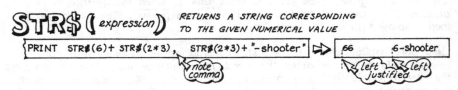

&00020206
   01

The first two hex digits above are 00 which signifies that @% is to apply only to PRINT statements, not to the STR$( ) function. But if the first two hex digits are changed to 01 then @% would be referred to by the STR$( ) function as well. Warning: when @% *does* apply to STR$( ), the field width specified by the last two digits is nevertheless ignored ⋙

Here is the inverse function:

VAL (*string*)   RETURNS THE NUMERICAL VALUE (IF ANY) REPRESENTED BY THE STRING ⟺ OTHERWISE RETURNS ZERO

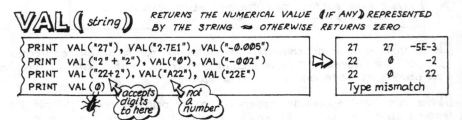

```
PRINT VAL ("27"), VAL("2.7E1"), VAL("-0.005")
PRINT VAL ("2" + "2"), VAL("0"), VAL("-002")
PRINT VAL ("22+2"), VAL("A22"), VAL("22E")
PRINT VAL (0)
```
accepts digits to here   *not a number*

⇨   27   27   -5E-3
    22   0   -2
    22   0   22
    Type mismatch

There is an important example covering the use of STR$( ) on page 96.

EXPRESSIONS AS STRINGS

There is, in BBC-BASIC, a function named EVAL( ) which requires for its argument a *string* and returns a numerical value. The value returned is derived assuming that the string represents an *expression* to be decoded.

Here is the definition:

EVAL (*string*) RETURNS THE NUMERICAL VALUE OF ITS STRING ARGUMENT, TREATING THIS AS A BBC-BASIC EXPRESSION

```
PRINT EVAL("6"), EVAL("6*3"), EVAL( "1+ SQR(4)")
```
6	18	3

Using this function it is possible for the *programmer* to allow the *user* of his or her program to write an item of data in the form of an expression. Here is a trivial example to illustrate this concept:

```
10 INPUT "Please type a number"; A$
20 LET N = EVAL ( A$)
30 PRINT "The square of "; A$; " is "; N^2
>RUN
Please type a number ? 2*PI/3
The square of 2*PI/3 is 4.38649084
>
```

Names of variables unknown to the program should not be quoted:

```
>LET X=5
>RUN
Please type a number ? X
No such variable at line 20
>
```

But it is allowable to quote the names of variables which are in the program:

```
>15 LET X= 5
>RUN
Please type a number ? X
The square of X is 25
```

If the user of a program is allowed to type expressions instead of numbers the programmer should trap the inevitable errors. The following example uses ON ERROR ; a statement defined in chapter 13

```
10 ON ERROR GOTO 60
20 PRINT "Please type a number "; A$ ◄
30 LET N = EVAL (A$)
40 PRINT "The square of "; A$; " is "; N^2
50 END
60 PRINT "Rotten expression: try again"
70 GOTO 20
>RUN
Please type a number? SQR(-3)
Rotten expression: try again
Please type a number?:
```

53

EXERCISES

1. Type the various examples to verify the results given on the right of each page.

2. Implement the Sexism program. Make the program more even handed by dealing with SHE and HER as well as HE, HIM, HIS.

3. Write a program to encode ≈ and subsequently decode ≈ messages typed in English. Spy stuff.

CONTROL

FLOW CHARTS

LOGICAL SHAPES FOR STRUCTURED PROGRAMS

The control statements of BBC-BASIC are introduced in earlier chapters; in this chapter they are defined formally and their characteristics explained.

The actions of control statements are depicted below as flow charts and informal diagrams.

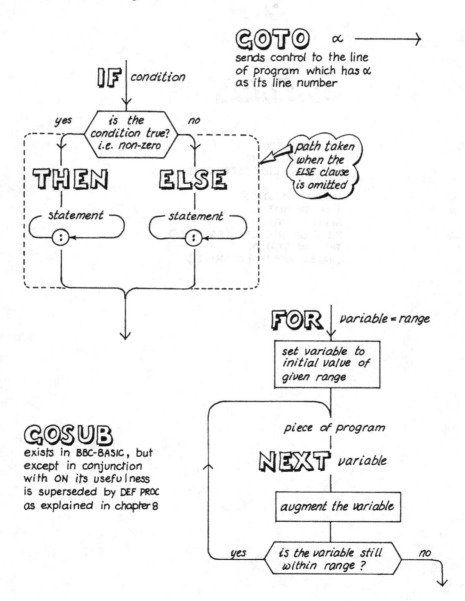

GOTO α ⟶

sends control to the line of program which has α as its line number

IF | *condition*

yes — is the condition true? i.e. non-zero — *no*

THEN   **ELSE**

path taken when the ELSE clause is omitted

statement   *statement*

FOR | *variable = range*

set variable to initial value of given range

GOSUB exists in BBC-BASIC, but except in conjunction with ON its usefulness is superseded by DEF PROC as explained in chapter 8

piece of program

NEXT *variable*

augment the variable

yes — is the variable still within range? — *no*

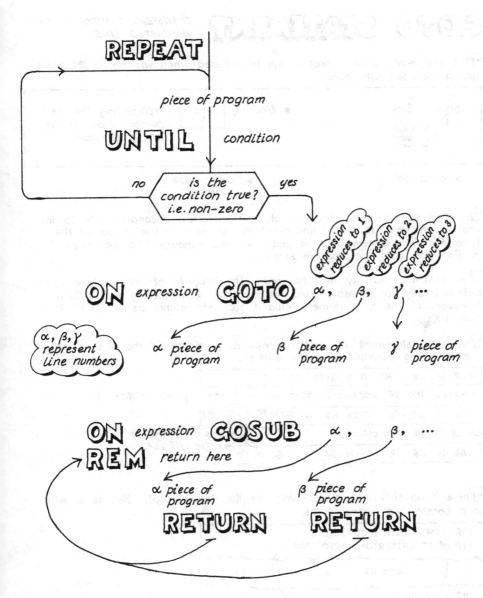

REPEAT

piece of program

UNTIL *condition*

no / is the condition true? i.e. non-zero \ yes

expression reduces to 1   *expression reduces to 2*   *expression reduces to 3*

ON *expression* GOTO α, β, γ ...

α, β, γ represent line numbers

α *piece of program*   β *piece of program*   γ *piece of program*

ON *expression* GOSUB α, β, ...

REM *return here*

α *piece of program*   β *piece of program*

RETURN   RETURN

The control statements END and STOP are almost synonymous; when either is obeyed the program stops. In the case of STOP, however, the screen displays the message: "STOP at line..." quoting the number of the line containing the relevant STOP statement.

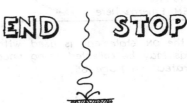

END   STOP

GOTO STATEMENT

This statement, which cannot always be avoided when writing in BBC-BASIC, should be used with care.

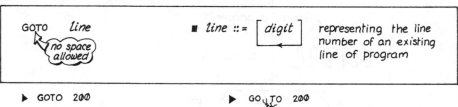

GOTO *line*   ■ *line* ::= [digit]   representing the line number of an existing line of program

(no space allowed)

▶ GOTO 200   ▶ GO TO 200

On obeying this statement control is transferred unconditionally to the line which has the given line number. If no such line exists at the time the GOTO statement is obeyed then the message "No such line..." is displayed and the program stops.

The RENUMBER facility may be used, the integrity of line numbers being automatically preserved during the process. Renumbering would fail, however, if the programmer included such statements as LET L = 250: GOTO L

The GOTO statement is used typically as a clause of the IF statement. The following example is given earlier:

```
40 IF C$ = "R" THEN GOTO 80
```

However, the IF statement does not need the keyword GOTO:

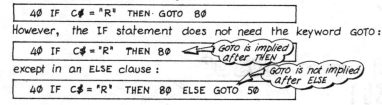

```
40 IF C$ = "R" THEN 80
```
GOTO is implied after THEN

except in an ELSE clause:
GOTO is not implied after ELSE

```
40 IF C$ = "R" THEN 80 ELSE GOTO 50
```

There is no structure in BBC-BASIC for the "while loop". Here is a while loop constructed using GOTOs.

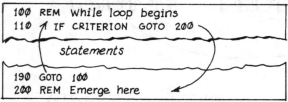

```
100 REM While loop begins
110   IF CRITERION GOTO 200

        statements

190 GOTO 100
200 REM Emerge here
```

When the ON statement is used with GOTO (rather than GOSUB) the loose ends may be collected using unconditional GOTOs. This technique is illustrated on page 65.

IF • THEN • ELSE STRUCTURE

The IF statement is all on one numbered line and has the form:

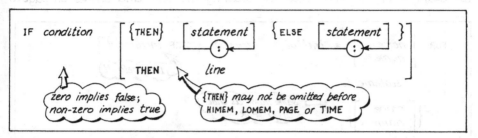

IF *condition* [{THEN} [*statement*] {ELSE [*statement*] }]
                                    (:)   (:)
         THEN   *line*

zero implies false; non-zero implies true

{THEN} may not be omitted before HIMEM, LOMEM, PAGE or TIME

- ▶ IF   PROFIT > LOSS THEN PRINT "Hooray!"
- ▶ IF   PROFIT > LOSS PRINT "Hooray!" ELSE PRINT "Bother"
- ▶ IF   FACILITY = 1Ø   THEN   HIMEM = HIMEM − 1Ø24
         obligatory THEN
- ▶ IF OK THEN 12ØØ ELSE GOTO 13ØØ
                         obligatory GOTO
- ▶ IF NAME$ > "K" AND   NAME$ < "S" PRINT "See L to R Directory"

When *condition* is evaluated, and its value turns out to be *non*-zero, then the statements following THEN are obeyed ≈ statements following ELSE being ignored. When *condition* is evaluated as zero (*false*) the statements following THEN are ignored; those following ELSE are obeyed. The flow chart on page 56 depicts this logic more clearly than words can describe it.

Be careful when nesting one IF statement within another. The flow chart below would *appear* to be correctly encoded as the following statement:

```
1ØØ IF C1 THEN  IF C2  THEN X=1 ELSE  X=2  ELSE  X=3
11Ø REM
```

but this would *not* give the results expected. When C1 *is false* the computer would seek and obey the *first* ELSE clause to follow the condition C1. So in this example the statement X=3 would *never* be obeyed: a false C1 would result in X=2.

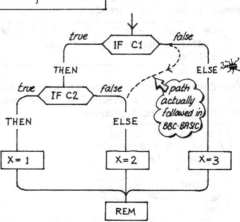

There may be any number of statements in a THEN clause or ELSE clause but they must all be on a single numbered line.

FOR • NEXT

These keywords are for constructing a loop as depicted on page 56. There is an example of FOR..NEXT loops for drawing the stars and stripes on page 22.

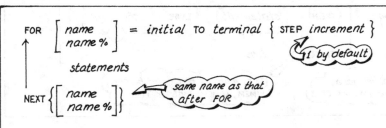

FOR $\begin{bmatrix} name \\ name\% \end{bmatrix}$ = *initial* TO *terminal* { STEP *increment* }

↳ *1 by default*

statements

NEXT $\left\{ \begin{bmatrix} name \\ name\% \end{bmatrix} \right\}$ ← *same name as that after FOR*

■ *name* is the name of a variable

■ *initial, terminal, increment* are expressions

In the first example below, the STEP clause has been omitted, therefore STEP 1 is assumed by default. The looping variable, BAH, is a real variable. Loops run more efficiently under the control of *integer* variables but in these examples the increase in speed would be unnoticeable.

```
FOR BAH = 1 TO 3
  PRINT "We wish you a merry Christmas"
NEXT BAH
```

The next example illustrates a decrement (negative increment) applied to an integer variable which controls the loop.

```
FOR I% = 39 TO 15 STEP -1
  PRINT STRING$( I%, "#")
NEXT I%
```
displays a trapezium made of # symbols

The next example illustrates the use of general expressions for *initial, terminal* and *increment*.

```
FOR THETA = -PI/2  TO  3*PI/2  STEP PI/3
  PRINT DEG(THETA); " degrees"
NEXT THETA
```

The final example illustrates nested loops. The I% has been omitted after NEXT on the final line. The omission is allowable but confusing and therefore bad practice.

```
FOR I% = Ø TO 24
  FOR J% = Ø TO 39
    PRINT "*";
  NEXT J%
  PRINT
NEXT
END
```
displays a screen full of stars

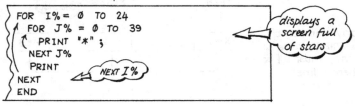 *NEXT I%*

60

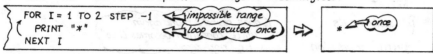

The FOR loop in BBC-BASIC displays some important characteristics:

- when control meets a FOR statement the FOR loop is executed *at least once* even if the specified range is meaningless:

```
FOR I = 1 TO 2 STEP -1     impossible range
   PRINT "*"                loop executed once
NEXT I
```
⇨ `*` ← once

- on emergence from a FOR..NEXT loop the controlling variable contains *the next value not used*. In the first example opposite, variable BAH would emerge from the loop containing 4. In the next example, variable I% would emerge from the loop containing 14. In the third example, variable THETA would emerge from the loop containing the numerical equivalent of $11\pi/6$ (*i.e.* $3\pi/2 + \pi/3$)

- once a FOR..NEXT loop has been entered, changes to the range have no effect on the number of times the loop is executed; the range is "frozen" on entry:

```
LET A=1:   B=3:   C=1
FOR K= A TO B STEP C     range frozen at 1 TO 3 STEP 1
   LET A=0
   LET B=99              changes
   LET C=-100            to range
   PRINT "*"
NEXT K
PRINT A,B,C,K
```
⇨
```
*
*
*
0  99  -100  4
```

- it is *allowable* to jump out of a FOR..NEXT loop, but there is a limit of 10 to the number of times it can be done without jumping back.

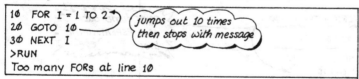

```
10  FOR I = 1 TO 2      jumps out 10 times
20  GOTO 10             then stops with message
30  NEXT I
>RUN
Too many FORs at line 10
```

- it is bad practice to tinker with the looping variable

```
FOR I = 1 TO 2
   PRINT "*" : I=I-1     program stuck in
NEXT I                   this loop forever
```

- a loop containing IF may not have NEXT on the same line

```
FOR I=1 TO 2 : IF I=1 PRINT "*" : NEXT I    fails
```

- it is more efficient to control a loop with an integer variable (*e.g.* I%) than with a real variable (*e.g.* I).

REPEAT · UNTIL

These keywords are for constructing the loop depicted on page 57. Every REPEAT should have precisely one matching UNTIL.

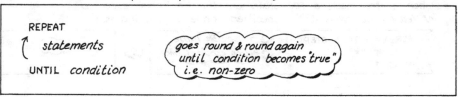

```
     REPEAT
        statements
     UNTIL  condition
```

goes round & round again until condition becomes "true" i.e. non-zero

The example below illustrates a REPEAT..UNTIL loop which is to be executed three times. In such circumstances it is simpler to employ a FOR..NEXT loop than a REPEAT..UNTIL loop.

```
LET BAH = Ø
REPEAT
   PRINT "We wish you a merry Christmas"
   BAH = BAH + 1
UNTIL  BAH = 3
```

Proper use of the REPEAT..UNTIL loop is illustrated opposite.

The next example illustrates an infinite loop

```
REPEAT
   PRINT "*";
UNTIL FALSE
```

condition can never be true

It is a mistake (when writing in BBC·BASIC) to jump out of a REPEAT..UNTIL loop unless you jump back in again without having executed any other control statements. The following innocent-looking "while" loop is *wrong*.

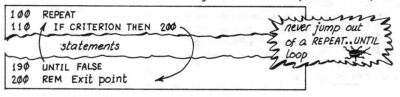

```
100   REPEAT
110   IF CRITERION THEN 200
         statements
190   UNTIL FALSE
200   REM Exit point
```

never jump out of a REPEAT..UNTIL loop

The desired effect of a "while" loop may be properly achieved only by using GOTO as already described but shown again below for completeness:

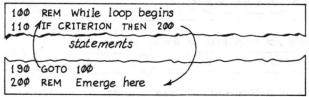

```
100   REM While loop begins
110   IF CRITERION THEN 200
         statements
190   GOTO 100
200   REM  Emerge here
```

RATE OF INTEREST

The program on page 17 computes the monthly repayment, M, of a mortgage loan of S at P per cent compound interest over N years. But here is a more difficult problem: a loan of S is to be repaid at M per month over N years; what rate of interest is being charged?

$$M = \frac{SR(1+R)^N}{12\left[(1+R)^N - 1\right]}$$

where $R = P \div 100$

The obvious approach is to try turning the equation round so that R is alone on the left-hand side. It can't be done.

But the equation can be solved by trial and error. Guess R; substitute in the formula and compute M1. If M1 is the same as the given value of M then the guess was correct. If M1 is too small it means that R was guessed too low; so multiply R by M/M1 to make it bigger and try again. Conversely, if M1 is too big it means that R was guessed too high; so multiply R by M/M1 to make it smaller and try again. In other words if M1 is not very close to M then multiply R by M/M1 and try again. Sooner or later it will get close enough to be acceptable as a solution to the equation.

This method works for well-behaved relationships in which an increase in one thing implies an increase in another. The method fails if the other fluctuates or there is a discontinuity such as a bankrupt mortgagee.

Here is the program:

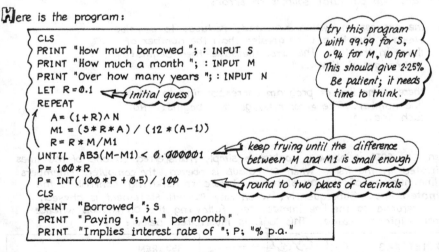

```
CLS
PRINT "How much borrowed "; : INPUT S
PRINT "How much a month "; : INPUT M
PRINT "Over how many years "; : INPUT N
LET R = 0.1          <- initial guess
REPEAT
   A = (1+R)^N
   M1 = (S*R*A) / (12*(A-1))
   R = R*M/M1
UNTIL ABS(M-M1) < 0.000001       keep trying until the difference
                                 between M and M1 is small enough
P = 100*R
P = INT(100*P + 0.5) / 100       round to two places of decimals
CLS
PRINT "Borrowed "; S
PRINT "Paying "; M; " per month"
PRINT "Implies interest rate of "; P; "% p.a."
```

try this program with 99.99 for S, 0.94 for M, 10 for N. This should give 2.25% Be patient; it needs time to think.

The ABS() function returns the absolute value of its argument. Thus ABS(0.005) and ABS(-0.005) both return 0.005.

To understand the rounding process, assume P works out at 3.45678. Then 100*P would be 345.678. Adding 0.5 gives 346.178. Taking the integral part gives 346. Dividing by 100 gives 3.46, which is the rounded value of 3.45678 to two decimal places.

THE ON STATEMENT

Apart from the use of ON to transfer control as described on this page, BBC-BASIC has the ON ERROR statement. The ON ERROR statement is defined separately on page 156.

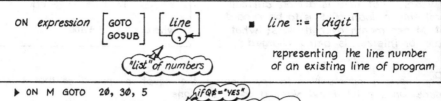

ON *expression* [GOTO / GOSUB] [*line* / ,]   ■ *line* ::= [*digit*]

"list" of numbers

representing the line number of an existing line of program

▶ ON M GOTO 2∅, 3∅, 5   *if Q$ = "YES"*
▶ ON (Q$ = "YES")+2 GOSUB 3∅∅, 2∅∅   *if Q$ ≠ "YES"*

When the ON statement is obeyed, the *expression* is evaluated. The resulting value is truncated, if necessary, to the nearest integer. If this integer is *unity*, control jumps to the line nominated *first*; if the integer is *two*, control jumps to the line nominated *second*, and so on.

For example, with ON M GOTO 2∅, 3∅, 5   if the value stored in M is 1 then control jumps to line 2∅; if the value in M is 2 then control jumps to line 3∅; if the value in M is 3 then control jumps to line 5.

There are two potential sources of error:

- the expression, when evaluated, reduces to a value which is less than 1 or greater than the number of items in the list. The error message then begins: "ON range at line ... "

- there is no line of program corresponding to a listed line number. The error message then begins: " No such line ... "

When ON..GOTO is obeyed, control is simply transferred to one of the lines nominated in the list. When ON..GOSUB is obeyed, the computer remembers the line number of the ON statement before transferring control to the nominated line. Subsequently, when any RETURN statement is obeyed, control returns to the line immediately following the ON..GOSUB whence control originally came. This logic is illustrated below:

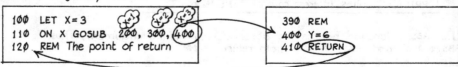

```
1∅∅  LET X = 3
11∅  ON X GOSUB  2∅∅, 3∅∅, 4∅∅
12∅  REM The point of return
```

```
39∅  REM
4∅∅  Y = 6
41∅  RETURN
```

The RENUMBER facility may be used, the integrity of line numbers being automatically preserved during the process.

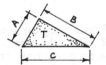

SHAPES AGAIN

AN EXAMPLE TO ILLUSTRATE
ON..GOTO AND ON..GOSUB

The program on page 20 illustrates control using IF and GOTO. Here is the same problem solved using ON..GOSUB and ON..GOTO.

After typing RUN and pressing RETURN the user of the program is invited to enter R (for a rectangle), T (for a triangle), or C (for a circle). The user is then asked for dimensions relevant to the shape selected. Finally the program prints the area of the shape.

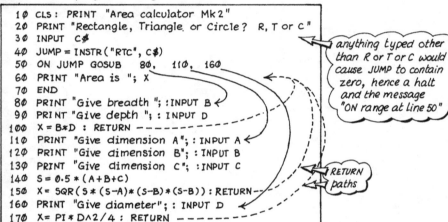

Here is the program using ON..GOSUB

```
10 CLS : PRINT "Area calculator Mk 2"
20 PRINT "Rectangle, Triangle or Circle? R, T or C"
30 INPUT C$
40 JUMP = INSTR ("RTC", C$)
50 ON JUMP GOSUB  80,  110,  160
60 PRINT "Area is "; X
70 END
80 PRINT "Give breadth "; : INPUT B
90 PRINT "Give depth "; : INPUT D
100 X = B*D : RETURN
110 PRINT "Give dimension A"; : INPUT A
120 PRINT "Give dimension B"; : INPUT B
130 PRINT "Give dimension C"; : INPUT C
140 S = 0.5 * (A+B+C)
150 X = SQR (S * (S-A)*(S-B)*(S-B)) : RETURN
160 PRINT "Give diameter"; : INPUT D
170 X = PI * D^2/4 : RETURN
```

anything typed other than R or T or C would cause JUMP to contain zero, hence a halt and the message "ON range at line 50"

RETURN paths

Here it is using ON..GOTO

```
10 CLS: PRINT "Area calculator Mk 3"
20 PRINT "Rectangle, Triangle or Circle? R,T or C "
30 INPUT C$
40 JUMP = INSTR ("RTC", C$)
50 ON JUMP GOTO  60,  90,  140
60 PRINT "Give breadth "; : INPUT B
70 PRINT "Give depth "; : INPUT D
80 X = B*D :  GOTO 160
90 PRINT "Give dimension A "; : INPUT A
100 PRINT "Give dimension B "; : INPUT B
110 PRINT "Give dimension C "; : INPUT C
120 S = 0.5 * (A+B+C)
130 X = SQR (S*(S-A)*(S-B)*(S-C)): GOTO 160
140 PRINT "Give diameter "; : INPUT D
150 X = PI * D^2/4
160 PRINT "Area is "; X
170 END
```

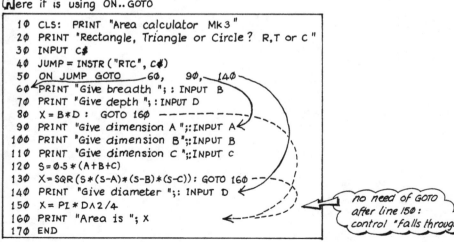

no need of GOTO after line 150: control "falls through"

65

EXERCISES

1. Implement the Rate of Interest program.

2. Write a program to discover how long it would take to repay a given sum of money. Use the formula on page 63; given S, M and P% compute N.

3. Implement either of the Shapes programs on page 65. Modify the program so that it offers to compute the area of another shape each time an area has been printed. Make the program recognize S (for Stop) as well as R, T and C.

7

ARRAYS

ARRAYS

ARRAYS OF ELEMENTS, EACH OF WHICH BEHAVES LIKE A VARIABLE

Recall that a variable is a named box which can store a single value. The type of value it stores is signified by the name of the box: the name ends with % if the type of value is *integer*, ends with $ if the type is *string*, has no special ending if the type is *real*.

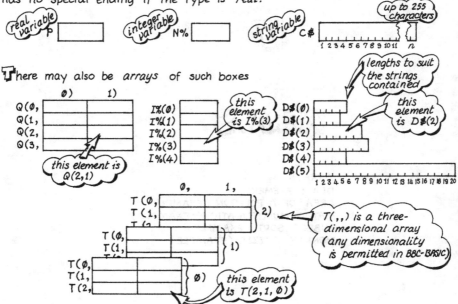

real variable P

integer variable N%

string variable C$ up to 255 characters
1 2 3 4 5 6 7 8 9 10 11   n

There may also be *arrays* of such boxes

Q(∅,   1)
Q(∅,
Q(1,
Q(2,
Q(3,
this element is Q(2,1)

I%(∅)
I%(1)
I%(2)
I%(3)   this element is I%(3)
I%(4)

lengths to suit the strings contained

D$(∅)
D$(1)
D$(2)   this element is D$(2)
D$(3)
D$(4)
D$(5)
1 2 3 4 5 6 7 8 9 10 11 12 13 14 15 16 17 18 19 20

∅,   1,
T(∅,
T(1,
T(2   } 2)

T(∅,
T(1,
T(2   } 1)

T(∅,
T(1,
T(2,   } ∅)
this element is T(2,1,∅)

T(,,) is a three-dimensional array (any dimensionality is permitted in BBC-BASIC)

The names P, N%, C$ are names of *variables*; Q, I%, D$, T are names of *arrays*. The suffix % or $ to the name of an array signifies *type* in the same way as for variables.

The terms Q(2,1), T(2,1,∅), I%(3), D$(2) identify *array elements* in the same way as P, N%, G$ identify *variables*. In many circumstances array elements may be used just as though they were variables:

```
LET  N% = 6  :  LET  I%(3) = 6
PRINT   N% ,  I%(3)
INPUT   P  :  INPUT  T(2,1,∅)
```
illustrating array elements used as though they were simple variables

Arrays are said to be one-dimensional, two-dimensional etc. as the above pictures suggest. The *dimensionality* of an array is the number of subscripts needed to refer to a single element thereof.

The term "dimension" ⇌ in the context of arrays ⇌ means the value of the largest subscript allowed in a particular position, not the number of rows or columns. Thus the array Q(,) shown above, which has 4 rows and 2 columns, has *dimensions* 3 and 1 respectively.

Arrays of any type, dimensionality and dimensions may be created using the DIM statement defined opposite.

DIM

An array does not exist until an appropriate DIM statement has been obeyed.

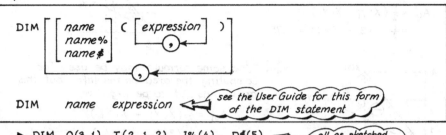

```
DIM  [ [ name   ( [ expression ]  )
         name%
         name$ ]
                    ( , )
```

DIM   name   expression ◄ *see the User Guide for this form of the DIM statement*

▶ DIM Q(3,1), T(2,1,2), I%(4), D$(5) ◄ *all as sketched on opposite page*

The effect of a DIM statement is to create arrays with the given names, dimensionalities and types. A further effect is to set all elements of the nominated numerical arrays to zero and of string arrays to *null* strings (*i.e.* strings of zero length).

Readers familiar with other computer languages should notice that the DIM statement in BBC-BASIC is *executable*. It is possible to re-dimension an array by a second DIM statement but doing so causes all elements of the re-dimensioned array to be set to zero or null in the process.

```
DIM  D$(5): LET D$(5)= "I exist"
DIM  D$(6): PRINT D$(5)
```
⇨   ◄ *prints null*

Once an array has been created its elements may be used in the same manner as variables. There would be no merit in doing this but for a vital facility:

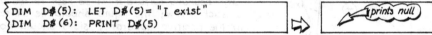

THE SUBSCRIPTS (*truncated to integer if non-integral*) **MAY BE VARIABLES AND EXPRESSIONS**

So it is easy to input and store a column of five (say) numbers ⇨

```
PRINT "How many integers?"
INPUT N
DIM I%(N)
FOR ROW= 1 TO N
  PRINT "Next integer please"
  INPUT I%(ROW)
NEXT ROW
PRINT N;" integers stored"
```

```
DIM I%(4)
FOR ROW= 0 TO 4
  PRINT "Next integer please"
  INPUT I%(ROW)
NEXT ROW
PRINT "Five integers stored"
```

◄ **I**t is usually more comprehensible to ignore the zeroth element and run subscripts from 1.

Here is a routine for seeking and printing the maximum and minimum of the integers stored by the second of the two programs above ⇨

```
LET MIN%=I%(1): MAX%=I%(1)
FOR ROW= 2 TO N
  IF I%(ROW)>MAX% THEN MAX%= I%(ROW)
  IF I%(ROW)< MIN% THEN MIN%= I%(ROW)
NEXT ROW
PRINT "Max= "; MAX%;" Min= "; MIN%
```

AREA OF A POLYGON

Consider the diagram on the right : ➡
The spotted area is given by A_{ij} where

$$A_{ij} = \tfrac{1}{2}(X_i Y_j - X_j Y_i)$$
$$= \tfrac{1}{2}(2 \times 3 - 2.5 \times 1) = 1.75$$

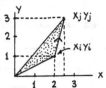

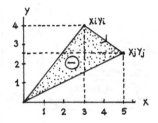

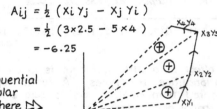

◄ The same formula may be used for computing the area on the left. But this area turns out to be *negative*:

$$A_{ij} = \tfrac{1}{2}(X_i Y_j - X_j Y_i)$$
$$= \tfrac{1}{2}(3 \times 2.5 - 5 \times 4)$$
$$= -6.25$$

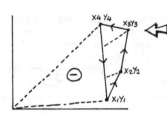

The formula may be applied to sequential sides of a polygon and the triangular areas summed to give the area shown here ➡

But if the polygon is *closed*, as shown on the left, the sum of the areas will be the area enclosed.

The bounded surface must be kept to the *left* of each arrow; the figure should lie entirely in the positive quadrant; sides should not cross as in a figure of eight.

Here is a program by which to input coordinates of boundary points and compute the area enclosed:

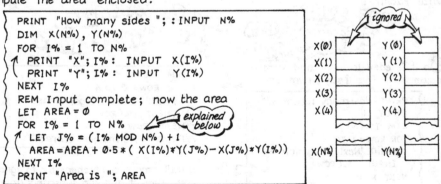

```
PRINT "How many sides ";:INPUT N%
DIM X(N%), Y(N%)
FOR I% = 1 TO N%
  PRINT "X";I%: INPUT X(I%)
  PRINT "Y";I%: INPUT Y(I%)
NEXT I%
REM Input complete; now the area
LET AREA = 0
FOR I% = 1 TO N%
  LET J% = (I% MOD N%)+1
  AREA = AREA + 0.5*( X(I%)*Y(J%) - X(J%)*Y(I%))
NEXT I%
PRINT "Area is "; AREA
```

Variable I% points to the pair of coordinates at the *tail* of the arrow; variable J% points to the *head* of the arrow. Thus J% is (I%+1) except when I% is pointing to the final pair of coordinates; then J% must revert to 1 so as to close the polygon. That is why J% is made (I% MOD N%)+1 instead of I%+1.

There is scope for improving this program with graphical display.

MATRIX MULTIPLICATION
NON-MATHEMATICIANS DON'T GO AWAY!

There are 3 salespeople each selling 4 products; their weekly achievement is tabulated like this

SALES PERSON	PRODUCT			
	PASTES	BRUSHES	FLOSS	PICKS
ATKINS	5	2	0	10
BLIMP	3	5	2	5
CALEY	20	0	0	0

WEEKLY SALES: FORM A(3,4)

The list of prices and sales commissions (in money, not as a percentage) is tabulated like this

PRICE LIST : FORM B(4,2)

PRODUCT	PRICE	COMMISSION
PASTES	1.50	0.20
BRUSHES	2.80	0.40
FLOSS	5.00	1.00
PICKS	2.00	0.50

So the money brought in is as follows:

ATKINS	$5 * 1.50 +$	$2 * 2.80 +$	$0 * 5.00 +$	$10 * 2.00 =$	33.10
BLIMP	$3 * 1.50 +$	$5 * 2.80 +$	$2 * 5.00 +$	$5 * 2.00 =$	38.50
CALEY	$20 * 1.50 +$	$0 * 2.80 +$	$0 * 5.00 +$	$0 * 2.00 =$	30.00

And the commissions earned are:

ATKINS	$5 * 0.20 +$	$2 * 0.40 +$	$0 * 1.00 +$	$10 * 0.50 =$	6.80
BLIMP	$3 * 0.20 +$	$5 * 0.40 +$	$2 * 1.00 +$	$5 * 0.50 =$	7.10
CALEY	$20 * 0.20 +$	$0 * 0.40 +$	$0 * 1.00 +$	$0 * 0.50 =$	4.00

To put this problem on the computer, employ two two-dimensional arrays for the data and one for the results:

$$A(1, \begin{matrix} 1) & 2) & 3) & 4) \\ 5 & 2 & 0 & 10 \\ 3 & 5 & 2 & 5 \\ 20 & 0 & 0 & 0 \end{matrix} \quad B(1 \begin{matrix} 1) & 2) \\ 1.50 & 0.20 \\ 2.80 & 0.40 \\ 5.00 & 1.00 \\ 2.00 & 0.50 \end{matrix} \quad R(1 \begin{matrix} 1) & 2) \\ 33.10 & 6.80 \\ 38.50 & 7.10 \\ 30.00 & 4.00 \end{matrix}$$

The part of the program that does the arithmetic is:

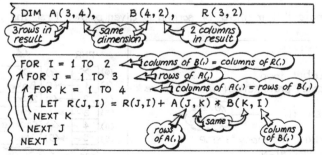

```
DIM A(3,4),      B(4,2),     R(3,2)
```
3 rows in result — same dimension — 2 columns in result

```
FOR I = 1 TO 2        columns of B(.) = columns of R(.)
  FOR J = 1 TO 3      rows of A(.)
    FOR K = 1 TO 4    columns of A(.) = rows of B(.)
      LET R(J,I) = R(J,I) + A(J,K) * B(K,I)
    NEXT K
  NEXT J
NEXT I
```
rows of A(.) — same — columns of B(.)

This operation is called "matrix multiplication". "Matrix" in this context is synonymous with "array".

71

BUBBLE SORT

Facilities yet to be revealed make sorting easier than as shown below, but the traditional bubble sort illustrates well the use of arrays and the manipulation of subscripts.

Take a list of names. Point to the first name and the one following. If the names pointed to are in the right order, leave them alone and advance the pointer one row. If they are in the wrong order swop them; then advance the pointer to the next row. Obviously this must stop before the end of the list so as to prevent the second arrow pointing off the end.

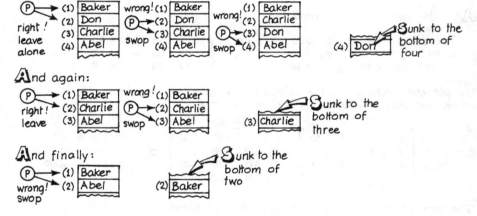

The names are not yet fully sorted. So apply the same process as before, stopping one short of the previous scan because Zebra is already in its correct position.

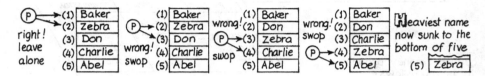

And again:

And finally:

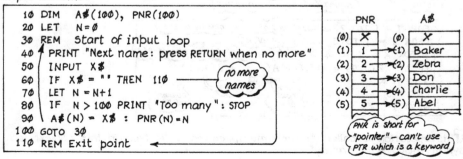

A program to automate this method of sorting is given below. First the input routine:

```
10 DIM   A$(100), PNR(100)
20 LET   N = 0
30 REM   Start of input loop
40 PRINT "Next name: press RETURN when no more."
50 INPUT X$
60 IF  X$ = "" THEN 110
70 LET  N = N+1
80 IF  N > 100 PRINT "Too many": STOP
90 A$(N) = X$ : PNR(N) = N
100 GOTO 30
110 REM Exit point
```

no more names

PNR			A$
(0)	X	(0)	X
(1)	1	(1)	Baker
(2)	2	(2)	Zebra
(3)	3	(3)	Don
(4)	4	(4)	Charlie
(5)	5	(5)	Abel

PNR is short for "pointer" – can't use PTR which is a keyword

72

The number of names to be sorted would now be contained in variable N. The vector (the usual word for one-column array) named PNR( ) is a vector of pointers into vector A$( ) as depicted opposite. Instead of swopping the names themselves we swop *pointers* to those names. This technique holds little merit in this particular example but becomes essential when sorting records each comprising name, address, profession, salary, sex, religion, hobbies, diseases and felonies. Only pointers need be moved when sorting on any one such sorting key.

The following routine employs the logic described opposite:

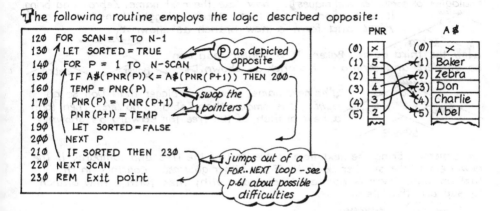

```
120  FOR SCAN = 1 TO N-1
130  LET SORTED = TRUE
140  FOR P = 1 TO N-SCAN
150  IF A$(PNR(P)) <= A$(PNR(P+1)) THEN 200
160  TEMP = PNR(P)
170  PNR(P) = PNR(P+1)
180  PNR(P+1) = TEMP
190  LET SORTED = FALSE
200  NEXT P
210  IF SORTED THEN 230
220  NEXT SCAN
230  REM Exit point
```

(P) as depicted opposite

swop the pointers

jumps out of a FOR..NEXT loop – see p.61 about possible difficulties

	PNR		A$
(0)	✕	(0)	✕
(1)	5	(1)	Baker
(2)	1	(2)	Zebra
(3)	4	(3)	Don
(4)	3	(4)	Charlie
(5)	2	(5)	Abel

The logical variable named SORTED is for efficiency. It is set *true* at the beginning of a scan but changed to *false* when a swop is made. Thus if SORTED contains *true* after a scan it means that all names are in the correct order, further scans being unnecessary.

Printing the sorted list is simple:

```
240  FOR ROW = 1 TO N
250  PRINT A$(PNR(ROW))
260  NEXT ROW
```

⇨

```
Abel
Baker
Charlie
Don
Zebra
```

Comparison of strings is explained on page 49.

The efficiency of the program could be improved by changing all real variables to integer variables and the real vector to an integer vector (e.g. change PNR to PNR% and N to N% etc.).

MONKEY PUZZLE

A "BINARY TREE" SORT, TO ILLUSTRATE ARRAYS & CONTROL

Take some names to sort:

Don, Zebra, Baker, Edward, Abel, Freddie, Charlie

Use the first name as the root of a tree (which grows upside down as do several analogies of computer techniques). Now take the next name, Zebra, and bring it to the root of the tree. Zebra is bigger than Don so go *right* and form a new branch as shown.

Now the third name, Baker. It is smaller than Don so go *left* and form a new branch as shown.

The next name, Edward, is bigger than Don so go *right*. It is smaller than Zebra so go *left*. Then form a new branch of the tree for Edward as shown.

In general: bring the next item to the root of the tree and compare. If the new item is the smaller go *left*; if the bigger go *right*. Continue in this fashion until there is no item to compare with; then form a new branch to support that item.

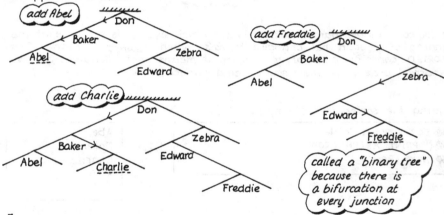

add Abel
add Freddie
add Charlie

called a "binary tree" because there is a bifurcation at every junction

At any stage the tree may be "stripped" (metaphors tend to get mixed in computer jargon) as shown below. Notice that the arrow runs through the names in alphabetical order.

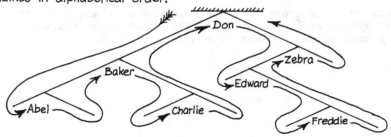

To organize this on a computer the items to be sorted are read into a vector (i.e. a one-dimensional array). Associated with each element are three *pointers*; one pointing back towards the root of the tree, one pointing left, one pointing right. Below is shown Baker with its back pointer pointing to Don, its left pointer pointing to Abel, its right pointer pointing to Charlie.

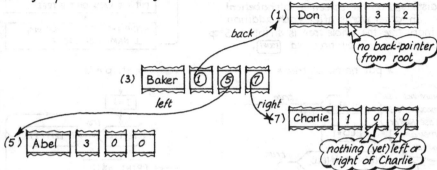

Whereas the back pointer from Abel points to Baker (following the direction of stripping) notice that the back pointer from Charlie does *not* point back to Baker, but to Don. See below. Charlie "steals" the pointer from Baker. In general: when a new item is established on the *left* branch its back-pointer is made to point straight back to the previous item. But when a new item is established on a *right* branch its back-pointer becomes a copy of the back-pointer of the previous item.

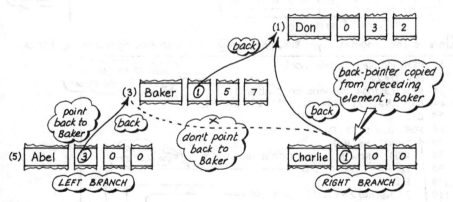

The arrays needed to store names and pointers are depicted below. The program is shown overleaf.

N$(1)	Don		BACK(1)			LEFT(1)			RIGHT(1)	
N$(2)	Zebra		BACK(2)			LEFT(2)			RIGHT(2)	
N$(3)	Baker		BACK(3)			LEFT(3)			RIGHT(3)	

etc.   etc.   etc.   etc.

MONKEY PUZZLE (CONTINUED)

The program is arranged according to the flow chart on the right. Each time you type a name, and press RETURN, all the names are displayed on the screen in alphabetical order. In other words after each addition to the binary tree the whole tree is stripped. Stop the demonstration by pressing ESCAPE.

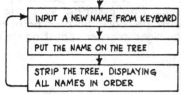

```
INPUT A NEW NAME FROM KEYBOARD

PUT THE NAME ON THE TREE

STRIP THE TREE, DISPLAYING
ALL NAMES IN ORDER
```

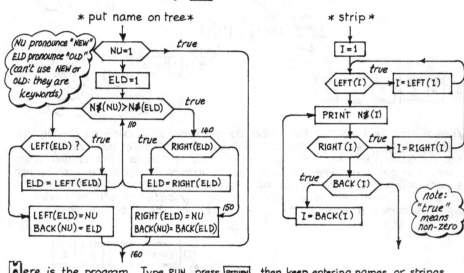

* put name on tree *

(NU pronounce "NEW"
ELD pronounce "OLD"
(can't use NEW or
OLD: they are
keywords)

NU=1 → true

ELD=1

N$(NU)>N$(ELD) → true

110

LEFT(ELD)? → true   true → RIGHT(ELD)   140

ELD=LEFT(ELD)   ELD=RIGHT(ELD)

LEFT(ELD)=NU   RIGHT(ELD)=NU   150
BACK(NU)=ELD   BACK(NU)=BACK(ELD)

160

* strip *

I=1

LEFT(I) → true → I=LEFT(I)

PRINT N$(I)

RIGHT(I) → true → I=RIGHT(I)

true → BACK(I)

I=BACK(I)

note:
"true"
means
non-zero

Here is the program. Type RUN, press RETURN, then keep entering names or strings.

```
10   REM Monkey puzzle sort
20   LET D=20                              allow 20 names so
30   REM Change dimension D at will        as to fit the screen
40   DIM N$(D), BACK(D), LEFT(D), RIGHT(D)
50   CLS
60   FOR NU = 1 TO D
70   INPUT N$(NU)
80     REM *Now put new name on tree *     GOTO 160
90     IF NU=1 GOTO 160                     on first item
100    ELD=1
110    IF N$(NU)>N$(ELD) GOTO 140
120    IF LEFT(ELD) THEN ELD=LEFT(ELD): GOTO 110
130    LEFT(ELD)=NU : BACK(NU)=ELD : GOTO 160
140    IF RIGHT(ELD) THEN ELD=RIGHT(ELD) : GOTO 110
150    RIGHT(ELD)=NU : BACK(NU)=BACK(ELD)
160    REM *Now strip*
170    I=1 : CLS
180    IF LEFT(I) THEN I=LEFT(I): GOTO 180
190    PRINT N$(I)
200    IF RIGHT(I) THEN I=RIGHT(I): GOTO 180
210    IF BACK(I) THEN I=BACK(I): GOTO 190
220  NEXT NU
```

make the program
more efficient by
changing to integer
variables
e.g. LEFT%(ELD%)
instead of
LEFT(ELD) etc.

8

FUNCTIONS AND PROCEDURES

GENERAL PRINCIPLES

A *function* called FNTH(,) is defined on page 23.

```
DEF FNTH ( F%, NTH%)
LET A% = 10 ∧ NTH%
= INT (10 * (F% − A% * INT (F% / A%))) / A%
```

which defines a function to return the N^{TH} digit 《 from the right 》 of integer F.

Such definitions may appear anywhere in a program ≈ on high- or low-numbered lines ≈ provided that the computer does not try to "obey" them as though they were assignments. The easiest way to prevent this is to group all functions and procedures after a final END statement of the main program. Another technique is to jump round them.

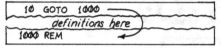

Single-line functions need no special location or treatment; they are immune from being "obeyed."

To use a function it should be *invoked* in the same manner as INT( ) or ABS( ).

IF FNTH(X%, I%) <> FNTH(Y%, J%) THEN 160   *invocation of a function*

A *procedure* called PROCLAIM is defined on page 24. Here it is again:

```
100 DEF PROCLAIM (X%, Y%)
110 LET BULLS% = 0 : COWS% = 0
120 FOR I% = 1 TO 4
130 FOR J% = 1 TO 4
140 IF FNTH (X%, I%) <> FNTH(Y%, J%) THEN 160
150 IF I% = J% THEN BULLS% = BULLS%+1 ELSE COWS% = COWS%+1
160 NEXT J%
170 NEXT I%
180 ENDPROC
```

definition of a procedure

procedure PROCLAIM invokes function FNTH (,)

The above defines a keyword, PROCLAIM, which may be used in a program as though it were just another statement of BBC-BASIC:

PROCLAIM (TARGET%, GUESS%)   *program invokes procedure PROCLAIM*

Notice how the program invokes PROCLAIM, PROCLAIM invokes FNTH, FNTH invokes INT. Procedures and functions may invoke each other indefinitely.

The ENDPROC, when a procedure is invoked, sends control back to the statement which directly follows the invocation. An equals sign in the definition of a function behaves in a similar way; when the relevant expression has been evaluated the result is handed back to the expression in the program from which the function was invoked. You can't get lost.

The syntax of statements for defining functions and procedures is set out in the following pages. The rest of this chapter explains the differences between dummy and actual arguments, deals with local variables, and introduces the concept of recursion.

DEF FN · LOCAL

The statements for defining a function are as follows:

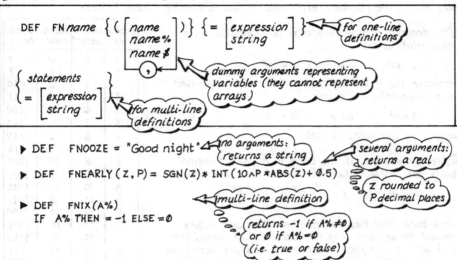

▶ DEF   FNOOZE = "Good night" *no arguments:
returns a string*

▶ DEF   FNEARLY (Z, P) = SGN(Z) * INT (10^P * ABS(Z) + 0.5) *several arguments:
returns a real*

*Z rounded to
P decimal places*

▶ DEF   FNIX (A%)
IF A% THEN = −1 ELSE = 0 *multi-line definition*

*returns −1 if A% ≠ 0
or 0 if A% = 0
(i.e. true or false)*

Local variables, as the name suggests, are variables local to the function being defined. Any variables in the main program having names identical to those of local variables are nevertheless distinct:

DEF FNTH (F% , NTH%)
LOCAL A%
LET A% = 10 ∧ NTH
= INT (10 * (F% − A% * INT (F%/A%)) / A%

*no connection with any A%
which might be in main program*

The statement for declaring local variables is defined as follows:

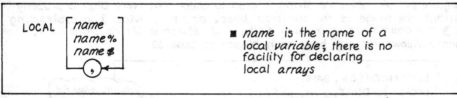

LOCAL [name
name%
name$]
(,)

■ *name* is the name of a
local *variable*; there is no
facility for declaring
local *arrays*

▶ LOCAL A%   ▶ LOCAL X, X%, A%, NAM$

Contents of all local variables evaporate on return to the invoking program.

The arrangement of statements in a multi-line function is:

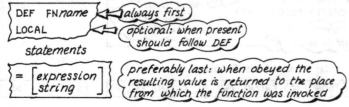

DEF FN*name* *always first*
LOCAL *optional: when present
should follow DEF*
    statements
= [expression
string] *preferably last: when obeyed the
resulting value is returned to the place
from which the function was invoked*

NUMBER BASES

There is nothing special about *ten*; numbers can be expressed in other bases. Here are some numbers expressed in four commonly used bases:

The decimal number 906 may be expressed as a polynomial in ten:

$$9 \times 10^2 \;+\; 0 \times 10^1 \;+\; 6 \times 10^0$$

Similarly the octal number 767 may be expressed as a polynomial in eight:

$$7 \times 8^2 \;+\; 6 \times 8^1 \;+\; 7 \times 8^0$$

which, in decimal, is 503.

More generally: if the base is b, and the final digits are $\phi\psi\omega$, then the number may be expressed:

$$\ldots \phi \times b^2 \;+\; \psi \times b^1 \;+\; \omega \times b^0$$

The base specifies the number of unique digits needed to express any number to that base. The digit with the biggest value is always one less than the base itself. For example, the ten digits 0 to 9 for base 10; the eight digits 0 to 7 for base 8.

Bigger bases than 10 need digits for values beyond 9, so letters A, B, C,... are pressed into service as digits as shown in the *hex* column.

base 16 hex	base 10 decimal	base 8 octal	base 2 binary
0	0	0	0
1	1	1	1
2	2	2	10
3	3	3	11
4	4	4	100
5	5	5	101
6	6	6	110
7	7	7	111
8	8	10	1000
9	9	11	1001
A	10	12	1010
B	11	13	1011
C	12	14	1100
D	13	15	1101
E	14	16	1110
F	15	17	1111
10	16	20	10000
11	17	21	10001
12	18	22	10010
13	19	23	10011
14	20	24	10100
15	21	25	10101
16	22	26	10110
17	23	27	10111

etc.

Given a string as the first argument; a base expressed in decimal as the second argument; here is a function to return the decimal value of the first argument. A *reference* string is used to check that every digit is properly within the range of the specified base, and to provide (on subtracting 1) the decimal value of each digit. The reference string stops at V, hence allows for any base from binary to base 32.

```
DEF  FNTEN ( S$ , BASE)
LOCAL  I, DIGIT, SUM, REF$, L
REF$ = "0123456789ABCDEFGHIJKLMNOPQRSTUV"      doesn't allow for
LET  SUM=0  : L= LEN( S$)                        + or − in front
FOR  I = 1 TO L                                  of number
   DIGIT = −1 + INSTR(LEFT$(REF$, BASE), MID$(S$,I,1))
   IF DIGIT < 0  THEN  = −1          not in range
   SUM = SUM + DIGIT * BASE ∧ (L−I)  of base : return
NEXT I          = expression         value of −1
= SUM           last to be obeyed
```

This function could be invoked as follows:

```
PRINT  FNTEN( "906", 10), FNTEN("767",8), FNTEN( "FF",16)        906  503  255
```

80

The function opposite is for finding the *decimal* value of a number given its base. What about converting a decimal number to a different base? Say binary or hex?

Take the decimal number 4397 and convert to *hex*. To do so, keep dividing by the base, 16, and noting the remainders:

```
16) 4 3 9 7
   16) 2 7 4   remainder 13 (i.e. D)       Read the result upwards
     16) 1 7    remainder  2                along the remainders:
       16) 1    remainder  1
           0    remainder  1                112 D
```

Here is a function to return a string representing a positive decimal argument to a new base. The first argument is the decimal number; the second is the new base expressed in decimal. The same reference string is used as in the function defined opposite.

```
DEF FNEWBAS ( DECNO, BASE )
LOCAL  A$, REF$, I
REF$ = "0123456789ABCDEFGHIJKLMNOPQRSTUV"
LET  A$ = ""        null
REPEAT
  A$ = MID$ ( REF$, 1 + ( DECNO MOD BASE), 1 ) + A$
  DECNO = DECNO DIV BASE
UNTIL  DECNO = 0
= A$
```

This function could be invoked as follows:

```
PRINT FNEWBAS (906,10), FNEWBAS(503,8), FNEWBAS(255,16)   ⇨   906 767 FF
```

To convert a number from one non-decimal base to another it is easiest to go via decimal representation using both the functions defined above. It is easiest because the standard arithmetic of BBC-BASIC is decimal arithmetic. Here is the generalized function:

```
DEF FNXBAS ( STRNG$, FROM, UNTO )
LOCAL  TEMPRY
LET TEMPRY = FNTEN ( STRNG$, FROM )     null
IF TEMPRY < 0 OR UNTO > 32 THEN = ""
= FNEWBAS ( TEMPRY, UNTO )
```

This generalized function could be invoked as follows:

```
PRINT  FNXBAS ( "FF", 16, 8 )               377
PRINT  FNXBAS ( "111111", 2, 8 )       ⇨    77
PRINT  FNXBAS ( "111111", 2, 10 )           63
```

where the first example converts FF from hex to octal; the second converts 111111 from binary to octal; the third converts 111111 from binary to decimal.

DEF PROC name • LOCAL • ENDPROC

The statements for defining a procedure are set out below:

```
DEF  PROC name { ( [ name    ] ) }
                   name%
                   name$
                     (,)
ENDPROC
```

dummy arguments representing variables (they cannot represent arrays)

- ▶ DEF PROCEED   ◁ *no arguments*
- ▶ DEF PROCRASTINATE (N)   ◁ *one argument*
- ▶ DEF PROCESSION (X , X%, X$)   ◁ *several arguments*

Local variables may be used in the definition of a procedure:

```
LOCAL [ name   ]
        name%
        name$
          (,)
```

■ *name* is the name of a local *variable* (there is no facility for declaring local *arrays*)

- ▶ LOCAL A%
- ▶ LOCAL Y, Y%, Y$

Any variables in the main program which have identical names to those of local variables are nevertheless distinct. The contents of all local variables evaporate on return to the invoking program.

There should be at least one ENDPROC among the statements of a procedure. When obeyed, ENDPROC sends control back to the invoking program. It makes for clarity if ENDPROC is arranged to come last. DEF PROC name always comes first. LOCAL, if used at all, should come straight after DEF PROC name.

An example of a procedure definition is:

```
DEF  PROCUP ( VERT$ )
LOCAL N
FOR N = 1 TO LEN ( VERT$ )
  PRINT MID$ ( VERT$, N, 1 )
NEXT N
ENDPROC
```

dummy argument VERT$

no connection with any N in main program

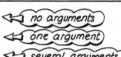

```
BROAD
T
A
L
L
```
screen

This makes PROCUP a keyword which may be invoked in much the same manner as PRINT:

```
PRINT " BROAD" : PROCUP ( "TALL")
```

Here is an example which anticipates the TIME function defined on page 97.

```
DEF  PROCRASTINATE ( N )
LOCAL T :  T = TIME
REPEAT : UNTIL TIME > T + N : ENDPROC
```

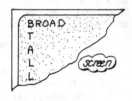

PROCRASTINATE (100) would delay 1 second – useful function for games

DUMMY versus ACTUAL ARGUMENTS

Consider the following function which returns the area of a circle given its diameter as an argument:

```
DEF FNAREA(D)
IF D<=0 THEN    =0 ELSE =PI*D*D/4          return the area
```
empty⤍ 𐒻—hole

Item D is a *name*, but not the name of a *variable*; it is the name of an empty hole. If the FNAREA() function were to be invoked as follows: /

```
LET D= -999
LET WEIGHT = 7.8 * 2500 * (FNAREA(2.5) - FNAREA(1.0))
PRINT D                                                    ⟹   -999
```

the function would not upset the value -999 stored in D which belongs to the invoking program. The name D in the function definition simply identifies an empty hole; it is a *dummy argument*. When a function is invoked, an *actual argument* is put into the empty hole and the calculation performed. In the example of invocation above, first the 2.5 is put into the empty hole; subsequently the value 1.0.

This same function may be invoked using names of variables as arguments:

```
LET  WEIGHT = DENSITY * LENGTH * (FNAREA(D1) - FNAREA(D2))
```

but this makes no difference to the concept introduced above; *values* found in the variables D1 and D2 are used in place of 2.5 and 1.0.

The actual argument supplied to a procedure or function must be of the same *type* as the corresponding dummy argument. Suppose, for example, the following introduced the definition of a procedure:

```
DEF  PROCESSION (X, X%, X$)          ⟻ dummy arguments
```

then any invocation of this procedure should specify a *real* argument followed by an *integer* argument followed by a *string* argument. All but the final example below would be correct:

```
PROCESSION ( 2.5, 7, "ME")            ⟻ actual arguments
PROCESSION ( A, B%, C$ )
PROCESSION ( A+2.5, B%+7, C$+"ME")
PROCESSION ( "ME", 2.5, 7)            ⟹  Argument⁊
```

It is not possible, in BBC-BASIC, for a function or procedure to change values of its arguments. In the jargon of computer science, arguments in BBC-BASIC are called by value, not by name. There is a further limit- ation; the name of an array is not allowed as an argument.

```
DEF  PROCSWOP (A, B)
LOCAL T:  T=A : A=B : B=T   ⟿ (WON'T WORK!)
ENDPROC
```

PROCEDURES *working on* ARRAYS

It is *not* possible in BBC-BASIC to make the name of an array an argument of a function or procedure, but it keeps a program tidy if statements which apply to an array can be parcelled up as a procedure. Here is the sorting program from page 72 re-cast as a program which invokes a procedure called PROCUBBLE(,). GOTO statements are unavoidable so line numbers must be shown.

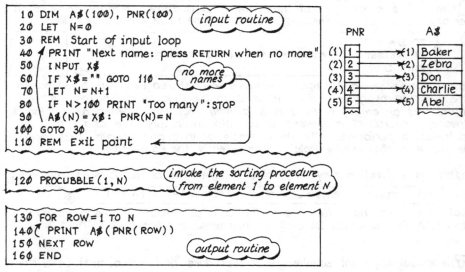

```
10 DIM A$(100), PNR(100)        input routine
20 LET  N=0
30 REM  Start of input loop
40 PRINT "Next name: press RETURN when no more"
50 INPUT X$
60 IF X$="" GOTO 110            no more names
70 LET N=N+1
80 IF N>100 PRINT "Too many":STOP
90 A$(N)=X$: PNR(N)=N
100 GOTO 30
110 REM Exit point
```

	PNR			A$
(1)	1	→	(1)	Baker
(2)	2	→	(2)	Zebra
(3)	3	→	(3)	Don
(4)	4	→	(4)	Charlie
(5)	5	→	(5)	Abel

```
120 PROCUBBLE (1, N)
```
invoke the sorting procedure from element 1 to element N

```
130 FOR ROW=1 TO N
140 PRINT A$(PNR(ROW))
150 NEXT ROW            output routine
160 END
```

Line 120 above simply nominates the procedure called PROCUBBLE. This procedure is for performing a bubble sort on array A$( ), with reference to pointers stored in array PNR( ), from element 1 as far as element N. Here is the definition of PROCUBBLE. This definition would be included as part of the program; say from line 1000 onwards.

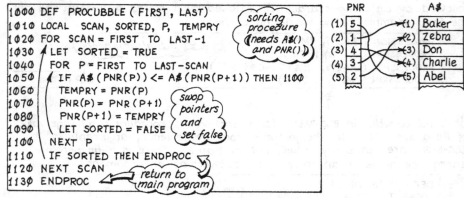

```
1000 DEF PROCUBBLE (FIRST, LAST)        sorting procedure
1010 LOCAL  SCAN, SORTED, P, TEMPRY     (needs A$() and PNR())
1020 FOR SCAN = FIRST TO LAST-1
1030 LET SORTED = TRUE
1040 FOR P = FIRST TO LAST-SCAN
1050 IF A$(PNR(P)) <= A$(PNR(P+1)) THEN 1100
1060 TEMPRY = PNR(P)
1070 PNR(P) = PNR(P+1)           swop pointers
1080 PNR(P+1) = TEMPRY           and
1090 LET SORTED = FALSE          set false
1100 NEXT P
1110 IF SORTED THEN ENDPROC
1120 NEXT SCAN
1130 ENDPROC            return to main program
```

	PNR			A$
(1)	5	→	(1)	Baker
(2)	1	→	(2)	Zebra
(3)	4	→	(3)	Don
(4)	3	→	(4)	Charlie
(5)	2	→	(5)	Abel

Notice that PROCUBBLE is not limited to sorting array A$( ) from its first element; any contiguous part of the array may be sorted.

RECURSION

Consider again the *first* scan of a bubble sort:

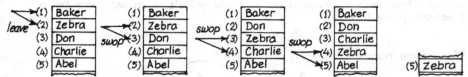

The initial scan makes the heaviest name sink to the bottom leaving those above unsorted. Begin implementing a general sorting procedure as follows:

```
1000 DEF PROCIPPLE(FIRST, LAST)
1010 LOCAL SCAN, SORTED, P, TEMPRY
1020 IF FIRST = LAST ENDPROC ←(nothing to sort)
1030 LET SORTED = TRUE
1040 FOR P = FIRST TO LAST−1
1050    IF A$(PNR(P)) <= A$(PNR(P+1)) GOTO 1100
1060      TEMPRY = PNR(P)              (swop
1070      PNR(P) = PNR(P+1)            pointers
1080      PNR(P+1) = TEMPRY            & set
1090      LET SORTED = FALSE          false)
1100 NEXT P
```

What remains to be done? Having sunk the heaviest name in a list of 5 it remains to sort all the names in a list of 5−1 = 4. In general, having sunk the heaviest name in a list from FIRST to LAST it remains to sort all the names in the list from FIRST to LAST−1. But we already have a procedure for doing this; it is called PROCIPPLE and its listing begins above. So the rest of the procedure is:

```
1110 IF NOT SORTED PROCIPPLE(FIRST, LAST−1)
1120 ENDPROC
```

It may seem strange for a procedure to invoke itself but it works. Try it by substituting PROCIPPLE for PROCUBBLE in the program opposite. The technique of self-invocation is called *recursion*.

When a procedure invokes itself it is as though the computer obeyed a *copy* of the procedure:

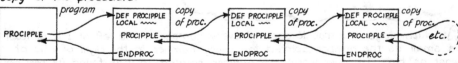

The way back is via ENDPROC statements. In this procedure the return journey would be started by either of the two ENDPROC statements in procedure PROCIPPLE.

Before the computer starts obeying each new copy it must store away the current values of arguments and local variables for possible re-use on return. This subject is enlarged upon after the next example.

QUICKSORT

The sorting method called Quicksort was devised by Prof. C.A.R. Hoare. This example has been formulated to illustrate principles rather than be a practical procedure.

Take some numbers to sort:

Set pointers I and J at each end of the list as shown. Move J towards I. If J points to a *bigger* number than I does, move J another step towards I.

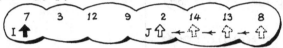

Now J points to a *smaller* number than I does. So swop the two numbers pointed to, and swop the pointers I and J as well:

Continue moving J towards I (which now means stepping rightwards instead of leftwards). If J points to a *smaller* number than I does, move J another step towards I. (Notice that the *condition* for continuing to move J towards I has been reversed.)

Now J points to a bigger number than I does. Swop numbers, pointers, direction and condition exactly as before:

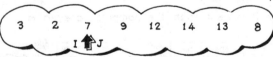

And so on, swopping if necessary (as already illustrated) until J meets I:

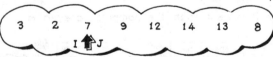

At which stage it is true to say that every number to the left of I is at least as small as the number pointed to; every number to the right of I is at least as big. In other words the number pointed to has found its resting place. The numbers to the left of I have not, however, been sorted; nor have those to the right of I. But, having described a procedure for locating a resting place which splits a group into two, it remains only to sort the groups to the left and right of I, starting out in each case as already described in detail above.

The logic is depicted below:

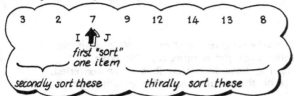

Recursion is applicable when a problem can be reduced to an identical problem ≈ or identical problems ≈ of smaller size. The recursive procedure must, of course, have an ENDPROC statement to be obeyed when the size of problem has been reduced enough. In the case of sorting this should be when the procedure is called upon to sort a single item.

Here is a Quicksort procedure that may be used in place of PROCUBBLE(,) or PROCIPPLE(,) to sort the names stored in A$( ):

```
1000 DEF PROCWIKSOT (FIRST, LAST)
1010 LOCAL I, J, T, JSTEP, CONDITION         ← nothing to sort
1020 IF LAST <= FIRST ENDPROC
1030 LET I = FIRST : J = LAST : JSTEP=-1 : CONDITION=TRUE
1040 REPEAT
1050    IF (A$(PNR(I)) <= A$(PNR(J))) = CONDITION THEN 1100
1060    T = PNR(I) : PNR(I) = PNR(J): PNR(J)=T  ← effectively swop items
1070    T = I : I = J : J = T              ← swop pointers
1080    LET JSTEP = -JSTEP                  ← reverse direction
1090    LET CONDITION = NOT CONDITION       ← reverse condition
1100    LET J = J + JSTEP
1110 UNTIL J = I
1120 PROCWIKSOT (FIRST, I-1)      ← recursive
1130 PROCWIKSOT (I+1, LAST)       ← invocations
1140 ENDPROC
```

Notice how the condition is switched between > and <= . The logical expression A$(PNR(I)) <= A$(PNR(I+1)) takes the value *true* or *false*. This logical value is compared with the value stored in the variable CONDITION which is made alternately *true* and *false* by the prefix NOT.

Every time PROCWIKSOT invokes itself the computer has to store away the values of arguments for possible re-use on return. A hackneyed example of recursion illustrates this well:

```
DEF FNACTORIAL (N)
IF N=1 THEN =1 ELSE =N*FNACTORIAL (N-1)
```
← "factorial" N!

With FNACTORIAL(4) the function says compute 4 * FNACTORIAL(3). So before invoking itself as FNACTORIAL(3) the computer must store away the 4 for use when control returns with 6 (which is the value of FNACTORIAL(3)) and so on.

The same applies to LOCAL variables; they are stored away on each invocation. Memory soon fills up. To sort long arrays using PROCWIKSOT (,) it might be necessary to remove T, JSTEP and CONDITION from the LOCAL statement ≈ but not, of course, I or J.

EXERCISES

1. Implement the three number-base functions. Write a simple program which asks the user for a number, the base in which it is expressed, the base to which it is to be converted. The program should print the result and offer another go.

2. Implement Area of a Polygon on page 70. Turn the program into a function; say FNPOLYGON(NSIDES). Then write a program to invoke the function.

3. Convert Matrix Multiplication into a procedure working always on the arrays A(,), B(,), R(,) but having dimensions as arguments. For example, begin:

   DEF PROCMATMUL(COLSA , ROWSB , COLSB)

4. If you are familiar with matrices write useful procedures for other matrix operations besides multiplication. For example: addition, scalar multiplication, transposition, translation, inversion.

5. Convert Monkey Puzzle into a procedure. When familiar with the algorithm you will notice that each element needs either a back pointer or a right pointer but not both. Therefore you can get by with two arrays of pointers instead of three. Back pointers and right pointers may be made to share the same array provided that one kind of pointer may be distinguished from the other. This distinction is easily achieved by making the back pointers negative or by adding 1 million as an offset. Modify your procedure to take advantage of these ideas.

6. Implement Quicksort and write a simple program to drive it.

9

INPUT AND OUTPUT

PRINT STATEMENT

AND THE HORRORS OF PUNCTUATION

The PRINT statement was used in earlier examples without formal definition. Here it is defined:

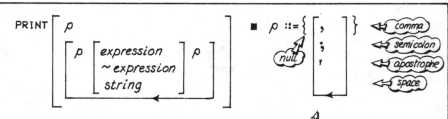

- p stands for punctuation as defined here ⤵
- ~ denotes *hex* notation and says "Print in hex"

▶ PRINT ⟵ start a new line
▶ PRINT X,Y,Z ⟵ print in separate "fields"
▶ PRINT X;Y;Z ⟵ print without separation
▶ PRINT X'Y'Z ⟵ print on separate lines

The rules of punctuation are described in detail below.

The screen is considered divided into fields, each of ten character positions. ⟨ Field width may be altered by setting the special variable @% as explained on page 94. ⟩

, *expression*
, ~*expression*

causes the value of the expression to be *right* justified in the next empty field. The ~ sign ⟨ displayed as ÷ in mode 7 ⟩ denotes *hex* notation

```
PRINT 3*5, -3*5, 9
PRINT ~3*5, ~9
```

⇨ | | 15 | -15 | 9 |
  | | F | 9 | |
  0   9   19   29

, *string*

causes the string to be *left* justified in the next empty field

```
PRINT "A", "B", "C"
```

⇨ | A | B | C |
  0   9   19   next empty field

A string may be wider than a single field:

```
PRINT "A","BEANSTALKER", "C"
```

⇨ | A | BEANSTALKER | C |
  0   9   19   29

Notice the effect of commas when a string follows a number and vice versa.

```
PRINT 5, "A", "B"
PRINT "A", 5, "B"
```

⇨ | | 5 A | B |
  | A | | 5 B |
  0   9   19   29

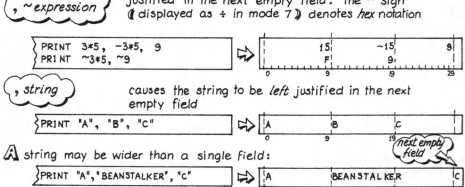
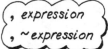

90

(''') one or more apostrophes signifies one new line for each apostrophe:

```
PRINT  6.5 ' ' "A"
```
new line   *new line*   *blank line*

	6.5	
A		

(; expression / ; string) ; causes the expression or string to be printed without leading spaces ≈ in other words right up against the previous item:

```
PRINT  6.5; 7.5; -8.5
PRINT  "A"; "B" ; "C"
PRINT  6.5; "B" ; -8.5
```

	6.5|7.5-8.5	
ABC		
	6.5|B-8.5	

(space or null) in general, space or null in front of an *expression* implies a *comma*:

```
LET  X=-8.5
PRINT  6.5  7.5 X
```

	6.5	7.5	-8.5

and, in general, space or null in front of a *string* implies a *semicolon*:

```
LET  Y$ = "C"
PRINT  "A"  "B" Y$
```

A BC		

WARNINGS + ODDITIES

A *null* between two quotations (e.g. between "A" and "B") makes the pair of strings represent a single string containing a single quote:

```
PRINT "A""B"
```

A"B		

A *space* or *null* between a string and an expression may imply a "displaced field" as illustrated here: *null or space*   *field width*

```
PRINT  "WOT" + "SIT" 4
```

WOTSIT	4	

However, a semicolon lurking anywhere to the left of the divide causes the gap to close:

```
PRINT  "WOT"; "SIT" 4
```
lurking   *null or space*

WOTSIT4		

so do not rely on implications of omission; punctuate explicitly.

A group of semicolons implies a single semicolon; likewise a group of commas implies a single comma:

```
PRINT "A",,,,"B"
```
ignored

A	B	*B should be here*

A comma at the end of a list is ignored (but a semicolon is honoured).

```
PRINT "A",
PRINT "B"
```
ignored

A	*B should be here*
B	

NEVER mix commas and semicolons (e.g. "A",;;;"B"). Results are unpredictable.

91

# PRINT~LIST FUNCTIONS
SPC( ), TAB( )
TAB(,)

There are three functions which may be used only in a PRINT list. These functions are defined below. Arguments are all *expressions*; the resulting value is automatically truncated to an integer if non-integral *e.g.* SPC(3.9) is treated as SPC(3).

SPC (expression) PRINT THE GIVEN NUMBER OF SPACES

```
PRINT "A"; SPC(5); "B"; SPC(5); 6.5
```
(N.B.) (N.B.) (N.B.) (N.B.)

⇨ | A | B | |6.5

Semicolons are shown separating SPC(5) from the strings and expressions to be printed. No other punctuation is recommended. SPC(5) has precisely the same effect as a string consisting of 5 spaces:

```
LET  S$ = "      "     (5 spaces)
PRINT "A"; S$; "B"; S$; 6.5
```
⇨ (precisely as above) A   B   6.5

Because SPC(5) has the same effect as S$ the warning given earlier about punctuation between strings and expressions applies also to SPC( ). The WOTSIT4 problem applies here too:

```
PRINT "WOT" + "SIT"  SPC(1) 4
PRINT "WOT" ; "SIT"  SPC(1) 4
```
⇨
```
WOTSIT      4
WOTSIT 4
```

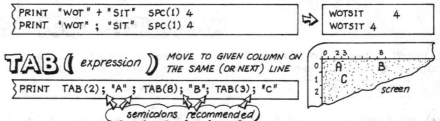

TAB (expression) MOVE TO GIVEN COLUMN ON THE SAME (OR NEXT) LINE

```
PRINT  TAB(2); "A" ; TAB(8); "B"; TAB(3); "C"
```
(semicolons recommended)

Columns and rows are numbered from zero as illustrated. If printing has already passed the nominated column then the subsequent item is printed in the nominated column on the *next line* as illustrated above.

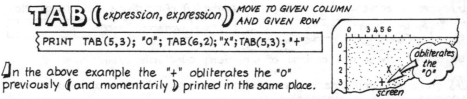

TAB (expression, expression) MOVE TO GIVEN COLUMN AND GIVEN ROW

```
PRINT  TAB(5,3); "O"; TAB(6,2); "X"; TAB(5,3); "+"
```

In the above example the "+" obliterates the "O" previously (and momentarily) printed in the same place.

Never use both TAB( ) and TAB(,) in the same piece of program; one messes up the other. The problem can be avoided by employing TAB(X,VPOS) in place of TAB(X). VPOS (which returns the Vertical POSition of the cursor) is explained opposite.

Punctuation on either side of TAB( ) or TAB(,) may be semicolon, colon, space or null ⇌ the function is not sensitive to punctuation. However, the semicolon is recommended for the sake of consistency. The semicolon says "No spaces for me!"

FIND THE CURSOR
FUNCTIONS POS, VPOS AND COUNT

The cursor belongs to the screen; it jumps automatically to the next row if the contents of a PRINT list overflow the current row of the screen. So it is not a trivial matter for the programmer to keep track of the cursor's position.   These functions help.

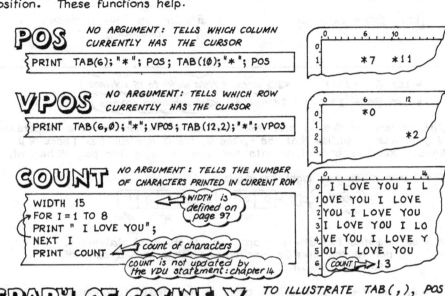

POS
NO ARGUMENT: TELLS WHICH COLUMN CURRENTLY HAS THE CURSOR

```
PRINT TAB(6); "*"; POS; TAB(10);"*"; POS
```

VPOS
NO ARGUMENT: TELLS WHICH ROW CURRENTLY HAS THE CURSOR

```
PRINT TAB(6,0); "*"; VPOS; TAB(12,2);"*"; VPOS
```

COUNT
NO ARGUMENT: TELLS THE NUMBER OF CHARACTERS PRINTED IN CURRENT ROW

```
WIDTH 15
FOR I=1 TO 8
PRINT " I LOVE YOU";
NEXT I
PRINT COUNT
```
WIDTH is defined on page 97

count of characters

COUNT is not updated by the VDU statement: chapter 14

GRAPH OF COSINE X
TO ILLUSTRATE TAB(,), POS AND VPOS

The following program plots the graph of cosine X for angles of 0° by increments of 15° to 165° (enough for one screen).

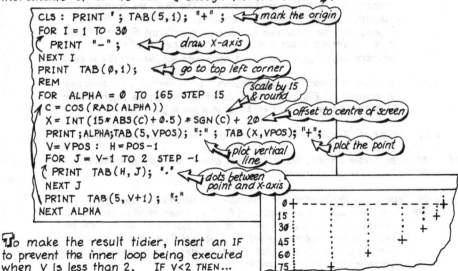

```
CLS : PRINT '; TAB(5,1); "+" ;          ← mark the origin
FOR I = 1 TO 30
  PRINT "-";          ← draw X-axis
NEXT I
PRINT TAB(0,1);          ← go to top left corner
REM
FOR ALPHA = 0 TO 165 STEP 15          scale by 15 & round
  C = COS(RAD(ALPHA))
  X = INT(15*ABS(C)+0.5)*SGN(C) + 20          ← offset to centre of screen
  PRINT ;ALPHA;TAB(5,VPOS); ":" ; TAB(X,VPOS); "+";          ← plot the point
  V= VPOS : H=POS-1          ← plot vertical line
  FOR J = V-1 TO 2 STEP -1
    PRINT TAB(H, J); "."          ← dots between point and X-axis
  NEXT J
  PRINT TAB(5, V+1); ":"
NEXT ALPHA
```

To make the result tidier, insert an IF to prevent the inner loop being executed when V is less than 2.   IF V<2 THEN...

The 'variable' named @% stores a coded number which specifies field width for subsequent PRINT statements and the format in which numbers are to be printed. This coded number may be assigned to @%

{LET} @% = *expression*   ■ @% contains &90A by default (2314 decimal)

▶ LET @% = &90F   ⟵ *increase field width to 15 columns*

▶ LET @% = 2 * 16^4 + 2 * 16^2 + 9   ⟵ *explained opposite*

The content of @% is best considered as a hex number. The ampersand (&) in &90F signifies that the F, the 9, the 0 are all hex (base 16) digits. Readers unfamiliar with hex numbers may find page 80 helpful.

The hex number has eight hex digits:

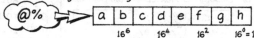

| a | b | c | d | e | f | g | h |

16^6 16^4 16^2 $16^0 = 1$

ab = 00 signifies that @% is to apply only to the print statement, not to the STR$( ) function ⟵ which adopts a code of &90A by default.

= 01 signifies that @% is to apply to the STR$( ) function as well as to the PRINT statement.

cd = 00 specifies "G-format" for printing. Whole numbers are printed without a decimal point; very small and very large numbers are printed in "E-format"; the rest are printed with a decimal point in the conventional way. In "G-format", ef specifies the maximum number of significant figures beyond which "E-format" becomes necessary. (e.g. for ef = 02 the numbers 9.9, 99, and 100 would appear as 9.9, 99 and 1E2 resply.)

= 01 specifies "E-format" for *all* numbers. In "E-format", ef specifies the number of figures to print, counting the single figure before the decimal point (e.g. 1.234E3 counts as 4).

= 02 specifies "F-format": ef specifies the number of decimal places.

ef = 00 to 09 see under cd = 00, cd = 01, cd = 02 above: ef has a different significance in each case.

gh = 00 to &FF specifies the number of character positions in each field (e.g. &0A signifies a ten-column field). When PRINT is used with commas in the list, each number is right-justified. When STR$( ) is used, the result of PRINT STR$( ) is left-justified, the field width being ignored. The useful function defined overleaf (p. 96) compensates for this difficulty.

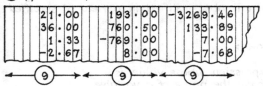

SETTING @%   TO ACHIEVE VARIOUS FORMATS AND LAYOUTS

Suppose output is to be tabulated as illustrated here:

21·00	193·00	-3269·46
36·00	760·50	133·89
1·33	-769·00	7·00
-2·67	8·00	-7·68

← 9 → ← 9 → ← 9 →

- every "field" is nine characters wide
- the format is "F" (digits 02 opposite)
- there are two places of decimals

For the sake of generality, assign these characteristics to variables as follows:

```
LET  FIELD = 9
LET  FMAT = 2      "F"
LET  PLACES = 2
```

Now it is a simple matter to specify the desired content of @% :

```
LET @% = FMAT * 16∧4 + PLACES * 16∧2 + FIELD
```

The above assumes that @% is not to be made applicable to the function STR$( ). If STR$( ) is to be affected, add 1∗16∧6 to the expression as shown later.

Here is a short program to demonstrate the effect illustrated above.

```
LET  RECALL = @%              "F"
LET  FIELD = 9 :  FMAT = 2 :  PLACES = 2
LET  @% = FMAT ∗ 16∧4 + PLACES ∗ 16∧2 + FIELD
FOR I = 1 TO 15
  X = (RND(1) − ·5) ∗ 100         RND(1) returns 0 to ·99...
  Y = (RND(1) − ·5) ∗ 1000        ∴ RND(1) − ·5 returns
  Z = (RND(1) − ·5) ∗ 500          − ·5 to + ·499...
  PRINT  X, Y, Z
NEXT I
@% = RECALL      restore original setting
END
```

it is worth trying this!

Consider a setting of @% which is sensitive to STR$( ). Here is an example:

```
LET @% = 1 ∗ 16∧6 + FMAT ∗ 16∧4 + PLACES∗ 16∧2 + FIELD
```

1∗16∧6 or &100000

If the PRINT line were also changed:

```
PRINT  STR$(X), STR$(Y), STR$(Z)
```

the result would *not* be the same as before. That is because STR$( ) is printed *left*-justified in its field ⇌ the setting of FIELD being effectively ignored. Over the page is a function which puts this right.

FNU (*VALUE, FORMAT, FIELD, PLACES*) A FUNCTION USEFUL FOR TABULATIONS

The FNU(,,,) function is defined below. The function returns a string having the value of the first argument *right*-justified in a field of specified width.

The arguments are used as follows:

VALUE is, in general, an expression whose value is to be printed; typically the name of a variable

FORMAT is "G" or "E" or "F" as defined on the previous double page

FIELD is an expression whose value specifies the desired field width (measured as character positions)

PLACES is an expression. For "F" and "E" formats the value specifies the number of places after the decimal point. For "G" format the value specifies the number of figures required (at least three less than field width to allow for spaces, sign and decimal)

Here is a program to demonstrate the function:

```
FOR  I = 1  TO  15
   X =(RND(1)−·5)∗100 :  Y= (RND(1)−·5)∗1000 : Z= (RND(1)−·5)∗500
   PRINT FNU(X,"F", 9, 2); FNU(Y, "G", 8, 5); FNU(Z,"E", 10, 2)
NEXT I
END
```

it is worth experimenting with this

N.B. *N.B.*

Format "F" may be used with the number of decimal places specified as zero (e.g. FNU(X,"F",9,0)), in other words to the nearest whole number. In such circumstances the trailing decimal point is automatically stripped off.

If the number would be too wide for its field, ### is printed in its place. Although information is thereby lost, a tidy layout is preserved.

Here is the function defined:

```
DEF FNU(X, SHAPE$, FIELD, PLACES )
LOCAL RECALL, Q, A$, L, D
RECALL = @%
Q = INSTR ("GEF", SHAPE$)−1      ← Q=0 for "G", 1 for "E", 2 for "F"
IF  Q<0 THEN = " "+ STRING$(FIELD−1, "∗")   ← ∗∗∗ if nonsense format
IF  Q=1 THEN PLACES = PLACES +1      1.123E3 counts as 4, not 3
LET  @% = 16^6 +Q∗16^4 + PLACES ∗16^2 + FIELD
A$ = STR$(X) : @% =RECALL :  L= LEN(A$)   ← restore @% after use
IF  Q=2 AND PLACES=0 THEN A$=LEFT$(A$, L−1)   ← "F" with 0 places: strip point
IF  L>FIELD THEN = " "+ STRING$(FIELD−1, "#")   ### if field too narrow
D = INSTR$ (A$ + " "," ")−1
= STRING$ ( FIELD−D," ")+LEFT$(A$,D)      ← right justify
```

96

MODE · WIDTH · TIME STATEMENTS

The MODE statement is needed for graphics but is introduced here for completeness. Using this statement it is possible to see the sizes and styles of *characters* displayed in the various modes.

MODE *expression*

> *don't use MODE in a FuNction or PROcedure*

■ *expression* should reduce to an integer from 0 to 7 to select a mode. Mode 7 is implied by default.

▶ MODE 6 ◀ *change to MODE 6*

Some models of computer do not work in modes 1 to 3.

The numbers of available rows and columns in each mode are tabulated on the right.

When the computer is switched on it adopts MODE 7 by default; likewise after pressing BREAK .

MODE	NUMBER OF ROWS	COLUMNS	STANDARD COLOURS
0	32	80	Black White
1	32	40	Black Red Yellow White
2	32	20	All 8 plus all 8 flashing
3	25	80	Black White
4	32	40	Black White
5	32	20	Black Red Yellow White
6	25	40	Black White
7	25	40	Teletext colours

▶ MODE 0 has rows 0 to 31, columns 0 to 79

The WIDTH of row may be reduced from the standard amount for the current mode (e.g. reduced from 0 ⇝ 39 in MODE 7) by using the WIDTH statement:

WIDTH *expression*

■ *expression* should reduce to the number of columns (character positions) desired

---

▶ WIDTH 12 ◀ *limit output to columns 0 to 11* ▶ WIDTH 40 ◀ *reset to standard width in MODE 7*

The computer has a clock which ticks once every centisecond (i.e. ticks a hundred times every second). The number of ticks since the clock was last set is held ⇝ and kept up to date ⇝ in a "pseudo variable" named TIME.

TIME

■ *pseudo variable*

▶ TIME = X ◀ *set the clock* ▶ LET T = TIME ◀ *read the clock*

```
INPUT "Hrs" H "Mins" M "Secs" S
LET TIME = ((H*60+M)*60+S)*100
```

```
LET S = (TIME DIV 100) MOD 60
LET M = (TIME DIV 6000) MOD 60
LET H = (TIME DIV 360000) MOD 24
PRINT H; ":"; M; ":"; S
```

Above is a clock *setting* routine; on the right is a clock *reading* routine.

And here is a procedure which causes a delay of a specified duration ⇝ measured in seconds.

```
DEF PROCRASTINATE (SECS)
LOCAL T: T=TIME : REPEAT UNTIL TIME>T+ SECS*100: ENDPROC
```

INPUT STATEMENT

The INPUT statement was used in earlier examples without formal definition. Here it is defined:

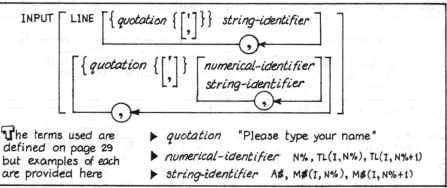

The terms used are defined on page 29 but examples of each are provided here

▶ *quotation* "Please type your name"
▶ *numerical-identifier* N%, TL(I,N%), TL(I,N%+1)
▶ *string-identifier* A$, M$(I,N%), M$(I,N%+1)

▶ INPUT "Type an integer" ' N% "Thanks"
▶ INPUT LINE A$ ⟵ equivalent ⟶ INPUTLINE A$
▶ INPUT "Three values please" A, B, C

Quotations are for display on the screen as "prompts" to the user of the program. When an INPUT statement is obeyed the computer displays the first prompt (if there is one) and waits for the user of the program to type a value and press ⟨RETURN⟩. The computer then stores the given value in the variable nominated next in the INPUT list. The computer then deals with the next prompt or the next variable (whichever is next encountered) and so on until the list is exhausted.

If the user of the program types a string when the INPUT list wants a number then the contents of the corresponding real or integer variable is made zero without an error message being displayed. Conversely, if the user types a number when the INPUT list wants a string then the corresponding string-variable is made to contain the typed digits as though they formed a string. Both cases described above are illustrated below.

If the user types 12.9 or –12.9 in response to INPUT K% then K% is made to contain 12 or –12.

A long list may be satisfied by typing each item and pressing ⟨RETURN⟩, alternatively by separating items by commas and finally pressing ⟨RETURN⟩ just once.

When responding to an INPUT statement do not treat a space as a separator; in a string it is just another character. But after a number, a space causes the rest of the line to be ignored:

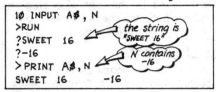

```
10 INPUT A$, N
>RUN
?SWEET  16          the string is
?-16                "SWEET 16"
>PRINT A$,N         N contains
SWEET  16    -16    -16
```

```
10 INPUT  N , A$
>RUN
?39 STEPS           STEPS is
? DAMMIT            ignored
>PRINT N,A$
        39DAMMIT
```

The INPUT LINE statement works differently; the entire response, including all spaces and commas, is treated as a single string:

```
10 INPUT LINE A$
>RUN
? writes; and, having writ, Moves on:
>PRINT A$
writes; and, having writ, Moves on:
```

The string may cover more than one row of the screen; it includes everything the user types in response to the prompt until [RETURN] has been pressed.

These four rules are useful for punctuating an INPUT list:

- *semicolon* behaves the same way as *comma*. A group of commas or semicolons or a mixture of both behaves the same way as a single comma. ⟨ *e.g.* INPUT A,,; B behaves as INPUT A,B ⟩

- *spaces* may be used to punctuate a list ⟨ *e.g.* INPUT "Next" Q$ X ⟩ and so may *null* where the syntax allows ⟨ *e.g.* INPUT "Next"Q$X⟩. *Null* has the same effect as *space*.

- each *apostrophe* causes the start of an extra line.

- unless an *apostrophe* or *quotation mark* precedes an identifier, a question mark is displayed on the screen as a prompt for that identifier. ⟨ *e.g.* A',B implies a question mark for B whereas B,'C implies *no* question mark for C. ⟩

Here are some INPUT statements to illustrate punctuation:

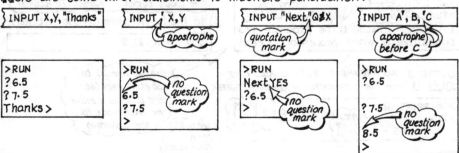

```
{ INPUT X,Y,"Thanks"      { INPUT ; X,Y           { INPUT "Next"Q$X        { INPUT A', B,'C
                                   apostrophe        quotation               apostrophe
                                                       mark                  before C

>RUN                      >RUN                    >RUN                     >RUN
?6.5                      6.5        no           NextYES                  ?6.5
?7.5                      ?7.5       question      ?6.5      no
Thanks>                   >          mark          >        question       ?7.5       no
                                                            mark           8.5        question
                                                                           >          mark
```

If these rules prove unhelpful, use trial and error to achieve the effects desired.

GET$ AND GET FUNCTIONS

The GET$ function is for returning any character typed by the user of a program whilst that program is running. The GET function behaves the same way but returns the ASCII code of the character rather than the character itself:

$$GET\$ \equiv CHR\$ (GET) \qquad GET \equiv ASC (GET\$)$$

When the function is invoked, the first character in the keyboard buffer is returned to the program. If the keyboard buffer is empty the computer waits until a character is put into it by pressing a key or keys. The keyboard buffer is, as its name suggests, a memory buffer between keyboard and processor. Everything typed goes into it; everything a program needs from the keyboard is taken out of it. The buffer may be "flushed" by executing *FX 21,0 as illustrated below and explained on page 174.

GET$
NO ARGUMENT: RETURNS FIRST CHARACTER IN KEYBOARD BUFFER

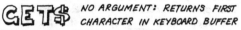

```
>10 LET X$= GET$
> RUN
```
buffer empty: waiting for a key → *press* [A] →
```
>10 LET X$=GET$
> RUN     run completed
>;_:
>PRINT X$
A
>;_:     print to verify
```

Notice that invoking GET$ does *not* make the screen display what was got; a PRINT statement is needed to verify that letter A was got correctly.

Here is a program to demonstrate that GET$ can get any visible character; GET$ is sensitive to space bar and shift key.

```
>10 REPEAT
>20 ( PRINT GET$;    note;
>30 UNTIL FALSE
>RUN
```
press [ESCAPE] *to leave program* ⇨

```
The program responds li
ke a word processor, ke
eping up with a fast ty
pist.
```

But the following example demonstrates what can happen if the keyboard buffer already contains characters when GET$ is invoked:

```
>10 FOR I=1 TO 10000: NEXT I
>20 REPEAT
>30 ( PRINT GET$;
>40 UNTIL FALSE
>RUN    from buffer    from keys
I FORGOT TO FLUSH ITThe program res
ponds like a word processor, keepi
```

This loop takes several seconds. After typing RUN, and whilst the computer is whizzing round the loop, type: I FORGOT TO FLUSH IT

Add the following line to flush the buffer:

```
>15  *FX 21,0
```

GET
NO ARGUMENT: RETURNS ASCII CODE OF FIRST CHARACTER IN KEYBOARD BUFFER

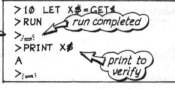

```
>10 PRINT GET
> RUN
    65    ASCII code for A
```
press [A]

change line 30 to >30 PRINT CHR$(GET); *and it should make no difference to the program*

see p.163 for all ASCII codes

This function behaves the same way as GET$ except that it returns the ASCII code of the character rather than the character itself.

INKEY$( ) • INKEY( ) FUNCTIONS

The INKEY$( ) function is for returning any character typed by the user of a program whilst that program is running. The function returns a character from the keyboard buffer in the same way as GET$, but the argument of INKEY$( ) specifies a maximum waiting time after which the function would return a null string saying "Time's up!" The INKEY( ) function behaves the same way as INKEY$( ) except that it returns the ASCII code of the character, or -1 when time is up.

$$INKEY(X) \equiv ASC(INKEY\$(X)) \qquad INKEY\$(X) \equiv CHR\$(INKEY(X))$$

The INKEY( ) function offers a further facility. Used with a negative argument to specify a particular key, INKEY( ) returns *true* if that key is currently depressed; otherwise *false*. The keyboard buffer is not consulted when INKEY( ) has a negative argument.

INKEY$ (wait)
- RETURNS FIRST CHARACTER IN KEYBOARD BUFFER OR "" IF BUFFER EMPTY & WAITING TIME EXCEEDED (null string)

INKEY ([wait / -key])
- RETURNS ASCII CODE OF 1ST CHARACTER IN KEYBOARD BUFFER OR -1 IF WAITING TIME EXCEEDED
- WITH NEGATIVE ARGUMENT RETURNS TRUE (i.e. -1) IF SPECIFIED KEY IS DEPRESSED, OTHERWISE FALSE (i.e. 0)

■ *wait* is an expression reducing to a positive value which specifies the maximum waiting time in centiseconds (1/100 sec.)

■ *-key* is an expression reducing to a negative value to signify any key on the diagram below:

▶ full example on page 104 ◀

```
>10  *FX 21,0
>20  PRINT INKEY$(360000)
>RUN
```
waits up to an hour for a key to be pressed: would simply stop if wait proved fruitless

INKEY(20) returns -1 if waiting time (1/5 sec.) is exceeded: NOT(-1) has the logical value FALSE (i.e. 0)

```
>10 PRINT "STRIKE A KEY...NOW!"
>20 IF NOT INKEY(20)PRINT "FAST REACTIONS" ELSE PRINT "TOO SLOW"
>RUN
```

```
>10 IF INKEY(-100) PRINT "YE"; ELSE PRINT "NO";
>20 GO TO 10
>RUN
```
-100 on diagram is V

prints YEYEYE... for as long as V is held down, otherwise NONONO... (worth trying)

101

TYPING SKILL

Choose a list of words or sentences to be the vocabulary: store them in the one-column array named VOC$( )

VOC$(1)	MAD DOG
VOC$(2)	CAT
VOC$(3)	BUDGERIGAR
VOC$(4)	HAMSTER
VOC$(5)	GERBIL

The program is to choose one of these words or phrases at random and display it on the screen. The player has to type the displayed word or phrase accurately without seeing letters appear on the screen and without pausing too long between letters. What constitutes "too long" must be set at the start of play. With each successful attempt this allowable delay gets shorter and shorter until impossibly short.

Here is the program. GOTO is unavoidable so line numbers have to be shown:

```
 10  CLS :  DIM VOC$(5)
 20  DATA  MAD DOG, CAT, BUDGERIGAR, HAMSTER, GERBIL
 30  FOR I=1 TO 5 :  READ VOC$(I) :  NEXT I
 40  REM
 50  INPUT '' "How many seconds between keystrokes" ' , P
 60  LET  WAIT = P * 100
 70  REPEAT : REM Main loop begins
 80  LET A$ = VOC$(RND(5)) :  L=LEN(A$)
 90  PRINT "Type "; A$; " now"
100  *FX 21,0
110  LET I=0 : REM Cycle the letters
120  I=I+1
130  IF  I>L PRINT "Jolly good" : WAIT = 0.95*WAIT : GOTO 190
140  K= INKEY(WAIT)
150  IF  K=-1 PRINT "Tardy" : GOTO 190
160  N= ASC(MID$(A$,I,1))
170  IF  K<>N PRINT "Mistake" : GOTO 190
180  GOTO 120
190  VDU7 :  REM a COMETO for GOTOs
200  T = TIME : REPEAT UNTIL TIME > T + 100
210  PRINT "Another go? Y/N"
220  *FX 21, 0
230  IF GET$ = "N" PRINT "Bye" : END
240  UNTIL FALSE
```

creates the array depicted above: DATA and READ are defined opposite

*FX 21,0 says flush keyboard buffer. ⇨p.174

VDU 7 says beep. ⇨p.162

delay 1 sec.

Flush again

everything counts as YES except N

Start the game by typing RUN and pressing [RETURN].

*FX 21,0 and VDU 7 are explained on pages 174 and 162 respectively.

Notice that the loop between lines 120 and 180 is not a FOR loop. That is because of the need to jump out of the loop without jumping back again. The FOR...NEXT loop would work, but not beyond the tenth try (*Too many FORs at...*).

The "IF K=-1" at line 150 may be replaced by "IF K=TRUE" but *not* by "IF K" alone. That is because *all* non-zero values after IF are treated as *true* in BBC-BASIC.

DATA · RESTORE · READ
AN INTERNAL FILE OF DATA

When BASIC was born in 1964 it had no INPUT statement; data had to be assembled in advance as a set of DATA statements *in the program itself.*

```
DATA    MAD DOG, CAT, BUDGERIGAR
DATA    HAMSTER, GERBIL
```
as the example opposite

To get such data into variables or array elements there had to be one or more READ statements:

```
READ    VOC$(1), VOC$(2), VOC$(3), VOC$(4)
READ    VOC$(5)
```

VOC$(1)	MAD DOG
VOC$(2)	CAT
VOC$(3)	BUDGERIGAR
VOC$(4)	HAMSTER
VOC$(5)	GERBIL

or, for a more succinct example: *either*

```
FOR    I = 1 TO 5 : READ VOC$(I) : NEXT I
```

The concatenation (*joining end to end*) of all DATA statements in a program constitutes an internal "file" of data; every time READ is obeyed the *next* item in this file is read. DATA statements may be anywhere in a program; before or after the READ. They need not be contiguous. But anything following a DATA statement on the same line *is ignored:*

```
DATA    100 : READ X     ignored
```

The DATA-file is "re-wound" when a RESTORE statement is obeyed; the next READ to be executed then takes data from the beginning of the internal file. If RESTORE nominates a line number then the file is positioned such that the next READ statement to be executed takes data from the beginning of the nominated line. If there is no DATA statement on the nominated line, execution ceases with the message "No such line ... "

If a number is read into a string variable it is read as a string. Thus DATA 17 followed by READ A$ would cause A$ to contain "17". But if a *string* is to be read into a numerical variable (*e.g.* DATA YES then READ N) execution ceases with the message "Type mismatch... "

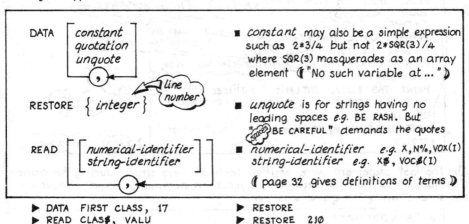

```
DATA   ⎡ constant    ⎤
       ⎢ quotation   ⎥
       ⎣ unquote     ⎦
            ⎝,⎠
                    line number

RESTORE  { integer }

READ   ⎡ numerical-identifier ⎤
       ⎣ string-identifier    ⎦
            ⎝,⎠
```

- *constant* may also be a simple expression such as 2*3/4 but not 2*SQR(3)/4 where SQR(3) masquerades as an array element (*"No such variable at ..."*)

- *unquote* is for strings having no leading spaces *e.g.* BE RASH. But "   BE CAREFUL" demands the quotes

- *numerical-identifier   e.g.* X, N%, VOX(I) *string-identifier   e.g.* X$, VOC$(I)

   (*page 32 gives definitions of terms*)

▶ DATA FIRST CLASS, 17
▶ READ CLAS$, VALU

▶ RESTORE
▶ RESTORE 210

REACTIONS

The following program is for testing a player's speed of assimilation and reaction. On typing RUN and pressing `RETURN`

- the screen is cleared

- after a pause (anything from 0·2 to 6·2 sec.) a capital letter appears somewhere on the screen at a spot randomly chosen by the computer

- the player is required to press the key labelled with that letter

- after finding and pressing that key the time taken (measured in milliseconds) is displayed at the bottom of the screen

- further tries are offered in this manner until the player has had ten tries

- the average time taken is then displayed.

The program is shown below. GOTO is unnecessary so the program may be listed below without the distraction of line numbers:

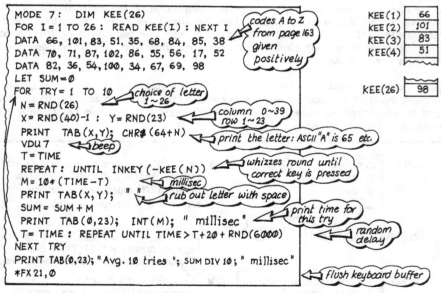

```
MODE 7 :  DIM KEE(26)
FOR I = 1 TO 26 : READ KEE(I) : NEXT I
DATA 66, 101, 83, 51, 35, 68, 84, 85, 38
DATA 70, 71, 87, 102, 86, 55, 56, 17, 52
DATA 82, 36, 54, 100, 34, 67, 69, 98
LET SUM=0
FOR TRY= 1 TO 10
N = RND(26)
X = RND(40)−1 :  Y = RND(23)
PRINT  TAB(X,Y); CHR$ (64+N)
VDU 7
T = TIME
REPEAT : UNTIL INKEY (−KEE(N))
M = 10*(TIME−T)
PRINT TAB(X,Y);  " "
SUM = SUM + M
PRINT  TAB(0,23);  INT(M);  " millisec "
T= TIME : REPEAT UNTIL TIME > T+20+ RND(6000)
NEXT TRY
PRINT TAB(0,23); "Avg. 10 tries "; SUM DIV 10; " millisec "
*FX 21, 0
```

Annotations (in speech bubbles):
- codes A to Z from page 163 given positively
- KEE(1) 66
- KEE(2) 101
- KEE(3) 83
- KEE(4) 51
- KEE(26) 98
- choice of letter 1~26
- column 0~39 row 1~23
- print the letter: ASCII "A" is 65 etc.
- beep
- whizzes round until correct key is pressed
- millisec
- rub out letter with space
- print time for this try
- random delay
- flush keyboard buffer

If the last statement were omitted then all keys struck during the game (perhaps more than ten had the player been nervous) would appear on the screen when the game was over:

```
>XPAOK DDFQRCI
```

COLOUR AND CLS

SPECIFY COLOUR OF TEXT AND BACKGROUND

The COLOUR statement may be used in modes 1 to 6, *not* in MODE 7.

The COLOUR statement is for specifying colour of text and colour of background. The CLS (CLear the Screen) statement is for clearing the text area of the screen to the current background colour and "homing" the cursor.

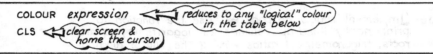

> COLOUR *expression* ⟵ *reduces to any "logical" colour in the table below*
> CLS ⟵ *clear screen & home the cursor*

Values in the body of the table are "logical" colours; each row of the table concerns an "actual" colour. When the computer is switched on, or when BREAK is pressed, or when VDU 20 (p.168) is executed, or when MODE is executed, then the logical colours of background and text become those encircled in the table below; *i.e.* the logical colour of the background becomes 128; the logical colour of the text becomes 1 for two-colour modes, 3 for four-colour modes, 7 for MODE 2.

ACTUAL COLOUR	LOGICAL COLOUR OF TEXT = t · · · LOGICAL COLOUR OF BACKGROUND = t + 128									ACTUAL COLOUR
	MODE 0	MODE 1	MODE 2 STEADY	MODE 2 FLASH	MODE 3	MODE 4	MODE 5	MODE 6	MODE 7	
0: black	0 (128)	0 (128)	0 (128)	8	0 (128)	0 (128)	0 (128)	0 (128)		0: black
1: red	1 129	—	1 129	9	—	—	1 129	—		1: red
2: green	*two-colour mode*	—	2 130	10	—	—	—	—		2: green
3: yellow		2 130	3 131	11	—	—	2 130	—		3: yellow
4: blue		*four-colour mode*	4 132	12	—	—	—	—		4: blue
5: magenta			5 133	13	—	—	—	—		5: magenta
6: cyan			6 134	14	—	—	—	—		6: cyan
7: white	(1) 129	(3) 131	(7) 135	15	(1) 129	(1) 129	(3) 131	(1) 129		7: white

(MODE 2 backgrounds do not flash. MODE 7 p.122 not applicable ~ see MODE 7 p.122)

The colour of text or background may be changed simply by quoting a different logical colour in the COLOUR statement and following with the CLS (CLear the Screen) statement. The new logical colour should be one of those tabulated for the current mode ≈ in other words from the same column of the table.

> MODE 5 ⟵ *see column 5 of table*
> COLOUR 1: COLOUR 130 : CLS ⟵ *change to red letters on yellow jolé!*
> COLOUR 2: COLOUR 131 : CLS ⟵ *change to yellow on white*
> COLOUR 3: COLOUR 129 : CLS ⟵ *change to white on red*

It is also possible to adopt a changed set of colours in each mode; in other words to take a logical colour out of its row of the table and put it in another. The statement is VDU 19 (p.168).

105

EXERCISES

1. Write programs to plot functions such as $Y = LN(X)$ or $Y = SIN(X)/EXP(X)$ on the same lines as $Y = COS(X)$ on page 93.

2. Implement FNU( ) on page 96. Use the function to print neatly lined up columns of logarithms, square roots, trigonometrical ratios etc. (The FNU( ) function is just as useful for tabulating columns of money, dates etc.)

3. Implement Typing Skill. Substitute your own dictionary of words or phrases to be typed. Line 20, asking if the player wants another go, could be omitted; it was included mainly to illustrate GET$.

4. Implement Reactions. There is scope for adding digits and symbols to the list of characters displayed.

10

GRAPHICS

MODE STATEMENT
RELEVANT VDU STATEMENTS
GCOL AND CLG STATEMENTS
PLOT STATEMENT
MOVE AND DRAW
PLOTTING
POINT FUNCTION
ARROW (USEFUL PROCEDURE)
XOX (GAME OF NOUGHTS & CROSSES)
AUTOMATON (GAME TO WATCH)
COLOUR PLANES
MODE 7 GRAPHICS
MODE 7 CHARACTER CODES

MODE STATEMENT

The MODE statement is defined also on page 97 with respect to text. Again:

MODE *mode*

~ *don't use MODE in a FuNction or PROCedure* ~

- *mode* is an *expression* reducing to an integer from 0 to 7 selecting one of the modes summarized below
- MODE 7 is implied by default

▶ MODE 5 ⟵ *change to MODE 5*

Some characteristics of the various modes are tabulated below. Some models of computer do not have all these modes.

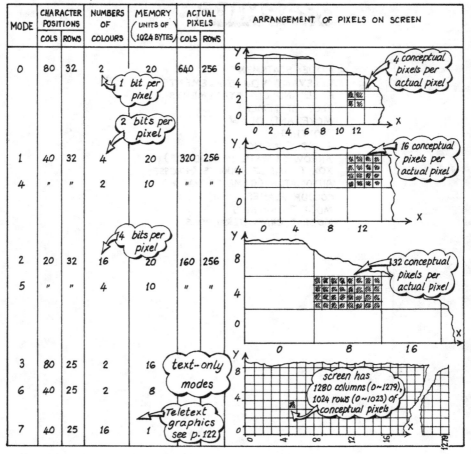

MODE	CHARACTER POSITIONS		NUMBERS OF COLOURS	MEMORY (UNITS OF 1024 BYTES)	ACTUAL PIXELS		ARRANGEMENT OF PIXELS ON SCREEN
	COLS	ROWS			COLS	ROWS	
0	80	32	2	20	640	256	*1 bit per pixel* — *4 conceptual pixels per actual pixel*
1	40	32	4	20	320	256	*2 bits per pixel* — *16 conceptual pixels per actual pixel*
4	"	"	2	10	"	"	
2	20	32	16	20	160	256	*4 bits per pixel* — *32 conceptual pixels per actual pixel*
5	"	"	4	10	"	"	
3	80	25	2	16			*text-only modes* — *screen has 1280 columns (0~1279), 1024 rows (0~1023) of conceptual pixels*
6	40	25	2	8			
7	40	25	16	1			*Teletext graphics see p. 122*

Coordinates are given with reference to the X and Y axis systems shown. All axes are graduated in conceptual pixels. The X axis is 1280 pixels long; the Y axis 1024 pixels high. It is a waste of computer time to plot more than one conceptual pixel falling inside any one actual pixel.

RELEVANT VDU STATEMENTS

The graphics screen comprises 1280 columns and 1024 rows of *conceptual pixels* as defined opposite.

The "graphics cursor" is the point of an invisible pen which draws all graphics. It rests on reaching the end of each line it has to draw; it does not move again until a PLOT or MOVE or DRAW statement is obeyed. (MOVE means draw an invisible line, so the cursor rests at the point "drawn" to.)

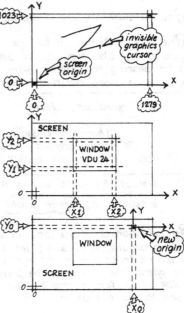

A graphics "window" may be created inside the screen area by VDU 24 (p. 170). The window behaves as a smaller screen except for the origin which remains at 0,0.

> VDU 24,   X1; Y1; X2; Y2; N; B;

Every time the graphics window is cleared by CLG the background is set to the colour specified by GCOL and the graphics cursor "homed" to the graphics origin 0,0.

However, the graphics origin may be moved to any desired point by VDU 29 (p. 170) after which CLG would "home" the cursor always to the new origin. The new origin may be located anywhere convenient.

> VDU 29,   XØ; YØ; N; B;

The text cursor may be made to ride on the back of the graphics cursor, and itself becomes invisible in the process. This is achieved by VDU 5 (p.166) which enables graphics to be annotated.

> VDU 5

The original position of the text cursor (its position before execution of VDU5) is remembered by the program as POS, VPOS. When a picture has been annotated the text cursor may be sent back to POS, VPOS by executing VDU4 which takes no argument:

> VDU 4

The effects of VDU24 and VDU29 may be wiped out simultaneously by VDU26 (p.167) which takes no arguments. Its effect is also to eliminate any *text* window created using VDU28 (p. 167).

> VDU 26

These statements are analogous to COLOUR and CLS respectively.

The GCOL statement is for specifying not only the colour of line and background but also the logic of applying the colours specified. The CLG statement is for clearing the graphics window ≈ which is the whole screen unless a smaller window has been defined using VDU24 (｢ p.170｣).

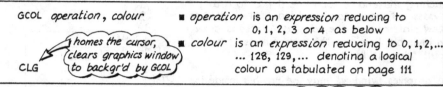

GCOL *operation, colour*
- *operation* is an *expression* reducing to 0, 1, 2, 3 or 4 as below
- *colour* is an *expression* reducing to 0, 1, 2,... ... 128, 129,... denoting a logical colour as tabulated on page 111

CLG ← *homes the cursor, clears graphics window to backgr'd by GCOL*

▶ MODE 0 : GCOL 0,1 : GCOL 0,128 ← *as implied by default in MODE 0*

▶ CLG ← *clear graphics window*

For definition of *operation*, let C denote the logical colour specified by the second argument of GCOL; let S denote the logical colour of a pixel in the path of a line to be drawn on the screen. The *operators* are OR, AND, EOR, NOT (｢ p.43｣). The *operations* which may be performed are: 1 for C OR S, 2 for C AND S, 3 for C EOR S, 4 for *inverse* S. Examples below are shown in binary to illustrate each logical operation:

0: disregard S and apply logical colour C

1: apply logical colour C OR S

(｢ 0101 OR 0011 gives colour 0111 ｣)

2: apply logical colour C AND S

(｢ 0101 AND 0011 gives colour 0001 ｣)

3: apply logical colour C EOR S

(｢ 0101 EOR 0011 gives colour 0110 ｣)

4: disregard C and apply inverse colour to S

(｢ reverse each bit: 0011 gives colour 1100 ｣)

Keen readers will notice that " inverse S" is not the same thing as "NOT S" because background colour codes have bit 7 set ≈ whether inverse or not.

The *logical colours* for use with GCOL are tabulated opposite. The table shows an *actual* colour associated with each *logical* colour when the computer is switched on. The encircled numbers in each column are those used for background and line when no specific GCOL statement is given; in other words "defaults are encircled."

The *logical* colours tabulated may be associated with different *actual* colours using VDU19 (｢ p.168｣). Changing an actual colour may be thought of as moving a logical colour from one row to another in a column of the table opposite. Defining a set of colours in this way is sometimes called "palette changing."

The following is a key to the table:

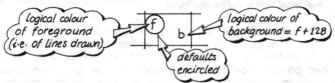

logical colour of foreground (i.e. of lines drawn) → f   b ← logical colour of background = f + 128

defaults encircled

ACTUAL COLOUR	MODE 0	MODE 1	MODE 2 STEADY	MODE 2 FLASHING	MODE 4	MODE 5	MODES 3 & 6	MODE 7
0 : black	0 (128)	0 (128)	0 (128)	8 136	0 (128)	0 (128)	no graphics in these modes	Teletext graphics ≈ p. 122
1 : red	—	1 129	1 129	9 137	—	1 129		
2 : green	—	—	2 130	10 138	—	—		
3 : yellow	—	2 130	3 131	11 139	—	2 130		
4 : blue	—	—	4 132	12 140	—	—		
5 : magenta	—	—	5 133	13 141	—	—		
6 : cyan	—	—	6 134	14 142	—	—		
7 : white	1 (129)	3 (131)	7 (135)	15 143	1 (129)	3 (131)		

The following examples of GCOL statements refer to MODE 1 (or MODE 5) which has four colours; black, red, yellow, white unless changed by VDU 19. For the following derivations of line colouring assume *no* previous changes by VDU 19 and assume every line to be drawn over an undisturbed area of the yellow background:

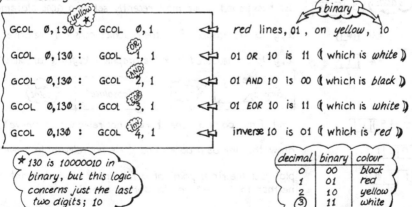

	GCOL 0, 130 :	GCOL 0, 1	⟵	red lines, 01 , on *yellow*, 10
	GCOL 0, 130 :	GCOL (OR) 1, 1	⟵	01 OR 10 is 11 (which is *white*)
	GCOL 0, 130 :	GCOL (AND) 2, 1	⟵	01 AND 10 is 00 (which is *black*)
	GCOL 0, 130 :	GCOL (EOR) 3, 1	⟵	01 EOR 10 is 11 (which is *white*)
	GCOL 0, 130 :	GCOL (inv) 4, 1	⟵	inverse 10 is 01 (which is *red*)

yellow ✱   binary

✱ 130 is 10000010 in binary, but this logic concerns just the last two digits; 10

decimal	binary	colour
0	00	black
1	01	red
2	10	yellow
③	11	white

When a GCOL statement defining a new background colour is obeyed in a program ≈ or typed as a direct command ≈ the graphics window does not change immediately to the new colour. The window is cleared to the new colour, and the graphics cursor "homed", only when CLG is obeyed.

PLOT STATEMENT

POINTS, FULL & BROKEN LINES,
COLOUR-FILLED TRIANGLES

The PLOT statement has a simple definition but complicated interpretation; it may be used to plot a point, draw a full or broken line from graphics cursor to a point, define a triangle with vertices comprising current point and the two points most recently visited by the graphics cursor.

PLOT *operation, x, y*

- *operation* is an *expression* reducing to a value built up as explained below

- *x* and *y* are *expressions* reducing to integer coordinates of a point

---

▶ PLOT 0+4, 640, 512 ⟵ move cursor to centre of screen (i)

▶ PLOT 1+4, 1280, 1024 ⟵ draw a diagonal to top right (ii)

The operation code is built up by adding a selection of feature codes as set out below. The operation code is best considered as a binary number of eight bits for this analysis.

In all cases the graphics cursor is transferred by the PLOT statement from where it is found to a new position defined by the arguments *x, y*. The two bottom bits of the operation code define the colour of line to be drawn.

```
128 64 32 16 8 4 2 1
[ 0 | 0 |  |  |  |  |  |  ]
```
ignored bits

start with one of these & add...

0 ⟦0|0⟧ use invisible colour ≈ in other words (move) to specified point

1 ⟦0|1⟧ use foreground colour most recently set by a GCOL statement

2 ⟦1|0⟧ use inverse colour of every pixel in the path of the line

3 ⟦1|1⟧ use background colour most recently set by a GCOL statement

+0 ⟦0⟧ *x, y* to be measured from the graphics *cursor* ("relative")

+4 ⟦1⟧ *x, y* to be measured from the graphics *origin* ("absolute")

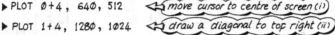

+8 ⟦1⟧ omit final point on line (+8 is not relevant to "move")

+16 ⟦0|0|1⟧ draw the line as a dotted line (+16 not relevant to "move")

+64 ⟦1|0|0⟧ plot just the final point of a full line (+64 is relevant neither to "move" nor to dotted lines)

+80 ⟦1|0|1⟧ colour fill a triangle with vertices *n, c, p*: *n* is the new point *x, y*; *c* is the current position of the graphics cursor; *p* is the previous location of cursor ≈ a location always remembered by the computer. The colour of fill is specified by the bottom two bits. (+80 not relevant to "move")

MOVE AND DRAW

The MOVE statement is a convenient synonymn for PLOT 0+4 ((PLOT 4)) and the DRAW statement for PLOT 1+4 ((i.e. PLOT 5)).

MOVE x, y	■ x and y are *expressions* reducing to the *ABSOLUTE* coordinates of a point
DRAW x, y	(($-32768 \leqslant x$ or $y \leqslant +32767$))

▶ MOVE 640, 512 ⟵ *as PLOT 0+4, 640, 512*
▶ DRAW 1280, 1024 ⟵ *as PLOT 1+4, 1280, 1024*

Several demonstration programs are given below to illustrate the effects of adding different feature codes ((+8, +16, *etc.*)) to the *operation code* of PLOT. All include +4 to signify *absolute* coordinates.

This program illustrates MOVE and DRAW. ⟹
The graphics cursor is moved to the middle of the screen, then 16 lines are drawn end to end, each in a different colour of MODE ((use MODE 5 if you do not have MODE 2. No need to alter 0 TO 15 because colours 4,5,6... become 0,1,2... automatically

```
10 MODE 2          or PLOT 0+4
20 MOVE 640, 512
30 FOR I = 0 TO 15
40 ⌐ GCOL 0, I
50 ⌐ DRAW RND(1279), RND(1023)
60 NEXT I          or PLOT 1+4
```

```
10 MODE 2
20 MOVE 640, 512
30 FOR I = 0 TO 15
40 ⌐ REM GCOL not referred to
50 ⌐ PLOT 6, RND(1279), RND(1023)
60 NEXT I   or PLOT 2+4
```

⟸ This program demonstrates PLOT 2+4 . The screen is black ((0000)) so lines are drawn in *inverse* black ((1111)) which, in MODE 2, is flashing white. An identical result may be obtained by changing line 40 to GCOL 4, 0 and line 50 to DRAW RND(1279), RND(1023).

This program illustrates PLOT 3+4 which picks ⟹ up the most recent background colour specified by GCOL. Notice, however, that the screen stays black because there is no CLG following GCOL 0, 128+I to make the screen adopt the newly specified background colour.

```
10 MODE 2
20 MOVE 640, 512
30 FOR I = 0 TO 15
40 ⌐ GCOL 0, 128 + I
50 ⌐ PLOT 7, RND(1279), RND(1023)
60 NEXT I   or PLOT 3+4
```

```
10 MODE 2
20 MOVE 640, 512   screen EOR green
30 FOR I = 0 TO 15
40 ⌐ GCOL 3, 2
50 ⌐ PLOT 13, RND(1279), RND(1023)
60 NEXT I   or PLOT 1+4+8
```

⟸ This program illustrates +8 for omitting the final point of a line. When lines are drawn end-to-end the final point of one becomes the initial point of the next. Such overlapping may be avoided by this facility. Run the program, then change PLOT 13 to PLOT 5 and run again. Notice that vertices become blunted because green EOR green is black.

This program demonstrates *dotted* lines. ⟹
This program is the same as the first program above except that DRAW ((which is equivalent to PLOT 1+4)) has been changed to PLOT 1+4+16.

More examples are given overleaf.

```
10 MODE 2
20 MOVE 640, 512        16 says
30 FOR I = 0 TO 15      dotted
40 ⌐ GCOL 0, I
50 ⌐ PLOT 1+4+16, RND(1279), RND(1023)
60 NEXT I
```

PLOTTING

This program demonstrates the facility of ➪ plotting individual points by adding +64 to the operation code. The program plots sixteen tiny points but the first cannot be seen because it blends with the background.

```
10 MODE 2
20 MOVE 640, 512          plot
30 FOR I = 0 TO 15        point
40   GCOL 0, I            only
50   PLOT 1+4+64, RND(1279), RND(1023)
60 NEXT 1
```

```
10  MODE 2
20  MOVE 640, 512
30  FOR I = 0 TO 15   triangles
40   GCOL 0, I
50   PLOT 1+4+80, RND(1279), RND(1023)
60  NEXT I
```

⟵ This program paints overlapping coloured triangles. Notice that the basic component of the operation code is 1+4 (i.e. use fore-ground colour and absolute coordinates) and not 0+4 which would generate *invisible* triangles.

Being more adventurous: wrap the demonstration program in a loop to execute twice; include X = RND(-1) to make the random-number generator produce an identical sequence of coordinates in each cycle; set the mode of GCOL to 3 (to signify EOR) and make the colour random. Finally increase the number of lines from 16 to 301.

```
10  MODE 2
20  FOR CYCLE = 1 TO 2
30   MOVE 640,512 : X = RND(-1)
40   FOR I = 0 TO 300
50    GCOL 3, RND(16)-1
60    PLOT 1+4, RND(1279), RND(1023)
70   NEXT I
80  NEXT CYCLE
```

⟵ When this program is run, more and more coloured lines appear. After a while they start to disappear until all have vanished. It is worth watching.

The secret lies in the EOR operation:

(b EOR c) EOR c is always b

POINT FUNCTION

The POINT(,) function returns the logical colour of any point on the screen given the coordinates of that point.

POINT (expression, expression)   RETURNS LOGICAL COLOUR OF POINT AT SPECIFIED COORDS. (OR -1 IF OFF SCREEN)

PRINT   POINT (1100, 920)   (assume screen is all red)   ➪   1 ⟵ red

The coordinates are specified with reference to the graphics origin. The coordinates are measured in the same units as for MOVE and DRAW.

If the coordinates refer to a point which is outside the screen area then the POINT(,) function returns -1.

The general shape of an arrow is shown here. The arrow head may be placed at the end of the shaft by setting ratio D to unity. The arrow head may be made sharper by increasing the ratio R. The breadth of the arrow head is twice W length units.

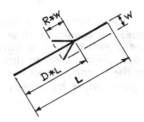

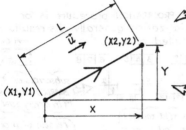

The arrow runs from X1,Y1 to X2,Y2 so its projections are:

$$X = (X2 - X1)$$
$$Y = (Y2 - Y1)$$

The length is given by L where $L = SQR(X^2 + Y^2)$. Divide X and Y by L and you have the projections of an arrow one unit long: a *unit vector* $\vec{u}$.

It is easy to find the projections of unit vector $\vec{v}$ at right angles to $\vec{u}$; swop the projections and change the sign of the second.

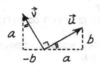

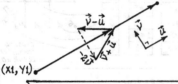

Employing these concepts the arrow may be drawn in the sequence shown here. Drawing starts at X1, Y1 and proceeds relatively.

(X1, Y1)

```
DEF PROCARO (X1, Y1, X2, Y2)
LOCAL D, W, R, X, Y, L, UX, UY, VX, VY
LET D = 0.97 :  W = 25 :  R = 3
X = X2 - X1 :  Y = Y2 - Y1
L = SQR( X^2 + Y^2)
UX = R*W*X/L :  UY = R*W*Y/L
VX = W*Y/L :  VY = -W*X/L
MOVE X1, Y1
PLOT 1,  D*X,  D*Y
PLOT 1,  VX-UX,  VY-UY
PLOT 0,  -2*VX,  -2*VY
PLOT 1,  VX+UX,  VY+UY
PLOT 1,  (1-D)*X,  (1-D)*Y
ENDPROC
```

alter these constants for different shapes of arrow

*form $\vec{u}$ and scale by R*W*

form $\vec{v}$ and scale by W

Demonstrate the procedure by drawing twenty arrows in white on a black screen (the default colours).

```
MODE 4
FOR I = 1 TO 20
  PROCARO ( RND(1279), RND(1023), RND(1279), RND(1023))
NEXT I
END
```

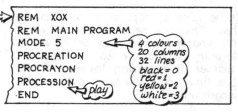

XOX A GAME OF NOUGHTS AND CROSSES (TICK-TACK-TOE)
TO ILLUSTRATE GRAPHICS AND PROGRAM DESIGN

Here is a program to play noughts and crosses. It comprises three main procedures: PROCREATION to initialize certain data, PROCRAYON to draw a board on the screen, PROCESSION to play the game move by move.

```
REM  XOX
REM  MAIN PROGRAM
MODE 5          4 colours
PROCREATION     20 columns
PROCRAYON       32 lines
PROCESSION      black = 0
                red = 1
.END    play    yellow = 2
                white = 3
```

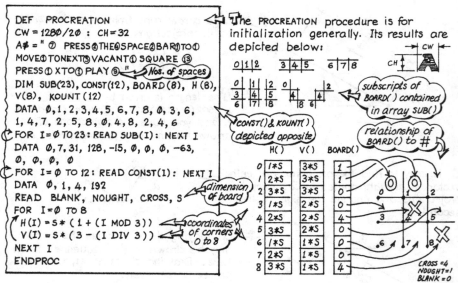

```
DEF   PROCREATION
CW = 1280/20 : CH = 32
A$ = " ⑦ PRESS④THE④SPACE④BAR①TO①
MOVE① TONEXT⑤ VACANT① SQUARE ⑬
PRESS① XTO① PLAY ⑨ "     Nos. of spaces
DIM SUB(23), CONST(12), BOARD(8), H (8),
V(8),  KOUNT (12)
DATA 0,1,2,3,4,5,6,7,8, 0,3,6,
1,4,7, 2, 5, 8, 0,4,8, 2, 4, 6
FOR I= 0 TO 23: READ SUB(I): NEXT I
DATA 0,7,31, 128, -15, 0, 0, 0, -63,
0, 0, 0, 0
FOR I= 0 TO 12: READ CONST(1): NEXT I
DATA 0, 1, 4, 192
READ BLANK, NOUGHT, CROSS, S
FOR  I= 0 TO 8
  H(I) = S * (1 + (I MOD 3))     coordinates
  V(I) = S * (3 - (I DIV 3))     of corners
NEXT  I                          0 to 8
ENDPROC
```

The PROCREATION procedure is for initialization generally. Its results are depicted below:

CONST() & KOUNT() depicted opposite
dimension of board

The PROCRAYON procedure is for drawing the board on the screen; red background; yellow noughts and crosses.

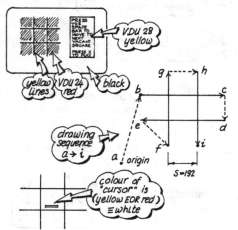

yellow lines   VDU 24 red   black

VDU 28 yellow

drawing sequence a → i

a : origin   S = 192

colour of "cursor" is (yellow EOR red) ≡ white

```
DEF   PROCRAYON
VDU 24, S; S; 4*S; 4*S;
GCOL 0, 128+1 : GCOL 0,2 : CLG
REM
VDU 28, 4.5*S/CW, 32-S/CH
6.5 *S/CW,  32-4*S/CH
COLOUR 128+2 : COLOUR 0 : CLS
PRINT A$          black letters
MOVE S, 3*S        on yellow
PLOT 1, 3*S, 0
PLOT 0, 0, -S
PLOT 1, -3*S, 0
PLOT 0, S, -S
PLOT 1, 0, 3*S
PLOT 0, S, 0
PLOT 1, 0, -3*S
REM              EOR
GCOL 3, 128+2         cursor
N=4 : PROCFLIP        switched
ENDPROC              on at
                     point 4
```

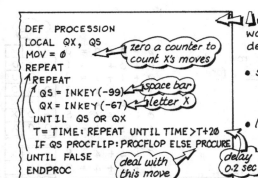

```
DEF PROCESSION
LOCAL QX, QS
MOV = 0          ← zero a counter to
REPEAT             count X's moves
  REPEAT
    QS = INKEY(-99) ← space bar
    QX = INKEY(-67) ← letter X
  UNTIL QS OR QX
  T = TIME: REPEAT UNTIL TIME > T+20 ← delay 0.2 sec
  IF QS PROCFLIP: PROCFLOP ELSE PROCURE ← deal with this move
UNTIL FALSE
ENDPROC
```

In PROCESSION the inner loop cycles, waiting for the first of two key depressions. To play, press:

- *space bar* to move the cursor into the next empty square of the board

- *letter X* to plant a cross in the square currently occupied by the cursor.

As soon as letter-key X is pressed the program invokes PROCURE. This procedure switches the cursor off and draws a big X in the same square. All X-moves are counted so as to detect a full board. On detection of a win or draw the procedure called PROCOFF is invoked and the program stops.

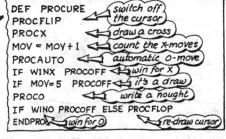

```
DEF PROCURE
PROCFLIP         ← switch off the cursor
PROCX            ← draw a cross
MOV = MOV + 1    ← count the X-moves
PROCAUTO         ← automatic 0-move
IF WINX PROCOFF  ← win for X
IF MOV = 5 PROCOFF ← it's a draw
PROCO            ← write a nought
IF WINO PROCOFF ELSE PROCFLOP ← win for 0 ... re-draw cursor
ENDPROC
```

```
730 DEF PROCAUTO
740 LOCAL P, SCORE, I, SUM
750 MAX = -1000 : WINX=FALSE : WINO=FALSE
760 FOR P = 0 TO 8
770   IF BOARD(P)<>BLANK GOTO 920
780   BOARD(P) = NOUGHT          ← "try"
790   FOR I = 0 TO 12 : KOUNT(I)= 0 : NEXT I
800   FOR I = 0 TO 21 STEP 3
810     TYPE = BOARD(SUB(I)) + BOARD(SUB(I+1))
              + BOARD(SUB(I+2))
820     KOUNT(TYPE) = KOUNT(TYPE)+1
830   NEXT I
840   IF KOUNT(3) WINO = TRUE
850   IF KOUNT(12) WINX = TRUE
860   SCORE = 0                   ← apply a formula
870   FOR I = 0 TO 8                explained overleaf
880     SCORE = SCORE + KOUNT(I)*CONST(I)
890   NEXT I                      ← remember P
900   IF SCORE > MAX MAX=SCORE: N=P
910   BOARD(P) = BLANK            ← "un-try"
920 NEXT P
930 ENDPROC    ← drop out with N pointing to the best square for NOUGHT
```

This procedure replies to X's move by placing a large O in a vacant square.

At 760 the program sets out to try a nought in each vacant square in turn, assessing the "value" of each try and subsequently adopting the best. At 770 the current square is tested for vacancy; if the test fails the next square is tested, and so on until a vacant square is found. A nought is put into this square as a trial ≈ it is not drawn on the screen.

With the trial NOUGHT in place the program, at 810, investigates the TYPE of every row, every column, each diagonal. For instance when I reaches 18, $SUB(I)$ holds 0, $SUB(I+1)$ holds 4, $SUB(I+2)$ holds 8; so TYPE at line 810 becomes $BOARD(0)+BOARD(4)+BOARD(8)$ for the diagonal

In every square there is a CROSS, NOUGHT or BLANK signified in array BOARD( ) by 4, 1 or 0 respectively. (Notice BOARD(P) = NOUGHT at line 780 and BOARD(P) = BLANK at line 910.)

(CONTINUED)

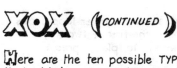

Here are the ten possible TYPEs of row, where it should be appreciated that $-|O|O$, for example, is of the same TYPE as: $O|O|-$ or $O|-|O$ or $\frac{O}{|O|}{O}$ etc.

Letter O has a value of [1] NOUGHT
" X " " " " [4] CROSS
blank - " " " " [0] BLANK

			TYPE
$0 + 0 + 0 = 0$	-	-	-
$0 + 0 + 1 = 1$	-	-	O
$0 + 1 + 1 = 2$	-	O	O
$1 + 1 + 1 = 3$	O	O	O
$0 + 0 + 4 = 4$	-	-	X
$0 + 1 + 4 = 5$	-	O	X
$1 + 1 + 4 = 6$	O	O	X
$0 + 4 + 4 = 8$	-	X	X
$1 + 4 + 4 = 9$	O	X	X
$4 + 4 + 4 = 12$	X	X	X

A score for the current position of the trial NOUGHT is given by the following formula:

$$SCORE = 7 * (\text{no. of rows of type 1})$$
$$+ 31 * (\text{no. of rows of type 2})$$
$$+ 128 * (\text{no. of rows of type 3})$$
$$- 15 * (\text{no. of rows of type 4})$$
$$- 63 * (\text{no. of rows of type 8})$$

This formula appears from time to time in computer magazines, being attributed to different sources, so I do not know whom I should acknowledge. As you ponder this formula its significance grows clearer. The very beginnings of a.i.

The diagonal sketched on the previous page might contain one NOUGHT, one CROSS, one BLANK as shown here ⇝ in which case TYPE becomes $1+4+0 = 5$. So the count of rows of type 5 should be bumped up by 1. This is done at line 820 by KOUNT(5) = KOUNT(5)+1 .

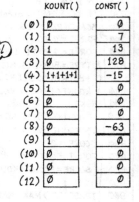

The loop at line 800 goes round eight times to deal with three rows, three columns, two diagonals. On completion, array KOUNT( ) might be as depicted here. ⇒

The formula is applied by the loop at line 870. SCORE is made to contain zero at line 860, then products of corresponding rows of KOUNT( ) and CONST( ) are added in. Accumulation need be taken no further than row 8.

	KOUNT( )	CONST( )
(0)	0	0
(1)	1	7
(2)	1	13
(3)	0	128
(4)	1+1+1+1	-15
(5)	1	0
(6)	0	0
(7)	0	0
(8)	0	-63
(9)	1	0
(10)	0	0
(11)	0	0
(12)	0	0

In this example SCORE would be $1*7 + 1*31 + 4*(-15)$ which is -22. Notice that MAX is initially set to -1000 (not to zero) so as to cope with negative scores.

The score for each trial position of NOUGHT is compared with the best obtained so far, and exchanged if better. When an exchange is made at line 900 the current position, P, is remembered by storing it in variable N. A winning row (type 3 or 12) is remembered by setting WINO or WINX to TRUE.

When each trial position has been evaluated, that square is again made blank (as shown at line 910) before trying the next.

This algorithm is imperfect; X can always win by unorthodox play: ⤳

XOX (FINAL PAGE)

The rest of the program comprises procedures for drawing the cursor, drawing a cross, drawing a nought, shutting off.

```
DEF PROCFLIP
MOVE H(N), V(N)
LOCAL C: C = INT (S/4)
PLOT Ø, C, C/2
PLOT 3, 2*C, Ø
ENDPROC
```

PLOT 3 implies background colour

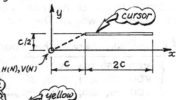

EOR *yellow*

The cursor is drawn under the influence of GCOL 3, 2 and so appears in the colour (*yellow EOR red background*) which is *white*. The cursor is drawn again before appearing in the next square. On the second drawing the colour becomes (*yellow EOR white*) which is *red*. In other words the cursor becomes invisible.

```
DEF PROCFLOP
REPEAT : N = (N+1) MOD 9
UNTIL BOARD(N) = BLANK
PROCFLIP
ENDPROC
```

This procedure is for advancing the cursor (having been switched off) to the next vacant square. As soon as N points to a vacant square, PROCFLIP is invoked to draw the cursor.

This procedure draws a cross in square N and records it in BOARD(N).

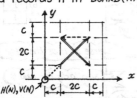

```
DEF PROCX
LOCAL C
MOVE H(N), V(N)
C = INT (S/4)
PLOT Ø, C, C : PLOT 1, 2*C, 2*C
PLOT Ø, -2*C, Ø : PLOT 1, 2*C, -2*C
BOARD(N) = CROSS
ENDPROC
```

```
DEF PROCO
LOCAL C, M
MOVE H(N), V(N)
C = INT(S/4) : M = INT (2*C/3)
PLOT Ø, C+M, C
PLOT 1, -M, M : PLOT 1, Ø, M
PLOT 1, M, M : PLOT 1, M, Ø
PLOT 1, M, -M : PLOT 1, Ø, -M
PLOT 1, -M, -M : PLOT 1, -M, Ø
BOARD(N) = NOUGHT
ENDPROC
```

This procedure draws a nought as an octagon in square N and records its presence in BOARD(N).

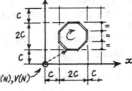

The final procedure provides a beep when the game is over, displays the result, and clears the keyboard buffer of all the Xs and spaces pressed during the course of the game.

```
DEF PROCOFF
VDU 7
*FX 21, Ø
IF WINX PRINT "X-WINS!" : END
IF WINO PRINT "O-WINS!" : END
PRINT "OX-DRAW" : END
ENDPROC
```

beep *flush buffer*

AUTOMATON

This is a game to watch, not play. A red triangle and a yellow triangle rebound off the walls of a squash court. When the triangles pass one another the red triangle passes *over* the face of the yellow triangle in an uncanny way. The trick is explained opposite.

First of all, here is the program:

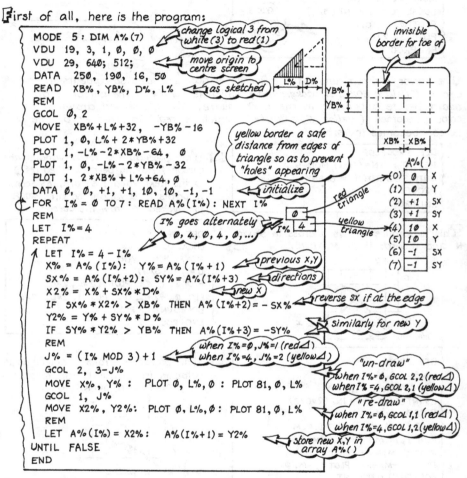

```
MODE  5 : DIM A%(7)              change logical 3 from
VDU  19, 3, 1, 0, 0, 0          white(3) to red(1)
VDU  29, 640; 512;              move origin to
DATA  250, 190, 16, 50          centre screen
READ  XB%, YB%, D%, L%           as sketched
REM
GCOL  0, 2
MOVE  XB%+L%+32, -YB%-16
PLOT  1, 0, L%+2*YB%+32
PLOT  1, -L%-2*XB%-64, 0        yellow border a safe
PLOT  1, 0, -L%-2*YB%-32        distance from edges of
PLOT  1, 2*XB%+L%+64, 0         triangle so as to prevent
DATA  0, 0, +1, +1, 10, 10, -1, -1   "holes" appearing
FOR  I% = 0 TO 7 : READ A%(I%) : NEXT I%   initialize
REM
LET  I%=4                       I% goes alternately
REPEAT                          0, 4, 0, 4, 0,...
  LET  I% = 4 - I%
  X% = A%(I%) :  Y% = A%(I%+1)          previous x,y
  SX% = A%(I%+2) : SY% = A%(I%+3)       directions
  X2% = X% + SX%*D%                     new X
  IF  SX%*X2% > XB%  THEN A%(I%+2)= - SX%   reverse sx if at the edge
  Y2% = Y% + SY%*D%
  IF  SY%*Y2% > YB%  THEN A%(I%+3)= -SY%    similarly for new Y
  REM                              when I%=0,J%=1 (red△)
  J% = ( I% MOD 3 )+1              when I%=4, J%=2 (yellow△)
  GCOL  2, 3-J%                    "un-draw"
  MOVE  X%, Y% :  PLOT 0, L%, 0 : PLOT 81, 0, L%   when I%=0, GCOL 2,2 (red△)
  GCOL  1, J%                      when I%=4,GCOL 2,1 (yellow△)
  MOVE  X2%, Y2%: PLOT 0, L%,0 : PLOT 81, 0, L%    "re-draw"
  REM                              when I%=0, GCOL 1,1 (red△)
  LET  A%(I%) = X2% :   A%(I%+1) = Y2%            when I%=4,GCOL 1,2 (yellow△)
UNTIL  FALSE                      store new X,Y in
END                               array A%( )
```

Labels in the sketched diagram: L% D%, YB%, YB%, XB% XB%, invisible border for toe of

A%( ) table:
(0)	0	X
(1)	0	Y
(2)	+1	SX
(3)	+1	SY
(4)	10	X
(5)	10	Y
(6)	-1	SX
(7)	-1	SY

red triangle — rows (0)-(3); yellow triangle — rows (4)-(7)

I% 0 / I% 4

Integer variables are used throughout the program because speed is desirable. Also, because of the need for speed, the rebounding shapes have been made as simple as possible and kept small. Despite these measures there is more flicker than would be acceptable in an arcade game. To make the program run faster it would be necessary to break out of BBC-BASIC (perhaps via indirection operators) and write crucial parts in assembly language. Nevertheless, games of the shoot-blast-kill variety may be written completely in BBC-BASIC; one technique is to compose moving parts from specially designed characters (page 169).

COLOUR PLANES

In the program opposite, the red triangle passes "over" the yellow one ⇒ obscuring any parts covered. How this is done is now explained.

In MODE 5 the logical colours are associated with actual colours as follows: 00 with black, 01 with red, 10 with yellow, 11 with white (values shown in binary). But in this program VDU 19 is used to sacrifice white for an extra red. After VDU 19, 3, 1, 0, 0, 0 the association of logical with actual colours becomes:

$$00 = black \qquad 01 = red \qquad 10 = yellow \qquad 11 = \{ red \}$$

The statement GCOL 2,... denotes the AND operation of the specified logical colour upon the screen pixel to be replaced; the statement GCOL 1,... similarly denotes OR. AND is appropriate to "un-drawing": OR is appropriate to "re-drawing."

Consider the red triangle; it may be "un-drawn" by drawing it again in the same place (in other words on a red background) but under the influence of GCOL 2,2. Here is why:

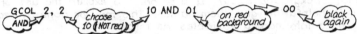

where the second argument of GCOL has 1 where the background has 0 and 0 where the background has ·1 (logical NOT). Similarly for undrawing the yellow triangle:

GCOL 2, 1 (AND) → choose 01 (NOT yellow) → 01 AND 10 → on yellow background → 00 → black again

Consider the red triangle once more; it may be "re-drawn" by plotting under the influence of GCOL 1, 1. The triangle may land entirely on black, entirely on yellow, or partly on each:

GCOL 1, 1 (OR) → choose 01 (R.H. bit = 1)
01 OR 00 → on black → 01 → red
01 OR 01 → on red → 01
01 OR 10 → on yellow → 11 → N.B. red

(Notice that red on red is included above for completeness although not demanded for the particular program opposite.)

Finally, consider the yellow triangle again; it may be "re-drawn" by plotting under the influence of GCOL 1, 2 whatever the background it lands on:

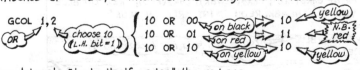

GCOL 1, 2 (OR) → choose 10 (L.H. bit = 1)
10 OR 00 → on black → 10 → yellow
10 OR 01 → on red → 11 → N.B. red
10 OR 10 → on yellow → 10 → yellow

So the yellow triangle "tucks itself under" the red one.

These principles may be applied to dramatic effect in MODE 2 in which *five* distinct colour planes are possible.

MODE 7 GRAPHICS

TELETEXT CODE

Graphics in MODE 7 are composed of characters: viz. letters, digits, punctuation marks; *also* special building blocks based on a grid of six squares as shown. The grid has the full width of letter A and the height of a row. All characters available in MODE 7 are tabulated on the next double page.

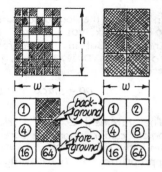

The building blocks in rows &A, &B, &E, &F of the table overleaf ‑ but not those in rows &2, &3, &6, &7 ‑ have codes derivable from their shape. The code is derived by adding the numbers (shown encircled) whose pixels are to be drawn in foreground colour ‑ and adding an additional 32+128. Thus the L‑shaped block shown here has the code 1+4+16+64+32+128=245.

The control codes shown in rows &8, &9 of the table overleaf are used to determine whether conventional characters or building blocks are to be displayed, whether characters should flash or not, what foreground colour to use, what background colour, and so on. To explain the use of control codes it is helpful to give them names. This may be done by reading control codes into named variables as follows:

```
10 REM   Give names to the control codes
20 REM
30 DATA  129, 130, 131, 132, 133, 134, 135
40 READ  RED, GRE, YEL, BLU, MAG, CYA, WHI
50 REM
60 DATA  16,       136, 137,   140,    141
70 READ  GRAPHICS, FLASH, STEADY, NHEIGHT, DBLHEIGHT
80 REM
90 DATA       152,  153,  154,  156,  157,  158,   159
100 READ CONCEAL, CONTIG, SEPAR, BLKBK, NEWBK, HOLD, RELEASE
```

defaults are:
VDU STEADY, WHI,
BLKBK, CONTIG,
NHEIGHT, RELEASE
at start of
every line

and appending this piece of program to the front of any program that uses names rather than codes. The rest of this explanation is given with reference to the names defined above.

In MODE 7 graphics a PRINT or VDU statement is used to send each row of characters to the screen. The following two lines of program, if obeyed, would send an identical line to the screen:

```
110 PRINT CHR$(BLU); CHR$(NEWBK); CHR$(RED); "RED ON BLUE"
120 VDU BLU, NEWBK, RED : PRINT "RED ON BLUE"
>RUN
```

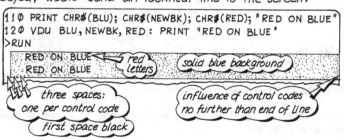

RED ON BLUE
RED ON BLUE

red letters — *solid blue background*

three spaces: one per control code

first space black

influence of control codes no further than end of line

NEWBK is explained opposite

122

A control code has influence on characters to its right, but this influence expires at the end of the current line. Every line is unique. Every line starts with standard white characters on black background. Control codes may be used to alter the line rightwards. Control codes may be used in combination (e.g. flashing together with double height letters) but are defined separately below.

GRAPHICS is set to 16. It is not a control code, but when *added* to a colour code it stipulates *graphics building blocks* in place of ordinary characters.

```
130 VDU GRAPHICS+RED,240,172,163: PRINT"p,£"
>RUN
```
one space — red stairs — equivalent: consult table overleaf

FLASH
STEADY

the flash code causes subsequent characters to flash; the steady code undoes this effect for characters to its right:

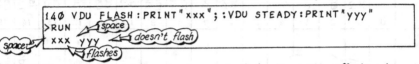

```
140 VDU FLASH:PRINT"xxx";:VDU STEADY:PRINT"yyy"
>RUN
xxx yyy
```
space — (space) — doesn't flash — flashes

DBLHEIGHT
NHEIGHT

the double-height code demands that characters affected be repeated on the next line:

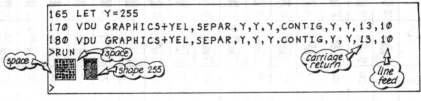

```
150 VDU DBLHEIGHT:PRINT"TALL";:VDU NHEIGHT:PRINT "not"
160 VDU DBLHEIGHT:PRINT"TALL";:VDU NHEIGHT:PRINT "bug"
>RUN
TALL not
>
```
space — (space) — ignores "bug"

SEPAR
CONTIG

the "separate" code causes each graphics building block to appear as a pattern of separate pixels rather than a solid shape. The "contiguous" code makes the pattern revert to a solid shape:

```
165 LET Y=255
170 VDU GRAPHICS+YEL,SEPAR,Y,Y,Y,CONTIG,Y,Y,13,10
180 VDU GRAPHICS+YEL,SEPAR,Y,Y,Y,CONTIG,Y,Y,13,10
>RUN
>
```
space — (space) — shape 255 — carriage return — line feed

NEWBK
BLKBK

the "new background" code causes the previous specification of colour (RED or GRE or YEL etc.) to apply to the *background*, not to the letters or building blocks themselves. The 'black background" code causes reversion to black background:

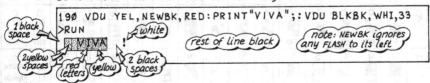

```
190 VDU YEL,NEWBK,RED:PRINT"VIVA";:VDU BLKBK,WHI,33
>RUN
VIVA !
```
1 black space — white — rest of line black — note: NEWBK ignores any FLASH to its left — 2 yellow spaces — red letters — yellow — 2 black spaces

CONCEAL
HOLD
RELEASE

these codes find application in data transmission using Teletext code.

123

SECOND HEX DIGIT

FIRST HEX DIGIT	Ø	1	2	3	4	5	6	7	8	9	A	B	C	D	E	F
&0		send given control code to printer, not screen	enable printer	disable printer			enable screen (if disabled by VDU 21)	beep	move text cursor one place left (do not delete)	move text cursor one place right	drop cursor one row (scroll if at bottom of screen)	raise cursor one row (scroll if already at top)	as CLS	cursor to left of current line	listings screenful by screenful, press SHIFT for next screen	cease listing by the screenful
	0	1	2	3	4	5	6	7	8	9	10	11	12	13	14	15
&1						DELETE...	as MODE but without changing HIMEM								home the cursor to top left corner of window	move text cursor to point with given coordinates
	16	17	18	19	20	21	22	23	24	25	26	27	28	29	30	31

those items shown in rows &0 and &1 are the same as for MODES 0≈6 (p.163)

foreground open ⇆ background shaded

FIRST HEX DIGIT	Ø	1	2	3	4	5	6	7	8	9	A	B	C	D	E	F
&2	space	!	"	#	$	%	&	'	(	)	*	+	,	-	.	/
	32	33	34	35	36	37	38	39	40	41	42	43	44	45	46	47
&3	0	1	2	3	4	5	6	7	8	9	:	;	<	=	>	?
	48	49	50	51	52	53	54	55	56	57	58	59	60	61	62	63
&4	@	A	B	C	D	E	F	G	H	I	J	K	L	M	N	O
	64	65	66	67	68	69	70	71	72	73	74	75	76	77	78	79
&5	P	Q	R	S	T	U	V	W	X	Y	Z	←	½	→	↑	
	80	81	82	83	84	85	86	87	88	89	90	91	92	93	94	95
&6	£	a	b	c	d	e	f	g	h	i	j	k	l	m	n	o
	96	97	98	99	100	101	102	103	104	105	106	107	108	109	110	111
&7	p	q	r	s	t	u	v	w	x	y	z	¼	‖	¾	÷	back-space delete
	112	113	114	115	116	117	118	119	120	121	122	123	124	125	126	127

CONTINUED OPPOSITE

MODE 7 CHARACTER CODES

α = alphanumeric
γ = graphic

FIRST HEX DIGIT	SECOND HEX DIGIT	0	1	2	3	4	5	6	7	8	9	A	B	C	D	E	F
&8		SHIFT f0 128	SHIFT f1 129	SHIFT f2 130	SHIFT f3 131	SHIFT f4 132	SHIFT f5 133	SHIFT f6 134	SHIFT f7 135	SHIFT f8 136	SHIFT f9 137	138	139	140	141	142	143
&8 (labels)		ǀ	α red	α green	α yellow	α blue	α magenta	α cyan	α white	flash on	show steady	ǀ	ǀ	normal height	double height		KEY
&9		144	145	146	147	148	149	150	151	152	153	154	155	156	157	158	159
&9 (labels)		ǀ	γ red	γ green	γ yellow	γ blue	γ magenta	γ cyan	γ white	conceal display	contiguous graphics	separated graphics	ǀ	black background	new background	hold graphics	release graphics
&A		space 160	! 161	" 162	£ 163	$ 164	% 165	& 166	' 167	(168	) 169	* 170	+ 171	, 172	- 173	. 174	/ 175
&B		0 176	1 177	2 178	3 179	4 180	5 181	6 182	7 183	8 184	9 185	: 186	; 187	< 188	= 189	> 190	? 191
&C		@ 192	A 193	B 194	C 195	D 196	E 197	F 198	G 199	H 200	I 201	J 202	K 203	L 204	M 205	N 206	O 207
&D		P 208	Q 209	R 210	S 211	T 212	U 213	V 214	W 215	X 216	Y 217	Z 218	← 219	$\frac{1}{2}$ 220	→ 221	↑ 222	# 223
&E		— 224	a 225	b 226	c 227	d 228	e 229	f 230	g 231	h 232	i 233	j 234	k 235	l 236	m 237	n 238	o 239
&F		p 240	q 241	r 242	s 243	t 244	u 245	v 246	w 247	x 248	y 249	z 250	$\frac{1}{4}$ 251	‖ 252	$\frac{3}{4}$ 253	÷ 254	block 255

CONTINUED

KEY: α → * 170

foreground open → background shaded

EXERCISES

1. Implement the little programs on pages 113-14. These demonstrate individually the various options of the operation code of the PLOT statement.

2. Implement the Arrow procedure on page 115. Vary the constants D, W, R to demonstrate arrows of different proportions. Add colour to the program which drives PROCARO( ).

3. Implement XOX, the game of noughts and crosses. Modify the main program so that it offers a new game when the current game is over. A challenge: make the program detect the tactics shown at the bottom of page 118 and behave more sensibly.

4. Implement the Automaton. Colour planes are explained in greater detail in "Advanced programming techniques for the BBC Micro" by Jim Mc Gregor & Alan Watt, published by Addison-Wesley, 1983. It is a mine of information for anyone determined enough to dig.

5. Compose a title screen for your favourite program using MODE 7 graphics. (This is the sort of thing Teletext graphics is intended for.)

MATCH - STIK
A GAME FOR ONE PLAYER
[PRESS F1 FOR DIRECTIONS]
BY PAT BOZ

11

SOUND

SOUND STATEMENT
MUSICAL NOTATION
TRANSLATION
PLAY THAT TUNE (EXAMPLE)
ADVAL FUNCTION
SYNCHRONIZATION
ENVELOPES
EXPERIMENT

SOUND STATEMENT

DEFINED FIRST OF ALL FOR SIMPLE MUSICAL SOUNDS

The computer has a loudspeaker fed by four sound *channels* numbered 0 to 3. Channel 0 carries hisses, scratches and grumbles; channels 1 to 3 carry musical notes.

Sounds are sent along a channel using the SOUND statement. This statement is defined below in the context of simple musical notes; the first two arguments have greater scope than indicated in this definition.

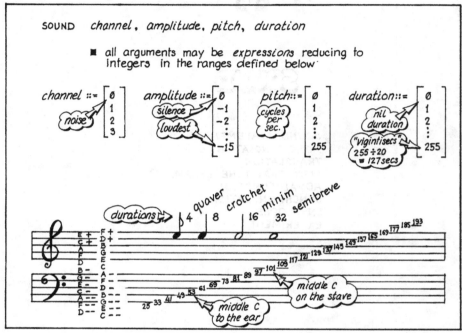

```
SOUND    channel, amplitude, pitch, duration
```

■ all arguments may be *expressions* reducing to integers in the ranges defined below

Here is a program to play just the notes with the pitches enumerated above. It is possible to go higher or lower.

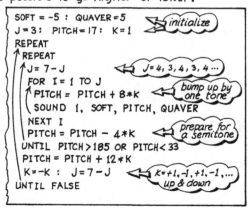

```
SOFT = -5 : QUAVER=5          initialize
J=3: PITCH=17: K=1
REPEAT
  REPEAT
    J=7-J                     J=4, 3, 4, 3, 4 ...
    FOR I=1 TO J
      PITCH = PITCH + 8*K     bump up by one tone
      SOUND 1, SOFT, PITCH, QUAVER
    NEXT I
    PITCH = PITCH - 4*K       prepare for a semitone
  UNTIL PITCH>185 OR PITCH< 33
  PITCH = PITCH + 12*K
  K=-K : J=7-J                K=+1,-1,+1,-1,...
UNTIL FALSE                   up & down
```

Notice the pattern of pitches on the stave. An octave from C to C goes: tone, tone, semitone, tone, tone, tone, semitone. The program starts at low F, generating a group of four notes a tone apart, then a semitone, then a group of three notes a tone apart, then a further semitone. This cycle is repeated. (A "tone" has a pitch difference of 8; a "semitone" of 4.)

MUSICAL NOTATION

AN UNORTHODOX NOTATION FOR
DEFINING ONE-FINGER TUNES

Here are the eight bars of "London's Burning":

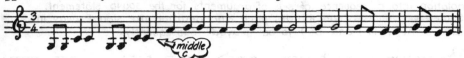

To make the computer play this tune ⪯ or any tune to be played with one finger ⪯ it is convenient to define a notation needing no stave so that the tune may be typed on the keyboard. Here is one idea:

- Each note is indicated by a capital letter A to G; a rest is indicated by R.   *middle c* ⟶ C

- Indicate the octave below middle C by appending a minus sign; two octaves by two minus signs. Indicate the octave of upper C and above by plus signs in a similar way.   *upper c* ⟶ C+

- Sharpen or flatten by appending # or $ as required   *upper c sharp* ⟶ C+#

- Indicate duration of note by W ((semiquaver)), Q ((quaver)), K ((crotchet)), M ((minim)), S ((semibreve)).   *crotchet in C sharp* ⟶ C+#K

- Signify a dotted note by a full stop.   *dotted crotchet in C sharp* ⟶ C+#K.

- Add an exclamation mark for emphasis.   *the whole works!* ⟶ C+#K.!

- To signify the end of a tune use RZ ((rest indefinitely)).

The symbols defining a note may be arranged in any order; the example above could be written +#KC!. if preferred. But the end-of-tune code, RZ, may not be rearranged or added to.

Here is "London's Burning" encoded in DATA statements by the rules set out above:

```
REM  London's Burning
DATA   GQ-, GQ-, CK!, CK, GQ-, GQ-, CK!, CK
DATA   DK, EK!, EK, DK, EK!, EK
DATA   GK, GM!, GK, GM!
DATA   GQ, FQ, EK!, EK, GQ, FQ, EK!, EK, RZ
```

And here is "Frère Jacques":

```
REM    Frere Jacques
DATA  FK!, GK, AK, FK, FK!, GK, AK, FK
DATA  AK!, B$K, C+M, AK!, B$K, C+M
DATA  C+Q!, D+Q, C+Q, B$Q, AK!, FK
DATA  C+Q!, D+Q, C+Q, B$Q, AK!, FK
DATA  FK!, CK, FM, FM!, CK, FM,  RZ
```

The program shown below can translate any tune expressed in the special notation into a sequence of sets of arguments for the SOUND statement. Successive values of amplitude, pitch and duration are stored away in arrays A( ), P( ) and D( ) to be "played" subsequently.

The program employs the arrays shown ➪ here for recognizing the letters in the encoded tune:

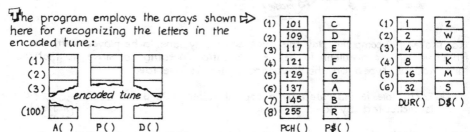

(1)	101	C
(2)	109	D
(3)	117	E
(4)	121	F
(5)	129	G
(6)	137	A
(7)	145	B
(8)	255	R

PCH( )   P$( )

(1)	1	Z
(2)	2	W
(3)	4	Q
(4)	8	K
(5)	16	M
(6)	32	S

DUR( )   D$( )

(1)
(2)
(3)
encoded tune
(100)

A( )   P( )   D( )

First set up the arrays needed for recognition:

```
REM Translate the musical notation
DIM A(100), P(100), D(100)
DIM PCH(8), P$(8), DUR(6), D$(6)
DATA 101, 109, 117, 121, 129, 137, 145, 255
FOR I = 1 TO 8 : READ PCH(I): NEXT I
DATA C, D, E, F, G, A, B, R
FOR I = 1 TO 8 : READ P$(I) : NEXT I
DATA 1, 2, 4, 8, 16, 32
FOR I = 1 TO 6 : READ DUR(I): NEXT I
DATA Z, W, Q, K, M, S
FOR I = 1 TO 6 : READ D$(I): NEXT I
```

The tune, encoded in DATA statements as already illustrated, is appended to the program (here or at the end) and processed as follows:

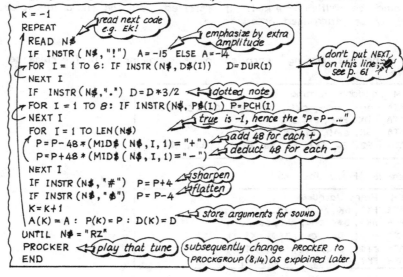

```
K = -1
REPEAT                     read next code e.g. Ek!
  READ N$
  IF INSTR(N$, "!") A=-15 ELSE A=-14      emphasize by extra amplitude
  FOR I = 1 TO 6: IF INSTR(N$, D$(I)) D = DUR(I)    don't put NEXT on this line; see p. 61
  NEXT I
  IF INSTR(N$, ".") D = D*3/2    dotted note
  FOR I = 1 TO 8: IF INSTR(N$, P$(I)) P = PCH(I)
  NEXT I                        true is -1, hence the "P=P-..."
  FOR I = 1 TO LEN(N$)
    P = P-48*(MID$(N$, I, 1) = "+")    add 48 for each +
    P = P+48*(MID$(N$, I, 1) = "-")    deduct 48 for each -
  NEXT I
  IF INSTR(N$, "#") P = P+4     sharpen
  IF INSTR(N$, "$") P = P-4     flatten
  K = K+1
  A(K) = A : P(K) = P : D(K) = D    store arguments for SOUND
UNTIL N$ = "RZ"
PROCKER        play that tune    subsequently change PROCKER to
END                              PROCKGROUP(8,14) as explained later
```

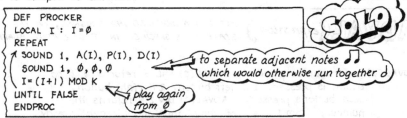

PLAY THAT TUNE

*FIRST WITH ONE FINGER, THEN
AS THREE "VOICES" IN A "ROUND"*

The program on the previous page ≈ together with the tune encoded as DATA statements ≈ is complete with the exception of the procedure named PROCKER. This is simple to define:

```
DEF PROCKER
LOCAL I : I = Ø
REPEAT
   SOUND 1, A(I), P(I), D(I)
   SOUND 1, Ø, Ø, Ø
   I = (I+1) MOD K
UNTIL FALSE
ENDPROC
```

SOLO ♫

*to separate adjacent notes
which would otherwise run together* ♩

*play again
from Ø*

The above procedure simply takes each row of values in turn ≈ A(I), P(I), D(I) ≈ and uses it as a set of arguments of the SOUND statement. When index I reaches K, I is automatically reset to Ø by (I+1)MOD K, so the tune begins all over again.

The tunes encoded earlier are singable as "rounds" which means that they stay in harmony as other singers join in at certain intervals ≈ in the case of "London's Burning" at two bars and four bars after the start. Because the tune is stored in the computer it is possible to send staggered copies of it along the three sound channels and so play a "round". Two problems arise: (a) all three "voices" must start together, and (b) the buffers belonging to the three channels must constantly be topped up. The solutions to these problems is explained later; here is a procedure called PROCKGROUP which does the job. Take PROCKER out of the program opposite, substitute PROCKGROUP(8, 14), and the program should play "London's Burning" as a "round" ⟨ but with all three voices going like mad from the start ⟩.

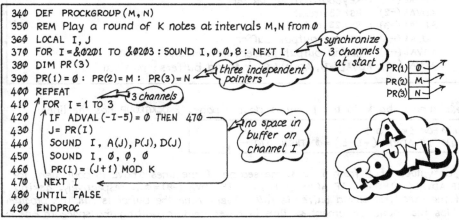

```
340  DEF  PROCKGROUP(M, N)
350  REM Play a round of K notes at intervals M, N from Ø
360  LOCAL I, J
370  FOR I =&Ø2Ø1 TO &Ø2Ø3 : SOUND I,Ø,Ø,8 : NEXT I
380  DIM PR(3)
390  PR(1) = Ø : PR(2) = M : PR(3) = N
4ØØ  REPEAT
41Ø    FOR I = 1 TO 3
42Ø      IF  ADVAL (-I-5) = Ø THEN  47Ø
43Ø      J = PR(I)
44Ø      SOUND I, A(J), P(J), D(J)
45Ø      SOUND I, Ø, Ø, Ø
46Ø      PR(I) = (J+1) MOD K
47Ø    NEXT I
48Ø  UNTIL FALSE
49Ø  ENDPROC
```

*synchronize
3 channels
at start*

*three independent
pointers*

3 channels

*no space in
buffer on
channel I*

PR(1) ⟨ Ø ⟩
PR(2) ⟨ M ⟩
PR(3) ⟨ N ⟩

A ROUND

By coincidence, a round of "Frère Jacques" demands the same arguments for PROCKGROUP(,) because the number of notes in the first *two* bars is the same as that in "London's Burning", likewise the number of notes in the first *four* bars of each tune. So change the tunes and play "Frère Jacques" as a round too.

The ADVAL( ) function returns information about a specified analogue input channel or the content of any input or output buffer. Here is the ADVAL function defined:

ADVAL(*expression*) RETURNS A DIGITIZED INPUT SIGNAL, OR THE STATE OF A SPECIFIED INPUT OR OUTPUT BUFFER

ADVAL($\emptyset$) is for games paddles. ADVAL($\emptyset$) AND 3 returns $\emptyset$ if *no* button is pressed, 1 if *left* button, 2 if *right* button, 3 if *both* buttons pressed. ADVAL($\emptyset$) DIV 256 returns the number, from 1 to 4, of the channel most recently ready with a reading converted from analogue signal to a digital value (jargon: A to D)

ADVAL(1) are typically for joysticks. ADVAL(1) measures and returns a
to   voltage from $\emptyset$ to 1.8 v on channel 1. The 1.8v is represented
ADVAL(4) in digital form as 65520; zero volts by $\emptyset$. (e.g. $\emptyset$.7v would be represented digitally as (0.7/1.8)∗65520 = 25472 ≈ always to the nearest multiple of 16.)

With negative arguments, ADVAL(-*n*) returns information about the buffer on channel *n*. In the case of input buffers the information returned is the number of *characters* currently in that buffer, so zero means *empty*. In the case of output buffers the information returned is the number of *free spaces*, so zero means *full*.

ADVAL(-1) : keyboard input buffer
ADVAL(-2) : RS423 input
ADVAL(-3) : RS423 output
ADVAL(-4) : printer output buffer
ADVAL(-5) : sound output buffer; non-musical
ADVAL(-6), ADVAL(-7), ADVAL(-8) : sound buffers; musical

Referring back to the previous double page, PROCKGROUP has the lines:

```
420 FOR I = 1 TO 3
430  IF ADVAL (-I -5) = Ø  THEN  470 ⟶
```

For values of I from 1 TO 3, the second of the lines above is equivalent to:
IF ADVAL(-6) = $\emptyset$ ...   IF ADVAL(-7) = $\emptyset$ ...   IF ADVAL(-8) = $\emptyset$ ... respectively, asking if the specified sound buffer is *full*. Every time the buffer is full the program skips the SOUND statement ≈ thus is never held up waiting for space in one buffer whilst another runs dry. In the case of "London's Burning" the IF statement never executes a jump to 470 because only crotchets and quavers are involved and every buffer has the capacity of five notes. However, with semiquavers in one channel and semibreves in another, the jump would have to be executed.

SYNCHRONIZATION

The first argument of the SOUND statement was earlier defined as an *expression* reducing to a channel number from 0 to 3. This definition is now extended to include extra information. To do so it is convenient to express the argument as a four-digit *hex* number:

The four *hex* digits are used as follows :

d   0 by default. Setting *d* to 1 signifies a dummy note which has no amplitude and no pitch but does have duration. For the specified duration the only sound on that channel would be the fade-away (release) sound of the previous note. "Release" is defined graphically overleaf.

s   0 by default. If this digit is set to 1 it means that the note would be delayed until another note on another channel (which also had *s* set to 1) was ready to play; then these two notes would start together. Similarly with *s* set to 2 the note would not sound until notes on both other channels (which also had *s* set to 2) were ready to play.

f   0 by default. Setting *f* to 1 means that the note would play as soon as it was sent to the buffer; it would "flush out" any other notes already in that buffer.

c   no default. This digit specifies the sound channel, 0 to 3, as previously defined.

Referring back to the previous double page, PROCKGROUP has the line:

```
FOR I = &0201 TO &0203 : SOUND I,0,0,8 : NEXT I
```

The effect of the above line is identical to that of the following three:

```
SOUND   &0201, 0, 0,8
SOUND   &0202, 0, 0,8
SOUND   &0203, 0, 0,8
```
(synch digit)

where the synchronizing digit for each channel ensures that the first note does not start until the other *two* are ready; then they all begin together. In this example all three notes are "rests" which make no noise for 8 vigintisecs (8÷20 seconds). The three "voices" stay synchronized thereafter because the number of beats in each bar has been made constant.

ENVELOPES

The SOUND statement defined on page 128 shows the second argument as a negative integer between -1 and -15. When this argument is given as a *positive* integer it denotes a sound *envelope* which specifies amplitude indirectly. This envelope is defined by the ENVELOPE statement as set out below. There may be as many as four envelope statements in a program; each may be referred to by different SOUND statements.

The sound envelope comprises two distinct envelopes, one to specify the variation of pitch with respect to time; the other to specify the variation of amplitude with respect to time.

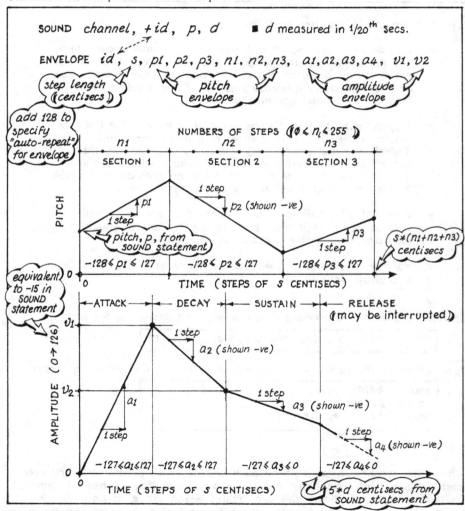

SOUND *channel, +id, p, d*   ■ *d* measured in 1/20th secs.

ENVELOPE *id, s, p1, p2, p3, n1, n2, n3, a1, a2, a3, a4, v1, v2*

▶ ENVELOPE 2, 3, 0, 0, 0, 0, 0, 0, 2, 0, -10, -5, -2, 120, 120
▶ ENVELOPE 3, 7, 2, 1, 1, 1, 1, 1, 121, -10, -5, -2, 120, 120

EXPERIMENT

Precede the music program with some envelopes. The following are envelopes suggested in the User Guide:

```
ENVELOPE 1, 1, 0, 0, 0,  0, 0, 0,  2, 0, -10, -5, 120, 0
ENVELOPE 2, 3, 0, 0, 0,  0, 0, 0, 121, -10, -5, -2, 120, 120
ENVELOPE 3, 7, 2, 1, 1,  1, 1, 1, 121, -10, -5, -2, 120, 120
ENVELOPE 4, 1, 0, 0, 0,  0, 0, 0,  61, 0, -10, -120, 120, 0
ENVELOPE   8, 1, -1, 1,  1, 1, 1, 121, -10, -5, -2, 120, 120
```

Next, insert a statement which asks for the numbers of two envelopes:

```
INPUT "Name two envelopes", EN1, EN2
```

And adjust the statement which deals with the exclamation mark. Change it from `IF INSTR(N$,"!") A=-15 ELSE A=-14` to:

```
IF INSTR(N$,"!") A=EN2 ELSE A=EN1
```

The resulting program becomes a test bed for envelopes:

```
>RUN
Name two envelopes ? 3,2
```

which causes "London's Burning" to be played using two sound envelopes. Notes marked with an exclamation mark are now played according to envelope 3, the remainder according to envelope 2.

To hear the effect of each envelope individually use procedure PROCKER rather than PROCKGROUP.

EXERCISES

1. Implement "London's Burning" as a solo and as a round.

2. Do the same with "Frère Jacques".

3. Experiment with sound envelopes as suggested on page 135.

4. Play a duet. This can be achieved by encoding the two parts sequentially and playing in the same manner as a round except that the music must be made to stop when the second pointer reaches the end of its tune.

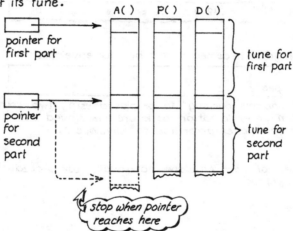

The music for a duet by J.S.Bach, and a great deal more information about music on the BBC Micro, is given in the book by McGregor & Watt referred to on page 126.

FILES

PROGRAM FILES
(SAVE, LOAD, CHAIN, !BOOT)
DATA FILES
THE CATALOGUE
(*CAT, *DELETE)
OPENOUT( ) • PRINT# • CLOSE#
OPENIN( ) • INPUT# • EOF# • CLOSE#
ADDRESS BOOK (EXAMPLE)
FILE FORMAT
FILE POINTER, PTR#
BPUT# AND BGET#

PROGRAM FILES

SAVE · LOAD · CHAIN

A program in the memory of the computer may be sent to the disk ⬱ or a cassette if no disk is fitted. The command to achieve this is defined below:

SAVE *string*	■ *string* denotes the name under which the program currently in memory is to be filed on cassette or disk.

▶ SAVE MYPROGRAM3   ▶ SAVE N$+"T"

The name chosen to identify a file (in computer jargon the *filename*) should start with a capital letter and comprise no more than ten capital letters and digits. Thus MYPROGRAM3 is as long as a filename is allowed to be. If a disk is fitted, however, the number of characters in a filename is limited to seven, but the characters of the name are not constrained to be letters and digits. The following rules, if followed, would ensure compatibility of filenames between installations equipped with cassette and those with disk:

- start the filename with a capital letter
- use only capital letters A to Z and digits 0 to 9
- make the filename no longer than seven characters

Notice that SAVE *string* is a *command* only; it does not work as a statement inside a program:

IF OK THEN SAVE "ME" ⤝🐜

To save a program on cassette: (1) rewind and set counter to ⟦0000⟧ (2) type SAVE "ME" ⟦RETURN⟧ (but using a proper name in place of "ME") (3) notice the message "RECORD then RETURN" on the screen (4) wind tape fast forward to where the program is to go and note the reading on the tape counter for future reference (5) press ⟦RECORD⟧ on the tape deck and ⟦RETURN⟧ on the keyboard (6) press ⟦ESCAPE⟧ to abandon the recording process if anything goes wrong.

A program filed on cassette or disk may be brought back into the memory of the computer by the command LOAD or the statement CHAIN :

LOAD ⟦*string* / " "⟧	■ *string* denotes the filename of a program file on disk or waiting on cassette

cassette only:
"load next program found"

▶ LOAD " "   ▶ LOAD "MYPROG3"   ▶ N$ = "MYPROG3" : LOAD N$

Notice that LOAD is a *command only*; it does not work as a statement:

IF OK THEN LOAD N$ ⤝🐜

138

The CHAIN statement has the effect of the command >LOAD followed by >RUN. It is defined below:

CHAIN [string] (cassette only: applies to next program found) ■ string denotes the filename of a program filed on disk or waiting on cassette

▶ 1040 CHAIN N$ ▶ > CHAIN N$

When a program file is loaded as a result of a LOAD command from the keyboard, or execution of a CHAIN statement in a program, the nominated program is brought into the memory of the computer obliterating the program previously there. The variables of the previous program are cleared ≈ apart from A% to Z% and '@% . The contents of these variables are retained, so offering means of communication between the previous and present programs.

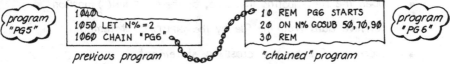

program "PG5"

```
1040
1050 LET N%=2
1060 CHAIN "PG6"
```

```
10 REM  PG6 STARTS
20 ON N% GOSUB 50,70,90
30 REM
```

program "PG6"

previous program   "chained" program

The sketches above illustrate communication between one program and another which is "chained" by the first. As soon as the "chained" program has been *loaded* it is automatically *run*, as though by >LOAD followed by >RUN.

!BOOT A SPECIAL PROGRAM FILE LOADED AND RUN BY PRESSING [CTRL] [SHIFT] (NOT WITH CASSETTE)

On pressing the control and shift keys the computer searches the disk on drive 0 for a program file having the special name !BOOT. Nothing happens if there is no such program filed on the disk, but if such a program is found it is automatically loaded and run as though by the two commands > LOAD "!BOOT" and >RUN.

Here is how to set up a file named "!BOOT" when using an Opus® disk drive:

```
>*BUILD  !BOOT
```

the computer now provides line numbers automatically:

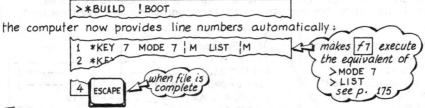

```
1 *KEY 7 MODE 7 |M LIST |M
2 *KE
```

(makes f7 execute the equivalent of >MODE 7 >LIST see p. 175)

4 ESCAPE (when file is complete)

The example illustrates a typical use of the file named "!BOOT" which is to "prime" the function keys with short programs useful to the work in hand. When developing a graphics program in MODE 5, for example, it is handy to have a function key which, when pressed, causes the computer to print a program listing in MODE 7.

 **DATA FILES**

So far this book has dealt with output to screen or printer and input from the keyboard. The rest of this chapter is concerned with output to ⇌ or input from ⇌ a file of data held on cassette or disk.

In general, to output data to a new file:

- open, and name, the file using the C=OPENOUT( ) function
- send data to the file by the PRINT#C statement
- close the file by the CLOSE#C statement.

To input data from an existing data file:

- open the file, quoting its name, by the C=OPENIN( ) function
- retrieve data from the file by the INPUT#C statement
- close the file by the CLOSE#C statement

It is not possible to send data to a file opened as a source of input, nor retrieve data from a file opened as a "sink" for output. But it *is* possible to close an output file, then re-open that file for input.

Details of the functions and statements mentioned above are given later in this chapter.

Filenames for data files should conform to the rules given for naming program files, namely:

- start the name with a capital letter
- employ only capital letters and digits Ø to 9
- make the name no longer than seven characters.

Data files offer a medium of communication between chained programs in addition to the variables A% to Z% and @%. Here is a trivial example to illustrate the mechanism of communication via both media:

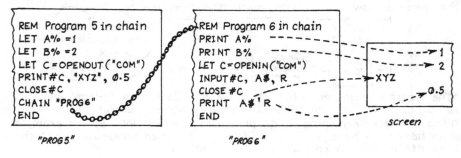

```
REM Program 5 in chain
LET A% =1
LET B% =2
LET C=OPENOUT("COM")
PRINT#C,"XYZ", Ø.5
CLOSE#C
CHAIN "PROG6"
END
```
"PROG5"

```
REM Program 6 in chain
PRINT A%
PRINT B%
LET C=OPENIN("COM")
INPUT#C, A$, R
CLOSE#C
PRINT A$,'R
END
```
"PROG6"

screen

THE CATALOGUE *CAT *DELETE

The catalogue is a list of names of files currently held on a cassette or disk. The list may be displayed by the command:

```
*CAT   ◄── no arguments
```

The resulting list comprises names of both *program* files and *data* files; there is no distinction in syntax.

To see the catalogue of files on cassette: (1) rewind (2) enter *CAT (3) play the tape (4) wait a long time as filenames are displayed. To obtain the catalogue for a disk simply enter *CAT; the list appears on the screen within a second.

When a disk is fitted, *CAT may be used as a statement in a program:

```
IF NOT OK THEN *CAT
IF NOT OK THEN STOP
```

Any file named in the catalogue may be deleted using the command:

```
*DELETE   filename   ◄── no quote marks
```

▶ DELETE MYFILE3

The *DELETE command should not be confused with DELETE (no star) which is employed to delete lines of a program during the editing process.

It is unnecessary to delete files from a cassette; simply record the next data file or program file on top of the unwanted one. The *DELETE command is intended for use with disks.

The *DELETE command may be included as a statement inside a program:

```
IF NOT OK THEN *DELETE  MYFILE3      statement with *
IF NOT OK THEN STOP                  must be the last
                                     on its line
```

and it is possible to commit suicide:

```
>1Ø REM Kamikaze
>2Ø *DELETE KAMI
>SAVE "KAMI"
>RUN
>*CAT        no sign of KAMI
             in the catalogue
```

It is impossible to delete a file connected to an open channel.

OPENOUT · PRINT# · CLOSE# FILES AS A SINK FOR OUTPUT

Communication with named files takes place through *channels*, of which no more than five may be open simultaneously.

Before data can be output to a file on cassette or disk, a *channel* must be opened. The function OPENOUT( ) is available for this purpose; its argument is the name of the file to which output is to go; the function returns a channel number allocated automatically by the computer. The function is defined as follows:

OPENOUT (*string*) RETURNS AN INTEGER TO IDENTIFY AN OUTPUT CHANNEL TO THE NOMINATED FILE

```
CHNL% = OPENOUT ( "MYFILE3") : PRINT CHNL%
```
⇨ 17 ⇐ *for example*

This function is invoked so as to open a *new* file to receive output. However, if an *existing* file is nominated then the content of that file is *lost*; a new and empty file is created with the given name. *N.B.*

Output is sent along the nominated channel by PRINT# :

```
PRINT# channel ,  [ numerical
                     string ]
                        ,
```
- *channel* is an *expression* reducing to an allocated channel number
- *numerical* is an *expression* treated as an *integer* if it reduces to a whole number in the range of an *integer†*, otherwise treated as a *real*.

▶PRINT#C, A$, "NO", −8192, 10*2*3, 10.0, INT(10.0), I%, R

treated as integer   *integer*   *real (exception)*   *integer*   *integer*   *real*

Reals occupy more space on file than integers. File structure is explained later.

When all desired output has been sent along a channel that channel should be closed; attempts to delete a file on an open channel evoke an error message.

```
CLOSE # channel
```
■ makes an end-of-file "mark" detectable by EOF#

▶ CLOSE #C

The following small program asks for names and addresses which it then files on cassette or disk. If using a cassette, locate the tape with the counter set at a round hundred; leave enough uncommitted tape ahead; make a note of the counter reading. Then run the following program:

```
INPUT "Name the new file ", F$
C% = OPENOUT ( F$)
REPEAT
  INPUT "Surname & initials " 'S$
  INPUT " No. & street " 'N$' "Town " 'T$
  PRINT#C%, S$, N$, T$
UNTIL S$ = ""
CLOSE #C%
```
open for output to a new file

close channel when user presses RETURN in response to all three questions

null

142

OPENIN · INPUT# · EOF# · CLOSE# FILES AS A SOURCE OF INPUT

For the computer to receive input from disk or cassette a channel to an existing file must first be opened. There is a function for this purpose; its argument is the name of a file already in the catalogue; the function returns a channel number allocated automatically.

OPENIN (string) RETURNS AN INTEGER TO IDENTIFY AN INPUT CHANNEL TO THE NOMINATED FILE

```
C = OPENIN ( "MYFILE3" ) : PRINT C        ⇨    14 ← for example
```

An error message is evoked if the nominated file is not on the disk.

Input is received through the nominated channel by INPUT# :

```
INPUT # channel,  ┌ numerical-identifier ┐      ■ channel is an expression
                  │ string-identifier    │        reducing to a channel number
                  └          ,           ┘        allocated by the computer
```

▶ INPUT #CH, N%, A(I), S$ ← an integer, then a real, then a string

At the end of the file is an end-of-file "mark" detectable by the function:

EOF# channel RETURNS TRUE IF THE EOF MARK HAS BEEN DETECTED

```
C = OPENOUT ("EG2")          ← file just two reals
PRINT #C, 2.0, 3.0 :  CLOSE #C    false                    true      0
C = OPENIN ("EG2")                                                  -1
INPUT #C, X :  PRINT EOF #C : INPUT #C, X :  PRINT EOF #C ⇨
```

When all required input has been received from the file the channel should be closed. Attempts to delete a file on an open channel evoke an error message.

```
CLOSE # channel        ■ channel is an expression reducing to a channel no.
```

▶ CLOSE #C

The following small program asks for the name of an existing file such as that created by the program opposite (a sequence of strings in threes) and displays the contents on the screen. An error message is evoked if the nominated file is missing from cassette or disk, also if an item other than a string is input from the file.

```
INPUT "Name of existing file please ", A$
C = OPENIN (A$) :  PRINT '' A$ '
REPEAT
┌ INPUT #C, NAM$, ST$, TN$   ← name, street, town
└ PRINT NAM$ ' ST$ ' TN$ ''
UNTIL EOF #C   ← detects "mark" against
CLOSE #C : END      final item on file
```

```
MYFILE3

JONES, D.
26 DRAGON ST.
CARDIFF

SMITH, A.
etc.
```

ADDRESS BOOK

The statements and functions defined on the previous double page are enough to implement the program opposite which maintains an address book in alphabetical order. To set up the initial address book:

- Run the BOOK program and answer "Name of file ?" by entering a name by which to identify the file which is to be your address book. Make the last character of the name a zero for reasons explained later. (*e.g.* FRENDSØ)

- Answer Y (for Yes) to the question "Is this a new file?"

- Answer A (for Add) to the selection Add, Delete, Quit

- Supply name, initials, street and town as prompted. Each sub-entry may be as long as desired.

- On making a mistake, finish the erroneous name and address by pressing RETURN . Then select D when Add, Delete, Quit appears.

- Answer Q (for Quit) to the selection Add, Delete, Quit to bring any session to an end.

To view the address book, run the utility program, VIEW, and supply the name of the address-book file. The number appended to the name is automatically bumped up by one every time the BOOK program is run. Thus if BOOK is given the file FRENDSØ it creates a new file named FRENDS1 etc.

To update the address book:

- Run the BOOK program and answer the first question (Name of file?) by entering the name of the file to be updated.

- Answer N (for No) to "Is this a new file? "

- Proceed with additions and deletions as already described above. A change of address is made by deleting an existing name and address followed by adding a new one.

- Execute *CAT to check the creation of an updated file. Delete previous copies using *DELETE *name* (*e.g.* when you have FRENDS1, FRENDS2, FRENDS3 in the catalogue it is probably time for > * DELETE FRENDS1 . This applies only to disk files.)

Here is the VIEW program:

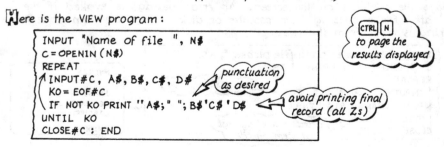

```
INPUT "Name of file ", N$
C = OPENIN (N$)
REPEAT
  INPUT#C, A$, B$, C$, D$          punctuation
  KO = EOF#C                        as desired
  IF NOT KO PRINT "A$;" "; B$'C$ 'D$     avoid printing final
UNTIL KO                                record (all Zs)
CLOSE#C : END
```

CTRL N
to page the
results displayed

The main BOOK program is simple:

```
REM Address book. Main program        change at will
LET  ND = 100                         (max. no. of names)
DIM A$(ND), INL$(ND), STREET$(ND)
DIM TWN$(ND), PNTR(ND)
PROCINCT : REM Preparation
PROCESSING: REM Process additions & deletions
END
```

	A$( )	INL$()	STREET$()	TWN$()
(1)	SMITH	W.H.	2 BOOK ST.	READING
(2)				
(ND)	ZZZZZZ	ZZZZZZ	ZZZZZZ	ZZZZZZ

The PROCINCT procedure interrogates for name of file and its status (new or old).

```
DEF PROCINCT
LOCAL N
Z$ = "ZZZZZZ"        special final record
REPEAT
 INPUT "Name of file? " NF$
  PRINT "Is this a new file?  ": N$ = GET$
  PRINT
 LET N = INSTR( "YNyn", N$)
UNTIL N>0 AND LEN(NF$)>1        at least two characters in file name essential
N = 1 + (N-1) MOD 2             N=1 when N$= "Y" or "y"
IF N=1 PROCREATE ELSE PROCRUSTES   N=2  "  "  = "N" or "n"
ENDPROC
```

Then *one* of the following two procedures is invoked; either:

```
DEF PROCREATE :  REM Create a final record
PRINT "New file"
K=1 :  A$(1) = Z$ :  INL$(1) = Z$      the last 3 items may be set
STREET$(1) = Z$ :  TWN$(1) = Z$        to any string; zzzzzz is
ENDPROC                                convenient
```

Or the procedure to reclaim existing data for extension or deletion:

```
DEF PROCRUSTES: REM Data for ext'n or delet'n
PRINT "Old file"
CHIN = OPENIN(NF$) : K=0    open a channel for input
REPEAT                      & initialize counter
 K=K+1
  INPUT#CHIN, A$(k), INL$(k), STREET$(k), TWN$(k)    input, name by name
UNTIL EOF#CHIN
CLOSE #CHIN        the final record will be zzzzzz
ENDPROC
```

The processing procedure invokes PROCADD, PROCROSSOUT, finally PROCOFF overleaf:

```
DEF PROCESSING
LOCAL  N, N$
REPEAT
 REPEAT
  PRINT "Add, Delete, Quit   ": N$= GET$
   N = INSTR("ADQa dq" , N$)
 UNTIL N>0                   N=1 when N$ =A or a
 N = 1 + (N-1) MOD 3              =2  "    D or d
 IF N=1 PRINT "Add a new name  ": PROCADD    =3  "    Q or q
 IF N=2 PRINT "Delete a name ": PROCROSSOUT
 IF N=3 PRINT "Batch complete ": PROCOFF : END
UNTIL FALSE
ENDPROC
```

(CONTINUED)

The following is for adding a name and address:

```
DEF PROCADD
INPUT "Surname   "A$(K)
INPUT "Initials  "INL$(K)
INPUT "Street    "STREET$(K)
INPUT "Town      "TWN$(K)
K=K+1
A$(K)=Z$ : INL$(K)=Z$ : STREET$(K)=Z$ : TWN$(K)=Z$
ENDPROC
```

these are written on top of the Z-record

then the Zs are written on the next row down

This procedure deletes by writing Z$ on top of the unwanted name:

```
DEF PROCROSSOUT
LOCAL  N, KO
IF K=1 PRINT "Nothing to delete" : ENDPROC
INPUT "Surname  " S$
INPUT "Initials " I$
KO = FALSE : N=0
REPEAT
  N=N+1
  IF N=K KO=TRUE : PRINT S$,I$, "not found"
  IF S$ = A$(N) AND I$= INL$(N) KO=TRUE : A$(N)=Z$
UNTIL KO
ENDPROC
```

when sorted, this name sinks to the bottom and so is ignored when file is saved on disk

both name AND initials must match

This procedure is invoked after Quit. It invokes a sorting procedure and sends the sorted data to the disk under an adjusted name.

```
DEF  PROCOFF
LOCAL  N, I
LET M$ =LEFT$(NF$,LEN(NF$)-1) + STR$(1+VAL(RIGHT$(NF$,1)))
CHOUT = OPENOUT (M$)
FOR N=1 TO K : PNTR(N)=N : NEXT N
PROCWIKSOT (1, K)
N = 0
REPEAT
  N=N+1 : I = PNTR(N)
  PRINT# CHOUT, A$(I), INL$(I), STREET$(I), TWN$(I)
UNTIL  A$(I) = Z$
CLOSE# CHOUT
ENDPROC
```

suppose NF$ is "FREND6" then LEN(NF$-1) is 5, so LEFT$(NF$,5) is "FREND"

suppose NF$ is "FREND6"; then RIGHT$(NF$,1) is "6", VAL("6") is 6, STR$(1+6) is "7"

invoke any convenient sorting procedure

get out on meeting the first of possibly several rows beginning ZZZZZZ

Finally a sorting procedure is needed. PROCWIKSOT (FIRST, LAST) on page 87. works well and is invoked as shown above. It is just as easy to invoke PROCBUBBLE (FIRST, LAST) which is listed on page 84 or PROCIPPLE (FIRST, LAST) as listed on page 85. As a general rule, bubble sorts are good when a list is almost in the right order before starting; Quicksort is better when the list is initially a jumble. The relative performance of different sorting procedures is a subject too big to go into in a book like this.

FILE FORMAT

HOW DIFFERENT TYPES OF DATA ARE FILED ≈ AND A PROGRAM TO LIST ANY DATA FILE

Files on cassette or disk are encoded in "internal format" as depicted below. For applications such as the address book it is unnecessary to know what the internal format looks like. If the computer obeys:

```
PRINT#C, I%, A, S$
```

and subsequently obeys:

```
INPUT #C, J%, B, T$
```

then the items on file are obviously in the correct sequence for re-input. The fact that integers, reals and strings on the file are of differing length is of no concern. It is obvious, however, that:

```
INPUT#C, T$, J%, B
```

would be an error because types would not match.

The forms of integers, reals and strings when filed are depicted below. The 1s and Øs in the boxes represent binary digits; digits underneath the boxes represent hex digits (for a description of hex notation see page 80).

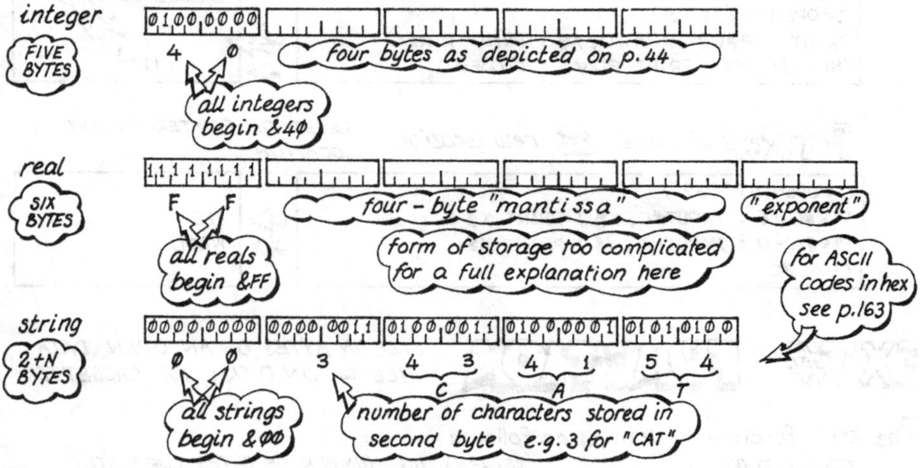

integer
FIVE BYTES
0100 0000
4 0
four bytes as depicted on p.44
all integers begin &40
real
SIX BYTES
1111 1111
F F
four-byte "mantissa"
"exponent"
all reals begin &FF
form of storage too complicated for a full explanation here
for ASCII codes in hex see p.163
string
2+N BYTES
0000 0000
0000 0011
0100 0011
0100 0001
0101 0100
0 0 3 4 3 4 1 5 4
C A T
all strings begin &00
number of characters stored in second byte e.g. 3 for "CAT"

The following program is useful for displaying the contents of *any* data file ≈ even if the sequence of integers, reals and strings is unknown. The program uses BGET#, EXT# and PTR# which are explained overleaf.

```
REM Display content of any data file
INPUT "Name the file "N$ :  C=OPENIN(N$)
REPEAT
  N=BGET#C : PTR#C=PTR#C-1
  IF N=&40  INPUT#C,I% : PRINT I%
  IF N=&FF  INPUT#C,R  : PRINT R
  IF N=&00  INPUT#C,A$ : PRINT A$
UNTIL EOF#C
PRINT "File has "; EXT#C; " bytes"
CLOSE#C
END
```

back-step the pointer

print no. of bytes in file

DISPLAY ANY DATA FILE HELD ON DISK

FILE POINTER • PTR#

Every open channel has a "pointer"; this is automatically set pointing to the first byte of the nominated file as the channel is opened. During *output* to a file the pointer moves so that it points to the byte immediately following the last item output; in other words it points to the place where the next item will go. During *input* from a file the pointer moves so that it points to the byte just after the last item input; in other words it points to the next item to come.

The behaviour of the pointer can be changed by manipulating PTR# (an abbreviation of *PoinTeR*). Used as a function, PTR# returns the current position of the pointer measured in bytes from 0 (e.g. LET N = PTR#C). Used as a special variable, the desired position of the pointer may be assigned to PTR#C (e.g. LET PTR#C = N).

PTR# *channel*   RETURNS THE NUMBER OF THE BYTE (COUNTING FROM 0) AT WHICH THE POINTER CURRENTLY POINTS

```
C = OPENOUT ("EG2")
PRINT#C, "ABCD" : PRINT#C, "EFG" : CLOSE#C
C = OPENIN ("EG2")
PRINT PTR#C : INPUT#C, X$ : PRINT PTR#C
INPUT#C, X$ : PRINT PTR#C : CLOSE#C
```
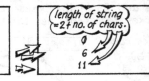
(length of string = 2 + no. of chars.)
0
6
11

PTR# *channel* ⊟ *new location*   RESET THE POINTER TO ANY LOCATION

```
C = OPENIN ("EG2")
PTR#C = 6 : INPUT#C, X$ : PRINT X$
PTR#C = 0 : INPUT#C, X$ : PRINT X$
CLOSE#C
```
EFG
ABCD

EXT# FUNCTION   SIZE IN BYTES OF AN OPEN DATA FILE ≈ ON DISK; NOT CASSETTE

The EXT# function is defined as follows:

EXT# *channel*   RETURNS THE NUMBER OF BYTES CURRENTLY CONTAINED IN A DATA FILE ON A DISK

```
C = OPENOUT ("EG3")
PRINT EXT#C
PRINT#C, "THIS LONG STRING" : PRINT EXT#C
PRINT#C, "PLUS", 120000, 0.5 : PRINT EXT#C
CLOSE#C
```
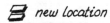 (2 + 16 bytes)
 (2 + 4) (5) (6 bytes)
0
18
35

When a file is opened for *input* its size, of course, remains constant:

```
C = OPENIN ("EG3")
PRINT EXT#C '
INPUT#C, A$, B$, I, R
PRINT EXT#C
CLOSE#C
```
35
35

BPUT# AND BGET#

The statement BPUT# and the function BGET# are for output and input of a single byte respectively. The # symbol introduces a channel number as for PRINT# and INPUT# respectively.

> BPUT# *channel, byte*
>
> ■ *channel* is an *expression* reducing to the number of an open channel
>
> ■ *byte* is an *expression* reducing to an integer in the range 0 ⩽ *byte* ⩽ 255

▶ BPUT#C, 255

The BGET# function is defined as follows:

BGET# *channel*

RETURNS THE SINGLE BYTE WHICH IS NEXT IN THE FILE CONNECTED TO THE NOMINATED CHANNEL

```
C = OPENOUT ("EG1")
BPUT#C, 255 :  CLOSE#C
C = OPENOUT ("EG1")
B% = BGET#C : PRINT B% : CLOSE#C
```

⇨   255

Because an integer on file occupies 5 bytes, a real occupies 6 bytes and a string occupies 2+N bytes, BPUT# and BGET# have few applications within the scope of BBC-BASIC. They are intended for use when the computer is connected to something other than the devices mentioned in this book. Nevertheless, BGET# finds a use in the program on page 147 to return the first byte of each item on the file of input. Once the type of item has been disclosed by this byte the appropriate INPUT# statement can be selected to input the complete item ⇌ the pointer having been stepped back by one byte ⟨ PTR#C = PTR#C - 1 ⟩ . This program is reproduced below for ease of reference.

```
REM  Display content of any data file
INPUT "Name the file "N$ : C = OPENIN (N$)
REPEAT
 N = BGET#C : PTR#C = PTR#C - 1
 IF N = &40 INPUT#C, I% : PRINT I%
 IF N = &FF INPUT#C, R  : PRINT R
 IF N = &00 INPUT#C, A$ : PRINT A$
UNTIL EOF#C
PRINT "File has "; EXT#C; " bytes"
CLOSE#C
END
```

EXERCISES

1. Implement the address book. Adjust the structure of each record according to need. For example, make the program ask for, and deal with, a telephone number in addition to name, initials, street and town.

2. If you have a disk make a !BOOT program to "program" the function keys usefully.

3. Use the Display program on page 147 to list the contents of various data files.

13

OPERATION
AND
ERROR HANDLING

EDITING COMMANDS
(NEW, OLD, CLS, LISTO, LIST,
   AUTO, DELETE, RENUMBER, SAVE)
EXECUTIVE COMMANDS
(CHAIN, MODE, CLEAR, RUN, GOTO)
TRACE COMMAND OR STATEMENT
ON ERROR
ERR • ERL • REPORT
ERROR REPORTS
JOINING PROGRAMS TOGETHER

EDITING COMMANDS

This chapter deals with operation; the commands needed to develop and run a program in BBC-BASIC. The subject of tracing errors and error handling in general is also covered in this chapter.

Several editing commands have been introduced by example earlier; in particular CLS, LIST, RENUMBER, RUN, SAVE in the introductory example of chapter 1. These, and other editing commands, are more formally defined below. One of these commands, CLS, may also be used as a statement in a program — the others may not.

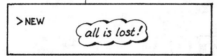

▶ NEW

Obliterate any program currently in the memory of the computer, retaining only the contents of variables A% to Z% and @%.

▶ OLD

Restore a program obliterated by NEW. This works only when no new statement has been introduced after execution of NEW or after pressing BREAK.

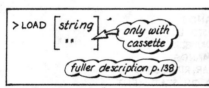

> LOAD [string ""] — only with cassette

(fuller description p.138)

▶ LOAD "MYPROG"

▶ N$ = "MYPROG" : LOAD N$

▶ LOAD "" — next program found on cassette tape

Obliterate the program in the memory of the computer, retaining only the contents (if any) of the variables named A% to Z% and @%. Then load the nominated program from cassette or disk into the computer's memory.

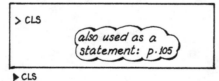

> CLS

also used as a statement: p.105

▶ CLS

Clear the text window (the whole screen by default of a window) painting it in the current background colour for text. Home the cursor to the top left corner of the window.

> LISTO i   ■ i is an expression reducing to an integer 0 ≤ i ≤ 7

▶ LISTO 0 — default

▶ LISTO 4+2+1 — all 3 options

▶ LISTO 1 — space after line nos., no indenting

Set the *style* of subsequent listings commanded by LIST. The argument, expressed in binary, has three bits:

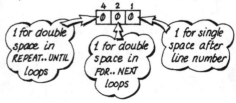

1 for double space in REPEAT..UNTIL loops

1 for double space in FOR..NEXT loops

1 for single space after line number

```
> LIST {  [ line
           line,
           , line
           line, line ] }
```

List all or part of the program in memory in the style set by LISTO. With no argument, LIST implies the whole program. For part of a program the first argument denotes the initial line; the second argument denotes the final line.

▶ LIST   ⊰ *whole program* ⟩

▶ LIST 100,   ⊰ *lines 100, 110, 120,...* ⟩

▶ LIST ,30   ⊰ *lines 10, 20, 30* ⟩   ⊰ *and, of course, any intermediate line numbers* ⟩

▶ LIST 30, 50   ⊰ *lines 30, 40, 50* ⟩

```
> AUTO {  [ line
            , inc
            line, inc ] }
```

Anstruct the computer to supply line numbers automatically, starting at *line* (which is 10 by default) and incrementing by *inc* (which is 10 by default). Escape from the facility by pressing ESCAPE .

▶ AUTO   ⊰ *10, 20, 30,...* ⟩

▶ AUTO 100   (or AUTO 100,)   ⊰ *100, 110, 120,...* ⟩

▶ AUTO ,2   ⊰ *10, 12, 14,...* ⟩

▶ AUTO 1,1   ⊰ *1, 2, 3, ...* ⟩

```
> DELETE  line, line
```

Delete lines from the program in memory. Both arguments must be given. Use 0 to signify the beginning of the program; use a very large integer to signify the end of the program.

▶ DELETE 140, 170   ⊰ *140, 150, 160, 170* ⟩   ⊰ *and, of course, any intermediate line numbers* ⟩

▶ DELETE 0, 30   ⊰ *10, 20, 30* ⟩

▶ DELETE 40, 32767   ⊰ *40, 50, 60,...* ⟩

▶ DELETE 50   ⊰ *just line 50* ⟩

```
> RENUMBER {  [ line
                , inc
                line, inc ] }
```

Renumber lines of the program in memory, the first to be numbered as *line* (10 by default) incremented subsequently by *inc* (also 10 by default). GOTO and ON statements are faithfully adjusted unless line numbers are not given as integers (GOTO L).

▶ RENUMBER   ⊰ *10, 20, 30,...* ⟩

▶ RENUMBER 100   ⊰ *100, 110, 120,...* ⟩

▶ RENUMBER ,1   ⊰ *10, 11, 12, ...* ⟩

▶ RENUMBER 100, 1   ⊰ *100, 101, 102,...* ⟩

```
> SAVE  string
```

fuller description, p. 138

Save the program in memory as a program file under the name given. If a file with the given name already exists, delete the existing file and replace it with a copy of the program in memory.

153

EXECUTIVE COMMANDS
CHAIN, MODE, CLEAR,
RUN, GOTO

The keywords defined as commands below may be used also as statements in programs; for example "10 MODE 5" might be the first statement.

For commands prefixed with a star such as *FX, *TAPE, *DISK, *MOTOR, see chapter 14. Commands with a star are handled directly by the computer's operating system and so are not, strictly speaking, commands of BBC-BASIC itself.

>CHAIN *string*

also used as a statement, p. 139

▶ CHAIN "PROG6"
▶ N$ = "PROG6" : CHAIN N$

Used as a command, CHAIN is equivalent to LOAD followed by RUN. In other words this command causes the nominated program to be loaded (obliterating everything in memory save the contents of variables A% to Z% and @%) and control passed to the first statement.

> MODE *n*

also used as a statement: p.108

■ *n* is an *expression* reducing to $0 \leqslant n \leqslant 7$

▶ MODE 7 ← *non-graphics*

Used as a command, MODE *n* switches the computer from one mode to another without disturbing the program currently in memory and without disturbing the values held in variables. The table on page 108 defines the characteristics of each mode.

> CLEAR

also used as a statement

▶ CLEAR
▶ 100 IF NOT OK THEN CLEAR

Used as a command, CLEAR makes all arrays and variables vanish. Exceptions are A% to Z% and @% which retain any values previously assigned to them. The command PRINT X, given after CLEAR, would evoke the message "No such variable."

>RUN

also used as a statement

▶ RUN ← *same as* >CLEAR >GOTO 1
▶ 100 IF OK THEN RUN ← *run thyself*

Used as a command, RUN has the effect of CLEAR followed by the transfer of control to the first statement of the program.

>GOTO *line*

also used as a statement

▶ GOTO 100
▶ CLEAR : GOTO 10 ← *same as RUN*

It is possible to transfer control from keyboard to any statement of the program in memory by using GOTO as a command.

TRACE COMMAND OR STATEMENT

In cases where the flow of control seems to have gone wrong it may be useful to trace the flow by displaying the number of every line the computer obeys. The TRACE command makes this possible.

```
TRACE [ ON  ]        ■ line is an expression reducing to the
        [ OFF ]          line number above which the display
        [ line ]         of line numbers is to be suppressed.
```

▶ TRACE ON   ▶ TRACE OFF   ▶ TRACE 1000

Whilst the trace is switched on, the number of each line encountered during execution is displayed between arrow symbols ⇔ or square brackets in MODE 0 to MODE 6. ⇨

```
10 REM
20 REM
30 END
>TRACE ON
>RUN
←10→ ←20→ ←30→ >
```

```
10 REM
20 REM     report suppressed
30 END
>TRACE 20
>RUN
←10→ >
```

Line numbers above a given value may be excluded from the report. This feature is useful when functions and procedures on high-numbered lines are thought not to be the cause of trouble.

In FOR..NEXT loops the FOR statement itself is considered as being executed only once at the beginning of the loop. ⇨

```
10 FOR X = 0 TO 2
20 ⌐ REM
30 NEXT X
>TRACE ON     once only
>RUN
←10→←20→←30→←20→←30→←20→←30→ >
```

```
10 FOR X = 0 TO 3
20 NEXT X
>TRACE ON
>RUN     once only
←10→←20→ >
```

And this happens: I don't know why.

The REPEAT line of a REPEAT..UNTIL loop is also considered as being executed only once, but every execution of the UNTIL line is reported. ⇨

```
10 X = 0
20 REPEAT: X = X+1
30 UNTIL X = 2
>TRACE ON
>RUN
←10→ ←20→←30→←30→←30→ >
```

It is permissible to use TRACE as a statement. TRACE may thus be switched on before execution of the piece of program thought to be in error and switched off in emergencies:

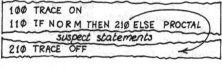

```
100 TRACE ON
110 IF NORM THEN 210 ELSE PROCTAL
        suspect statements
210 TRACE OFF
```

The trace switches itself off automatically on meeting an error or STOP or END.

ON ERROR

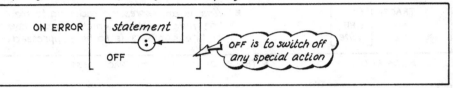

FOR TRAPPING ERRORS WHEN THE PROGRAM IS RUNNING

The ON ERROR statement is for trapping errors that would otherwise cause the program to stop ≈ having displayed an error message. This statement should be placed where it would be obeyed before meeting any error; preferably right at the beginning of the program.

```
ON ERROR ┌─ statement ─┐
         │      :       │        OFF is to switch off
         └─   OFF      ─┘        any special action
```

▶ ON ERROR PRINT "Oh dear" : LET KOUNT = KOUNT+1 : GOTO 10

▶ ON ERROR OFF

If ON ERROR is not used at all then errors detected by the computer during execution result in error messages on the screen and a halt to execution. This result can be avoided by using the ON ERROR statement. Instead of a message being displayed ≈ and the program coming to a halt ≈ the computer obeys the statements following ON ERROR.

The statement ON ERROR OFF, when obeyed, makes the computer ignore any action previously specified for dealing with errors. It is as though the ON ERROR statement had never been used in the first place.

Here is an example of ON ERROR added as lines 45 and 55 to the programs on page 65.

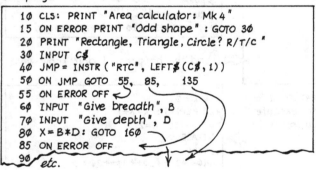

```
10 CLS: PRINT "Area calculator: Mk 4"
15 ON ERROR PRINT "Odd shape" : GOTO 30
20 PRINT "Rectangle, Triangle, Circle? R/T/c "
30 INPUT C$
40 JMP = INSTR ("RTC", LEFT$(C$, 1))
50 ON JMP GOTO 55, 85,    135
55 ON ERROR OFF
60 INPUT "Give breadth", B
70 INPUT "Give depth", D
80 X = B*D : GOTO 160
85 ON ERROR OFF
90 etc.
```

Assume a user of this program typed RUN and responded to INPUT C$ by typing Q. At line 50 the Q would not be found in string "RTC", therefore the variable named JMP would be set to zero. Line 50 is now impossible to obey because JMP does not contain 1 or 2 or 3. Without line 15 this would result in the message "ON range at line 50". But because of line 15 the standard error message and halt is circumvented; the message "Odd shape" is displayed and control goes to line 30 offering another try. If the user now typed R, control would find its way to line 55 and switch the special error treatment off. Similarly for T or C.

ERR · ERL · REPORT

In dealing with an error the functions ERR and ERL, and the statement REPORT, may be useful. Here they are defined:

ERR — RETURNS THE ERROR NUMBER OF THE ERROR WHICH CAUSED THE PROGRAM TO TRANSFER CONTROL VIA "ON ERROR"

```
10 ON ERROR GOTO 1000
```

```
1000 IF ERR<>18 PRINT "Error no."; ERR : STOP
1010 X = 1E30 : GOTO 120
```
GOTO somewhere suitable for carrying on

ERL — RETURNS THE LINE NUMBER OF THE STATEMENT IN WHICH THE PRESENT ERROR WAS DETECTED

```
10 ON ERROR GOTO 2000
```

```
2000 IF ERR<>18 PRINT "Error"; ERR; " line"; ERL: STOP
2010 X=1E30: PRINT "Infinity @ line "; ERL : GOTO 130
```

Every possible error number that could be returned by function ERR is listed overleaf; so is the standard error report associated with each error. This report may be displayed using the REPORT statement:

```
REPORT          ▪ Display the error report appropriate to the
                  most recent error, or the word "Escape"
                  in the absence of errors ( see overleaf for
                  all error reports )
```

▶ REPORT

The following trivial program illustrates the use of all three facilities defined above:

```
10 ON ERROR PRINT "Oh dear, "; :GOTO 60
20 REM Quick divisions
30 INPUT "Numerator & Denominator please " N, D
40 PRINT "Quotient is "; N/D
50 GOTO 20
60 REM Deal with mistakes
70 IF ERR=18 PRINT " infinity." : GOTO 20
80 PRINT " mistake "; ERR; " at statement "; ERL
90 REPORT: END
>RUN
Numerator & Denominator please    2, 5
Quotient is 0.4
Numerator & Denominator please    2, 0
Quotient is Oh dear, infinity.
Numerator & Denominator please    2, 1E512
Oh dear, mistake 20 at statement 40
Too big          result of REPORT
>
```

Error handling in BBC-BASIC involves a lot of GOTOs. Even in structured languages like Pascal, error handling becomes untidy unless the programmer takes particular care.

157

ERROR REPORTS

All error reports are listed below in alphabetical order. Those stemming from assembly-language routines are not elaborated. Those concerned with loading and recording on cassette tape have a brief note appended. The remaining errors may be made when coding BBC-BASIC; below is a minimal program against each of these errors. Running the program should evoke the corresponding error report ≈ appended with the line number at which the error occurred e.g. Accuracy lost **at line 10**.

23 Accuracy lost
```
10 X=SIN(1 E 10)
```

31 Arguments
```
10 PROCA(3)
20 DEF PROCA(X,Y)
30 ENDPROC
```

14 Array
```
10 A(1)=0
```

30 Bad call
```
10 PROC X
```

10 Bad DIM
```
10 DIM X(-3)
```

28 Bad HEX
```
10 X=&ff
```

25 Bad MODE *(main program only)*
```
10 DEF PROCA
20 MODE 7
30 ENDPROC
```

— Bad program *(possibly 10 ?A=X where A is an address in program area)*

218 Block? *(rewind some tape: try again)*

2 Byte *(assembly-language error)*

33 Can't match FOR
```
10 FOR I=0 TO 2
20 FOR J=0 TO 2
30 NEXT J
40 NEXT J
```

222 Channel *(unopened channel to file on cassette)*

216 Data? *(rewind some tape: try again)*

11 DIM space
```
10 DIM X(9000)
```

18 Division by zero
```
10 X=1/0
```

223 Eof *(premature end of cassette tape)*

17 Escape *(ESCAPE pressed)*

24 Exp range
```
10 X=EXP(88+2)
```
(limit is 88)
```
10 X=EXP(88+1)
```
(for some reason this gives error no. 20)

— Failed *(there is no line 2)*
```
1 GOTO 2
>RENUMBER
```

219 File? *(unexpected filename on cassette)*

34 FOR variable
```
10 FOR 5=1 TO 2
20 NEXT
```

217 Header? *(rewind some tape: try again)*

3 Index *(assembly-language error)*

— LINE space *(program too long)*

22 LOG range
```
10 X=LOG(0): Y=LOG(-1)
```

5 Missing ,
```
10 X$= LEFT$("ABC")
```

9 Missing "
```
10 X$ = "ABC
```
(X$ = ABC" evokes error 26)

27 Missing)
```
10 X = SIN(0.2
```

4 Mistake
```
10 BASE RATE = 9%
```
(errors 26 & 16 predominate for gibberish)

21 —ve root
```
10 i = SQR(-1)
```
(also occurs with ASN( ) & ACS( ))

38 No GOSUB
```
10 RETURN
```

7 No FN
```
10 =5
```

32 No FOR
```
10 NEXT
```

13 No PROC
```
10 ENDPROC
```

43 No REPEAT
```
10 UNTIL FALSE
```

0 No room *(adjust HIMEM or LOMEM)*

29 No such FN/PROC
```
10 X = FNTASTIC
```

41 No such line *(there is no 20)*
```
10 GOTO 20 : END
>
```

26 No such variable | `10 X=Y`

(Occurs when reference is made to an unset variable, but also occurs as a consequence of all sorts of other errors like X$=LEFT$(,"ABC") and X=SIN(A$) where more accurate diagnosis might be expected.)

36 No TO | `10 FOR I=1,3` *(TO)* / `20 NEXT I`

12 Not LOCAL | `10 LOCAL N`
(allowed only inside FNs and PROCs)

40 ON range | `10 X=3` / `20 ON X GOTO 30,40`

39 ON syntax | `10 X=1` / `20 ON X TAB(20), 30`

42 Out of DATA | `10 DATA 1.0` / `20 READ X,Y`

`10 DATA 1.0 : READ X,Y`
(not reported: see p. 103)

1 Out of range *(assembly-language error)*

– Silly *(zero inc.)* | `>AUTO 10, 0` / `>RENUMBER 10,0`

220 Syntax *(with cassette files: possibly a bad *OPT command)*

19 String too long *(limit 255 chars.)* | `10 X$ = "A"` / `20 FOR I=1 TO 7` / `30 X$=X$+X$` / `40 NEXT I`

15 Subscript | `10 DIM X(2)` / `20 Y = X(3)`

16 Syntax error | `10 X = 12,13`

(error 26 occurs more often as result of bad syntax)

20 Too big | `10 X = 1E20 ^ 2`

35 Too many FORs *(max. 10 nested)* | `10 FOR X=0 TO 1` / `20 GOTO 10` / `30 NEXT X`

37 Too many GOSUBs *(max. 26 nested)* | `10 GOSUB 20` / `20 GOTO 10`

44 Too many REPEATs *(max. 20 nested)* | `10 REPEAT` / `20 GOTO 10`

6 Type mismatch | `10 A$ = 3` / `20 A = "3"`

8 $ range | `10 $40 = "trespass"`

(overwriting forbidden area <&100: refer p. 178)

Note: these programs have been tried only on the BBC Microcomputer Model B.

ERROR REPORTS
(NUMERICAL ORDER)

0 No room	26 No such variable
1 Out of range	27 Missing)
2 Byte	28 Bad hex
3 Index	29 No such FN/PROC
4 Mistake	30 Bad call
5 Missing ,	31 Arguments
6 Type mismatch	32 No FOR
7 No FN	33 Can't match FOR
8 $ range	34 FOR variable
9 Missing "	35 Too many FORs
10 Bad DIM	36 No TO
11 DIM space	37 Too many GOSUBs
12 Not LOCAL	38 No GOSUB
13 No PROC	39 ON syntax
14 Array	40 ON range
15 Subscript	41 No such line
16 Syntax error	42 Out of DATA
17 Escape	43 No REPEAT
18 Division by zero	44 Too many REPEATs
19 String too long	216 Data?
20 Too big	217 Header?
21 –ve root	218 Block?
22 LOG range	219 File?
23 Accuracy lost	220 Syntax
24 EXP range	222 Channel
25 Bad MODE	223 Eof

JOINING PROGRAMS TOGETHER

Whilst a program is typed at the keyboard, each new statement which has a unique line number adds to the program in memory, whereas a new statement with a non-unique line number *replaces* the corresponding statement in memory. This process is called "merging"; the lines being typed are *merged* with the program in memory.

It is also possible to merge programs when both are on cassette or disk. The shorter is loaded in the conventional way; the longer is merged using the commands *SPOOL and *EXEC as explained in the User Guide. This merging procedure is complicated, hence prone to error and best avoided.

Programs may be *joined* end to end by the quick procedure described below. It is essential when joining programs to ensure that the biggest line number in the first program is less than the smallest line number in the second program. This requirement should be obvious. To meet this requirement it is only necessary to load and renumber each program before joining them:

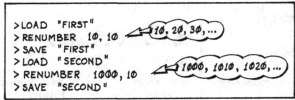

```
>LOAD "FIRST"
>RENUMBER 10, 10      ←── 10, 20, 30, ...
>SAVE "FIRST"
>LOAD "SECOND"
>RENUMBER 1000, 10    ←── 1000, 1010, 1020, ...
>SAVE "SECOND"
```

where it is assumed that the number of the final line of "FIRST" would be less than 1000.

Having properly adjusted the line numbering, the joining may be achieved as follows:

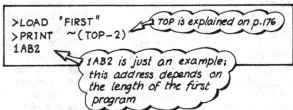

```
>LOAD "FIRST"          ←── TOP is explained on p.176
>PRINT ~(TOP-2)
1AB2
```
1AB2 is just an example; this address depends on the length of the first program

Now use this hex address as the base address of the second program as follows:

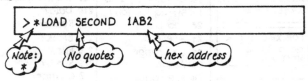

```
>*LOAD SECOND 1AB2
```
Note: *   No quotes   hex address

The *LOAD statement is not defined in this book; it may be taken on trust for the purpose described above.

14

BACKDOOR BASIC

VDU STATEMENT

The VDU statement is for controlling the cursor, enabling and disabling the printer, changing colours, defining windows, and other things for which the authors of BBC-BASIC decided not to introduce specific keywords. VDU is a "back door" to BASIC. It is defined syntactically as follows:

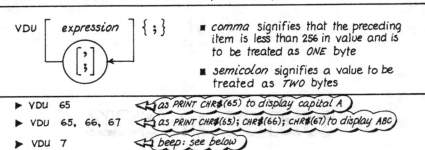

VDU [expression] {;}

```
      [ , ]
      [ ; ]
```

- **comma** signifies that the preceding item is less than 256 in value and is to be treated as *ONE* byte
- **semicolon** signifies a value to be treated as *TWO* bytes

▶ VDU 65 — as PRINT CHR$(65) to display capital A

▶ VDU 65, 66, 67 — as PRINT CHR$(65); CHR$(66); CHR$(67) to display ABC

▶ VDU 7 — beep: see below

The VDU statement is equivalent to PRINT CHR$( ) except that PRINT augments COUNT (p. 93) whereas VDU does not:

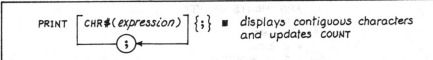

PRINT [CHR$(expression)] {;} ■ displays contiguous characters and updates COUNT

```
      (;)
```

▶ PRINT CHR$(65); CHR$(66); CHR$(67)

Consider the statement PRINT CHR$(65). The 65 is ASCII code for capital A. Therefore executing >PRINT CHR$(65) as a command, or including PRINT CHR$(65) in a program, causes a capital A to be displayed on the screen. But the table opposite shows that capital A may also be displayed by pressing [SHIFT][A], or by executing >VDU 65 or by including VDU 65 as a statement in a program.

Now consider PRINT CHR$(7). The 7 is an ASCII code but *not* that of a displayable character; instead it causes something to happen; a short beep on the loudspeaker. Therefore executing >PRINT CHR$(7), or including PRINT CHR$(7) as a statement of a program, would cause a short beep. The table opposite shows that pressing [CTRL][G], or executing >VDU 7, or including VDU 7 as a statement in a program would also cause a beep.

The following key shows how to read the table opposite:

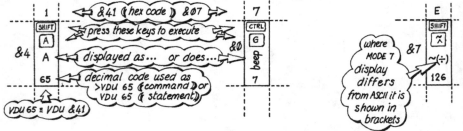

162

SECOND HEX DIGIT

	0	1	2	3	4	5	6	7	8	9	A	B	C	D	E	F
&0	CTRL @	CTRL A — send given control code to printer (↑ not screen)	CTRL B — enable the printer	CTRL C — disable the printer (↑ p.165)	CTRL D — reclaim text cursor and send it back to VPOS, POS	CTRL E — make text cursor join graphics cursor (↑ p.166)	CTRL F — enable screen (↑ if disabled by VDU 21)	CTRL G — beep	CTRL H — move text cursor one place left (↑ dont delete)	CTRL I or TAB — text cursor one place right	CTRL J — drop text cursor one row (↑ scroll if at bottom)	CTRL K — raise text cursor one row (↑ scroll if already at top)	CTRL L — as CLS	CTRL M or RETURN — cursor to left of current line	CTRL N — listing screenful by screenful, pressing SHIFT for next	CTRL O — cease listing by the screenful (↑ p.165)
	0	1	2	3	4	5	6	7	8	9	10	11	12	13	14	15
&1	CTRL P — as CLG	CTRL Q — as COLOUR	CTRL R — as GCOL	CTRL S — change colour scheme (↑ p.168)	CTRL T — reset colour schemes to defaults	CTRL U — as DELETE DELETE DELETE... (↑ p.167)	CTRL V — as MODE but without changing HIMEM	CTRL W — define a special character (↑ p.169)	CTRL X — define graphics window (↑ p.170)	CTRL Y — as PLOT	CTRL Z — reset both windows (↑ p.170)	CTRL [↑	CTRL ↓↑ — define a text window (↑ p.167)	CTRL ↓↑ — define the graphics origin (↑ p.170)	CTRL ↑↑ — home the text cursor to top left of window	CTRL ↑↑ — move text cursor to the point with given coords.
	16	17	18	19	20	21	22	23	24	25	26	27	28	29	30	31
&2	space bar	SHIFT 1! !	SHIFT 2" "	SHIFT 3# #	SHIFT 4$ $	SHIFT 5% %	SHIFT 6& &	SHIFT 7' '	SHIFT 8((	SHIFT 9))	SHIFT :* *	SHIFT ;+ +	<, ,	= =	>. .	?/ /
	32	33	34	35	36	37	38	39	40	41	42	43	44	45	46	47
&3	0 Ø	1! 1	2" 2	3# 3	4$ 4	5% 5	6& 6	7' 7	8(8	9) 9	:* :	;+ ;	SHIFT <, <	SHIFT = =	SHIFT >. >	SHIFT ?/ ?
	48	49	50	51	52	53	54	55	56	57	58	59	60	61	62	63
&4	@ @	SHIFT A A	SHIFT B B	SHIFT C C	SHIFT D D	SHIFT E E	SHIFT F F	SHIFT G G	SHIFT H H	SHIFT I I	SHIFT J J	SHIFT K K	SHIFT L L	SHIFT M M	SHIFT N N	SHIFT O O
	64	65	66	67	68	69	70	71	72	73	74	75	76	77	78	79
&5	SHIFT P P	SHIFT Q Q	SHIFT R R	SHIFT S S	SHIFT T T	SHIFT U U	SHIFT V V	SHIFT W W	SHIFT X X	SHIFT Y Y	SHIFT Z Z	[↑ [(←)	↓↑ \ (½)	↓↑] (→)	↑↑ ^ (↑)	£ — (—)
	80	81	82	83	84	85	86	87	88	89	90	91	92	93	94	95
&6	SHIFT £ £	A a	B b	C c	D d	E e	F f	G g	H h	I i	J j	K k	L l	M m	N n	O o
	96	97	98	99	100	101	102	103	104	105	106	107	108	109	110	111
&7	P p	Q q	R r	S s	T t	U u	V v	W w	X x	Y y	Z z	SHIFT [↑ { (¼)	SHIFT ↓↑ ¦ (¦¦)	SHIFT]↑ } (¾)	SHIFT ↑↑ ~ (÷)	DELETE back space & delete
	112	113	114	115	116	117	118	119	120	121	122	123	124	125	126	127
	0	1	2	3	4	5	6	7	8	9	A	B	C	D	E	F

FIRST HEX DIGIT

ARGUMENTS OF VDU

b, ≡ ONE BYTE
bb; ≡ TWO BYTES

Most VDU statements have a single argument. For example, VDU 7 has the single argument of 7. VDU 7 signifies 'beep'. Entering >VDU 7, 65 is equivalent to >VDU 7 ⟨beep⟩ followed by >VDU 65 ⟨display capital A⟩. However, >VDU 22, 3 does *not* mean >VDU 22 followed by >VDU 3 ≈ it means the same thing as >MODE 3. The code VDU 22 is incomplete; it requires an *extra* argument to specify a mode number. Several applications of VDU demand extra arguments such as this.

Most extra arguments occupy a single byte ⟨values 0 to 255⟩ but others may have bigger values and so require a pair of bytes for storage. To signify a single byte, the argument should be followed by a comma ⟨or by nothing if it is last in the line⟩. To signify a *pair* of bytes the argument should be followed by a semicolon. For example:

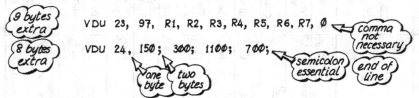

⟨9 bytes extra⟩   VDU 23, 97, R1, R2, R3, R4, R5, R6, R7, ∅ ← ⟨comma not necessary⟩

⟨8 bytes extra⟩   VDU 24, 150; 300; 1100; 700; ← ⟨semicolon essential⟩ ⟨end of line⟩
                        ↑one byte ↑two bytes

Below is a table showing where extra bytes are needed: b signifies one byte, bb signifies a pair of bytes; ∅ signifies b which must have a value of zero.

VDU ∅	VDU 8	VDU 16	VDU 24, bb; bb; bb; bb;
VDU 1, b	VDU 9	VDU 17, b	VDU 25, b, bb; bb;
VDU 2	VDU 10	VDU 18, b, b	VDU 26
VDU 3	VDU 11	VDU 19, b, b, b, ∅, ∅, ∅	VDU 27
VDU 4	VDU 12	VDU 20	VDU 28, b, b, b, b
VDU 5	VDU 13	VDU 21	VDU 29, bb; bb;
VDU 6	VDU 14	VDU 22, b	VDU 30
VDU 7	VDU 15	VDU 23, b, b, b, b, b, b, b, b, b	VDU 31, b, b

⟨must be zero bytes⟩

⟨nine bytes⟩

Any of the above arguments may be given in the form of an expression; for example: VDU 28, X, Y, 2*X+3, Y/2

PRINTER: VDU 2: VDU 1, b: VDU 3

To "enable" the printer means to ensure that output from PRINT statements goes not only to the screen but also to the printer:

> >VDU 2 ⊲ *enable the printer*

The printer may offer a range of type faces, sizes and spacings. Choice is made by sending appropriate character codes to the printer (if for example, sending &ØE to an Epson MX-80 printer signifies double-width characters).

> >VDU 1,&ØE ⊲ *character as specified in user's manual for particular printer*

To "disable" the printer means to prevent it responding to PRINT statements when a program is run. Output then goes only to the screen.

> >VDU 3 ⊲ *disable printer*

PAGING: VDU 14: VDU 15

On listing a long program its text scrolls by too quickly to be read, leaving only the final twenty or so statements to be studied. Executing VDU 14, however, causes the listing process to stop every time a screen is full. After perusing such a screen the operator may press SHIFT to display the next screenful.

> >VDU 14 ⊲ *listings screenful by screenful*

To revert to listing without paging use VDU 15:

> >VDU 15 ⊲ *continuous listings again*

CURSORS : *VDU 31,b,b : VDU 8~11 : VDU 127 : VDU 13 : VDU 30 : VDU 5~4*

The text cursor may be moved to any character position in its window; the position is defined by coordinates X,Y relative to the top left corner of the window.

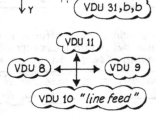

> `>VDU 31,7,4`   *move text cursor to col. 7 row 4*

The text cursor may be moved one position left, right, up, down, according to this diagram. If the cursor is already in the top row when called upon to go up, the window scrolls down to accomodate it. The converse applies when the cursor is already at the bottom.

VDU 11

VDU 8 ← → *VDU 9*

VDU 10 "line feed"

> `>VDU 9,9,9,9`   *text cursor 4 places right*

The cursor does *not* delete the character it moves to when moved by VDU 8 to VDU 10; deletion is the property of VDU 127 as made by pressing DELETE .

The text cursor may be moved to the left of the next row by pressing RETURN (or by pressing CTRL M which has precisely the same effect). But with:

> `100 VDU 13`   *text cursor to left of current line: "carriage return"*

the effect, when obeyed, is to move the text cursor in its current row to the left of its window. The cursor is not moved down to the next row as by pressing RETURN . *carriage return & line feed*

From wherever it is, the text cursor may be "homed" to the top left corner of its window:

> `200 VDU 30`   *text cursor to 0,0 of window*

The same effect may be achieved by pressing CTRL $\tilde{x}$.

In addition to the text cursor there is an invisible "graphics cursor" which is located at the last point moved to or drawn to. For example, if a line is drawn to the middle of the window *there* will be the graphics cursor also. To display letter X in the middle of the window the *text cursor* must somehow be moved to a position on top of the graphics cursor. This may be achieved by:

> `300 VDU 5`   *move text cursor to where graphics cursor is*

Subsequent drawing of lines now causes a text cursor to ride around the screen stuck to the graphics cursor. Conversely, subsequent printing of text moves the graphics cursor also. The mutual embrace may be severed by:

> `400 VDU 4`   *return the text cursor to POS,VPOS*

after which the text cursor returns to where it was before the union. This is the position to which POS and VPOS continually point whilst the cursors are joined.

Text may be "printed" in any character position appropriate to the current mode. For example, in MODE 7, columns 0 to 39, rows 0 to 24. However, the available area may be reduced to a "window" within the original confines. A window behaves as a smaller screen, the cursor and text remaining always within its boundaries, a screen within a screen. ((A "graphics window" may also be created as explained later.))

```
LET X1=5 :   X2=25
LET Y2=4 :   Y1=16
VDU 28, X1, Y1, X2, Y2
```

Less circuitously: (btm left) (top right)

```
VDU 28, 5, 16, 25, 4
```

The text window ((only what is *inside* it)) may be cleared using CLS.

An erroneous line of input, if spotted before RETURN, may be deleted by holding down DELETE and letting it repeat. Alternatively, press CTRL U and the whole erroneous line vanishes at once. However, the following piece of program:

```
100 VDU 21          (disable the screen)
```

would disable the screen when statement 100 was obeyed. Disabling the screen has practical application when implementing a password system or devising adventure games. The screen may be re-enabled by pressing CTRL F or typing VDU 6 ((which would not, of course, be seen on the disabled screen)) or from a program as follows:

```
200 VDU 6           (enable a disabled screen)
```

The window may be changed back to its original shape ≈ covering the whole screen and with origin at the top left corner ≈ by executing VDU 26. ((VDU 26 has the additional effect of restoring the original *graphics* window.))

```
300 VDU 26          (restore windows to
                     original ((default)) dimensions)
```

CHANGE COLOUR SCHEME: $VDU\ 19,b,b,0,0,0$: $VDU\ 20$

The full lines depict two columns from the table of logical colours on page 111. Broken lines are explained below.

Suppose the colour scheme for MODE 5 is to be changed from:

black⁰, red¹, yellow³, white⁷

to:

red¹, green², cyan⁶, blue⁴.

This is equivalent to rearranging the rows of column 5 as shown by broken lines.

MODE 5	MODE 5	ACTUAL COLOUR
0 (128)	0 (128)	0: black
1 129	1 129	1: red
2 130	3 131	2: green
	2 130	3: yellow
3 131		4: blue
		5: magenta
		6: cyan
		7: white

The rearrangement may be achieved using VDU 19 defined as follows:

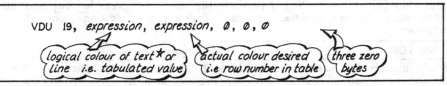

VDU 19, *expression, expression*, 0, 0, 0

(logical colour of text * or line i.e. tabulated value) (actual colour desired i.e. row number in table) (three zero bytes)

The example depicted above could be encoded as follows:

```
MODE 5
VDU  19,  0,  1,  0,0,0
VDU  19,  1,  2,  0,0,0
VDU  19,  2,  6,  0,0,0
VDU  19,  3,  4,  0,0,0
```
(logicals) (actuals)

The screen would initially show blue letters (or lines) on a red background — i.e. ③ on ⑫⑧ — but a COLOUR (or GCOL) statement may be used to select foregrounds and backgrounds among the four new colours.

This statement may be used to put *more than one* logical colour in a single row. For example:

```
MODE 5                 (revert to white on black)
VDU 19, 0, 1,  0, 0,0
VDU 19, 3, 3,  0, 0,0   (yellow letters on red)
```

which leaves logical colours 0 and 1 both red, logical colours 2 and 3 both yellow. This facility may be exploited in the field of animation as illustrated on page 121.

The effect of VDU 19 may be undone by executing VDU 20.

* giving (t + 128) produces same result as t.

168

SPECIAL CHARACTERS Я : *VDU 23, b, b, b, b, b, b, b, b*

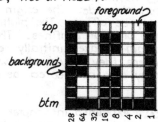

Special characters may be defined in modes 1 to 6; *not in MODE 7.*

Any of the visible characters shown in the table on page 163 may be given a new shape composed of dots on an 8×8 square grid as shown here.

For example the Cyrillic Я ≈ pronounced "ya" by Russians ≈ may be modelled by laterally transposing the Roman R.

This Я may be made to overwrite a standard character such as "a" ((ASCII code 97)) or be given a unique code in the range 244 to 255. The code number is given as the first argument of VDU 23; then come precisely eight values, each representing a row of the grid in binary. Their order is from top to bottom. A background square is represented by Ø; a foreground square by 1. Thus the top row is:

binary ⟹ | Ø | Ø | 1 | 1 | 1 | 1 | 1 | Ø |
|---|---|---|---|---|---|---|---|
| 128 | 64 | 32 | 16 | 8 | 4 | 2 | 1 |

⟹ 32 + 16 + 8 + 4 + 2 ⟹ 62 *decimal*

Here is the definition of Я to replace "a" :

```
>LET R1 = 32+16+8+4+2 :  R2= 64+32+4+2:  R3=R2
> LET R4= R1 :  R5=32+16+4+2:  R6=R2:   R7=R2
>VDU 23, 97, R1, R2, R3, R4, R5, R6, R7, Ø
```
there must be 8 terms even if the last is zero

Now type "Here we Яre ЯgЯin, HЯppy Яs cЯn be". The Я looks better on the screen ((try MODE 4)) than in the over-sized grid shown above.

This Я looks different in the various modes because of the different proportions of pixel. The following sketches show the eight by eight character grid in each graphics mode:

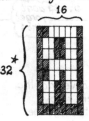

MODES Ø & 3

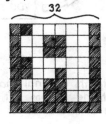

MODES 1, 4 & 6

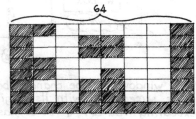

MODES 2 & 5

✳ all modes Ø to 6

GRAPHICS WINDOW : *VDU 24,bb; bb; bb; bb: VDU 29,bb;bb; : VDU 26*

Lines may be drawn all over the screen to a resolution appropriate to the current mode. The origin of axes is initially at the bottom left corner but may be offset. The plotting area may be reduced to a "window" within the original confines. This window behaves as a smaller screen, its origin of axes initially remaining where it was. Lines are "clipped" where they would otherwise run outside the edges. (A "text" window may also be created as explained earlier.)

As explained in chapter 10, the axes X and Y are assumed to be 1279 and 1023 units long (counting from zero) respectively, allowing for finer resolution than can, in fact, be achieved. Here is a window defined:

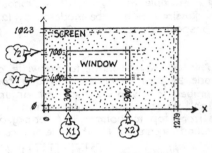

```
LET  X1 = 300 :   X2 = 900
LET  Y1 = 400 :   Y2 = 700
VDU 24,  X1; Y1; X2; Y2;
```

less circuitously:

```
VDU 24, 300; 400; 900; 700;
```
don't forget

The graphics window (only what is inside it) may be cleared using CLG.

The origin of axes remains at the bottom left corner of the screen. Call this point 0, 0 . The origin of X and Y may be relocated by specifying coordinates measured from 0, 0 . The new origin may be inside or outside the window or screen; the only limitation is that every coordinate must always lie in the range -32768 to +32767 (the capacity of two bytes) .

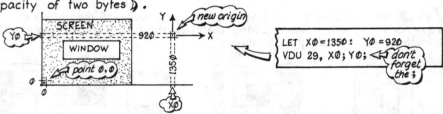

```
LET  X0 = 1350 :   Y0 = 920
VDU 29, X0; Y0;
```
don't forget the ;

The window may be changed back to its original shape ≈ covering the whole screen and with its origin at the bottom left corner ≈ by executing VDU 26. (VDU 26 has the additional effect of restoring the original *text* window.)

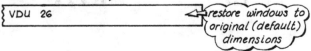

```
VDU 26
```
restore windows to original (default) dimensions

✻STAR PREFIX

Statements beginning *FX, *KEY *etc.* may be included in a BBC-BASIC program but are not, strictly speaking, statements of the language BBC-BASIC. Their function is to adjust the response of a program to keyboard and other peripheral devices.

Not all *commands are described; only those of immediate service to a programmer writing in BBC-BASIC on an installation with keyboard, screen and optionally cassette or disk or both.

The operating system in control of BBC-BASIC has rules of syntax different from those of BBC-BASIC itself. In particular the colon is not recognized as a separator of statements; a command is terminated by end-of-line. Because all statements beginning with a star are handled by the operating system it follows that any such statement in a BASIC program must be the final statement on its line. The tidiest approach is to make it the *only* statement on its line.

TAPE AND DISK SYSTEMS

To enable the tape deck when the installation has a disk:

```
*TAPE      ⟵ if 120 characters per sec. (1200 baud)
*TAPE3     ⟵ if 300 baud
```

To switch the motor of the tape deck on and off:

```
*MOTOR  1  ⟵ turn on
*MOTOR  0  ⟵ turn off
```

To revert to disk after switching to tape:

```
*DISK      ⟵ or *DISC
```

To raise or lower the picture on the screen:

```
*TV  2     ⟵ 2 lines up
*TV  254   ⟵ 256 - 254 = 2 lines down
```

*FX COMMANDS : SYNTAX

The syntax of *FX commands is defined below. The first argument of *FX determines how many ≈ if any ≈ arguments should follow. To give too many arguments may cause curious effects.

```
*FX [ integer ]        ▪ expressions not allowed
          └─,─┘           e.g.  *FX 9, 2*35 ≈✻
```

EDITING KEYS   *FX 4,1 : *FX 4,2 : *FX 4,0

The five editing keys `COPY` `←` `→` `↑` `↓` are usually employed for controlling the cursor. However, it is possible to disable control of the cursor and make each of these keys deliver a code in the same manner as `@`, for example, delivers 64 in response to the GET statement. Response from the arrow keys is useful in games for which a vehicle has to be manoeuvred left, right, up and down.

The editing function is disabled by:

```
*FX 4,1
```

after which the editing keys, when pressed, deliver codes 135 to 139 as below:

`COPY`	`←`	`→`	`↑`	`↓`
135	136	137	138	139

It is also possible to turn the editing keys into function keys ≈ to be employed in the same manner as `f6` to `f9`. Cursor control is disabled by:

```
*FX 4,2
```

whereupon the editing keys effectively become:

`f11`   `f12` `f13` `f14` `f15`

Cursor control is re-established by executing *FX 4,0

DESTINATION OF OUTPUT   *FX 5,0 : *FX 5,1 : *FX 6,ch

When developing a program it is sometimes useful to send output to a "sink" instead of the screen or printer. A sink behaves as a fast printer in the sense that the printer buffer is rapidly emptied so as to avoid a "hang". A sink is defined by:

```
*FX 5,0
```

Output may be directed back to the printer once again by one of the following

```
*FX  5,1
*FX  5,2
```
← Centronics® parallel printer
← RS432 serial printer

Any character destined for the printer may be suppressed by:

```
*FX  6,10
```
← ASCII code of character to be suppressed

For example, some printers perform a line feed automatically on receiving a carriage return signal. Therefore the line-feed character (ASCII 10) must be suppressed unless double-line spacing is required. But a line feed may still be transmitted when needed by VDU 1,10 (p.165).

FLASH RATE   *FX 9, colour : *FX 10, complement

Flashing colours apply only to MODE 2. A flashing object changes between specified colour and complement. All complements are tabulated here ⇨

During a single cycle the duration of colour is measured in fiftieths of a second. Similarly for the duration of the complement. Each duration is set at 25 (½ second) by default. The durations of colour and complement may be independently adjusted as illustrated below:

FLASH	
COLOUR	COMPLEMENT
black	white
red	cyan
green	magenta
yellow	blue
blue	yellow
magenta	green
cyan	red
white	black

```
> MODE 2
> COLOUR  9        ⟵ for example, red letters flashing
> *FX 9, 50        ⟵ 1 sec. for red
> *FX 10, 100      ⟵ 2 secs. for cyan
```

Setting a duration to zero makes permanent the corresponding colour or complement:

```
*FX 9, 0          ⟵ make colour permanent
*FX 10, 0         ⟵ make complement permanent
*FX 9, 0          ⟵ make colour permanent again
```

AUTO REPEAT   *FX 11, delay : *FX 12, rate

When any key of the keyboard is held down there is a pause, after which the key behaves as if it were struck repeatedly and rapidly. This effect continues until the key is released. The pause before repetition may be made longer or shorter. It is measured in hundredths of a second.

```
*FX 11, 100       ⟵ makes the pause one full second
```

The pause may be made infinitely long by giving a value of zero:

```
*FX 11, 0         ⟵ switch off auto repeat
```

The rate of effective key strikes may also be adjusted. The value to give is the time between strikes measured in hundredths of a second.

```
*FX 12, 20        ⟵ 1/5 sec. (i.e. 20/100)
                    between strikes
```

Setting the time between strikes to zero has the effect of cancelling any change made by *FX 11 and reverting to the default delay and default rate of strike:

```
*FX 12, 0         ⟵ revert to default delay
                    and strike rate
```

ANALOGUE TO DIGITAL   *FX 16, channel : *FX 16, Ø

The computer has four channels in which an applied analogue voltage can be converted to a digital value. These are called ADC channels and are typically used to sense movements of joysticks. A conversion from analogue to digital takes 10 milliseconds so there are 40 milliseconds between readings on one channel when all four channels are enabled. However, it is possible to enable just the channels required:

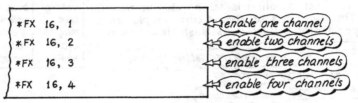

```
*FX  16, 1              enable one channel
*FX  16, 2              enable two channels
*FX  16, 3              enable three channels
*FX  16, 4              enable four channels
```

All channels may be disabled by:

```
*FX  16, Ø              disable all channels
```

The voltage intensity 0 to 1.8v is returned as an integer from 0 to 65520 by function ADVAL (channel) as described on page 132.

FLUSHING BUFFERS   *FX 15, Ø : *FX 21, buffer

Input and output are managed via buffers. For example, when keys of the keyboard are pressed the codes they generate are put into the keyboard buffer to be abstracted by INPUT or GET or INKEY statements. There is also a buffer of characters on their way to the printer; other buffers are for sound and RS432 port (typically a modem).

Sometimes it is necessary to flush a buffer. An example of flushing the keyboard buffer is shown on page 104.

The commonly used buffers may be flushed as below:

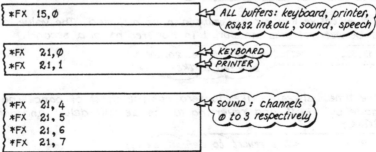

```
*FX 15,Ø                ALL buffers: keyboard, printer,
                        RS432 in&out, sound, speech
```

```
*FX  21,Ø               KEYBOARD
*FX  21,1               PRINTER
```

```
*FX  21,4               SOUND : channels
*FX  21,5               Ø to 3 respectively
*FX  21,6
*FX  21,7
```

The number of free spaces in a buffer is returned by function ADVAL( ) with a negative argument (p.132).

FUNCTION KEYS   *KEY string : *FX 18

The ten red keys along the top row of the keyboard are called "function keys" and are labelled f0 to f9. It is possible to make any such key deliver a sequence of characters as though those characters were typed on the keyboard. For example, f9 may be made to deliver the word RUN when pressed. The word RUN would appear on the screen as:

>RUN   just as though it had been typed on the keyboard.

The command to "program" a function key is defined as follows:

*KEY f [{|!} {| control } {character}]

> f is an integer from 0 to 9 to denote a function key (also from 10 to 14 if the editing keys have been disabled by *FX 4,2 as explained on page 172)

> |control is |A or |B etc. to denote one of the control codes in the ASCII range 1 to 31 as tabulated on page 163. (Example: |M specifies 13 which implies RETURN)

> |! says add 128 to the ASCII control code which follows. (Example: |! |V implies a control code of 128+22 =150 which says "graphics cyan" in MODE 7 as shown on page 125.)

> character is a character of the string to be delivered when key f is pressed

▶ *KEY 0 CLS |M ⟵ press f0 to clear the screen
▶ *KEY 1 CLS |M LIST |M ⟵ press f1 to list a program
▶ *KEY 7 MODE 7 |M |N LIST |M ⟵ press f7 to list page by page in MODE 7
▶ *KEY 5 MODE 5 |M RUN |M ⟵ press f5 to switch off paging & run in MODE 5
▶ *KEY 9 FOR I=1TO30: PRINT "*":NEXT |M |G ⟵ press f9 to print stars down left margin & beep

The above examples should be enough to illustrate the power and usefulness of *KEY. If you have a disk, put a selection of handy key settings in a program and file under the name !BOOT. Execute *OPT 4 3. Then whenever you press SHIFT BREAK the !BOOT program will be run and the function keys "programmed".

```
10 *KEY 1 CLS |M LIST |N
20 *KEY 7 MODE 7 |M |N LIST |M
30 *KEY 5 |O MODE 5 |M RUN |M
40 REM File this as program !BOOT
```

Cancel all key settings by executing *FX 18.

POKING AROUND
DIRECT ACCESS TO MEMORY VIA INDIRECTION OPERATORS

This book is about BASIC as a "high level" language, not about poking around in the computer's memory. Nevertheless BBC-BASIC offers certain operators and pseudo-variables which provide direct access to the computer's memory so that machine-code routines may be inserted and used. These facilities are described below.

SPACE IN MEMORY: PSEUDO-VARIABLES: PAGE, TOP, LOMEM, HIMEM

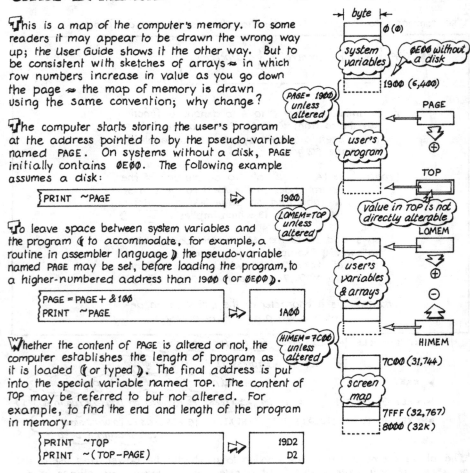

This is a map of the computer's memory. To some readers it may appear to be drawn the wrong way up; the User Guide shows it the other way. But to be consistent with sketches of arrays ≈ in which row numbers increase in value as you go down the page ≈ the map of memory is drawn using the same convention; why change?

→| byte |←

∅ (∅)

system variables

∅E∅∅ without a disk

1900 (6,400)

PAGE

The computer starts storing the user's program at the address pointed to by the pseudo-variable named PAGE. On systems without a disk, PAGE initially contains ∅E∅∅. The following example assumes a disk:

PAGE = 1900 unless altered

user's program

```
PRINT ~PAGE
```
⇨ 1900.

TOP

Value in TOP is not directly alterable

To leave space between system variables and the program (to accommodate, for example, a routine in assembler language) the pseudo-variable named PAGE may be set, before loading the program, to a higher-numbered address than 1900 (or ∅E∅∅).

LOMEM = TOP unless altered

LOMEM

```
PAGE = PAGE + &100
PRINT ~PAGE
```
⇨ 1A00

user's variables & arrays

Whether the content of PAGE is altered or not, the computer establishes the length of program as it is loaded (or typed). The final address is put into the special variable named TOP. The content of TOP may be referred to but not altered. For example, to find the end and length of the program in memory:

HIMEM = 7C00 unless altered

HIMEM

7C00 (31,744)

screen map

```
PRINT ~TOP
PRINT ~(TOP-PAGE)
```
⇨ 19D2
D2

7FFF (32,767)

8000 (32k)

The variables and arrays of the program are stored from the location pointed to by LOMEM. Unless altered, LOMEM points to the same address as TOP. But a space may be left between the program and its variables by setting LOMEM to a higher address than that contained in TOP. This should be done after loading and before running the program:

```
LOMEM = TOP + &200
PRINT ~LOMEM
```
⇨ 1BD2

The space for variables and arrays is cleverly used from both ends at once. But it is allowable to leave space between the variables and the part of memory devoted to the screen. This is achieved by reducing the value stored in the pseudo-variable named HIMEM to a value below 7C00 :

```
> PRINT ~HIMEM
HIMEM = HIMEM - &200
> PRINT ~HIMEM
```
⇨
```
7C00

7A00
```

A curiosity : if the keyword LET is used in the above examples (e.g. LET HIMEM = HIMEM - &200) the error messages "Syntax error" and "Bad program" are evoked. This is a mystery ➤

INDIRECTION OPERATORS *SUPERSEDING THE TRADITIONAL PEEK & POKE*

There are three "indirection operators": ? for bytes; ! for words; $ for strings. These may be used to copy or change the content of any byte or bytes in the memory map shown opposite.

If the computer's memory be considered an array of bytes ≈ much as DIM A(300) declares an array of reals ≈ then the question mark is analogous to the name of the memory array as depicted below.

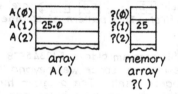

array
A( )

memory
array
?( )

Much as A(1) = 25.0 assigns a real number to A(1), so does ?(1) = 25 assign integer 25 to ?(1). The memory address may be written without brackets as ?1 = 25 .

Likewise, much as X = A(1) assigns the content of A(1) to X, so does Y = ?(1) assign the content of ?(1) to Y. The address may be written without brackets as Y = ?1 .

The analogy with arrays may be extended to relative addressing. Consider part of array A( ) as depicted here: ⇨ The analogous byte locations of the memory array may be addressed as depicted on the right of A( ). An alternative (and confusing) syntax is ?I, I?1, I?2, I?3,... but the term on the left of the question mark must be a name (I?3 not 3?I ➤).

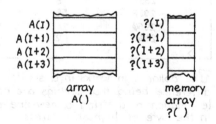

array
A( )

memory
array
?( )

Below is a command to display the program currently in memory as a sequence of bytes. For each byte its hex address is displayed followed by its value, both as a decimal and a hex number.

```
> FOR I=PAGE TO TOP-1: PRINT ~I, ?(I),~?(I): NEXT I

6400     13     D      ⟵ typical result
6401      0     0
6402      5     5
```

The exclamation mark ((officially "pling"; often pronounced "shriek")) works in the same way as the question mark but applies to *words* rather than *bytes*. Here is the analogy with arrays:

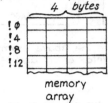

Notice that memory is still depicted as *bytes*; the address goes up in increments of four because there are four bytes to the word.

And below is depicted some relative addressing, but avoiding the confusing notation !1, I!4, I!8,...

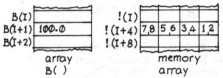

An assignment to the four bytes starting at !(I+4) is analogous to an assignment of a real number to B(I+1):

```
B(I+1) = 100.0
!(I+4) = &12345678
```

Notice that the bytes of &12345678 ((namely [1 2] [3 4] [5 6] [7 8])) are stored in memory with the least significant byte first. This pattern of storage is not universal among computers.

```
10 M = TOP + &1000
20 !(M+4) = &12345678
30 FOR J = 0 TO 3
40 (  PRINT ~M+4+J , ~?(M+4+J)
50 NEXT J
>RUN
       295E          78
       295F          56
       2960          34
       2961          12
>
```

This program places &12345678 in the memory space well beyond the program itself. The program then prints the separate bytes and their addresses in hex.

The addressing has been made more complicated than necessary only to show that general expressions are permitted as addresses; in particular ~?(M+4+J)

The dollar sign works in a similar way to ? and ! in locating strings; the difference being that strings are not all the same length. To mark the termination of a string a new-line character ((0D)) is automatically placed in the byte of highest address.

Indirection operators offer an escape from the restrictions imposed by a high-level language. However, the programmer who makes more than occasional use of them should not be writing in BASIC in the first place.

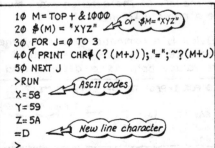

```
10 M = TOP + &1000          or $M="XYZ"
20 $(M) = "XYZ"
30 FOR J = 0 TO 3
40 (  PRINT CHR$(?(M+J)); "="; ~?(M+J)
50 NEXT J
>RUN          ASCII codes
X = 58
Y = 59
Z = 5A
=D            New line character
>
```

QUICK REFERENCE

The keywords of BBC-BASIC are classified under four headings and arranged alphabetically in each classification. The groups are headed

- Keywords not dealt with
  (these are explained in the User Guide; they go beyond BASIC)

- Operators

- Functions and pseudo-variables

- Statements and commands

KEYWORDS NOT DEALT WITH (BEYOND THE SCOPE OF BASIC)

CALL	LINE	OPT	USR

OPERATORS

```
                                                              page
AND | t | f   43,45   EOR | t | f   43,45   NOT | t | f   43,45    +,−,*,/,↑   36
 t  | t | f            t  | f | t            f  | f | t
 f  | f | f            f  | t | f           OR  | t | f   43,45    ?,!,$      177
                                             t  | t | t
DIV        36         MOD        36          f  | t | f          = , > , >= ,
                                                                 <> , < , <=   42,49
```

FUNCTIONS AND PSEUDO-VARIABLES

Abbreviations: e = expression , i = expression truncated if not integral, s = string

ABS(e)	37	EVAL(s)	53	LN(e)	37	RND(i)	41
ACS(e)	38	EXP(e)	37	LOG(e)	37	SGN(e)	37
ADVAL(i)	132	EXT#i	148	LOMEM	176	SIN(e)	38
ASC(s)	48	FALSE ←0	42	MID$($s,i,i$)	50	SPC(i)	92
ASN(e)	38	GET	100	OPENIN(s)	143	SQR(e)	37
ATN(e)	38	GET$	100	OPENOUT(s)	142	STR$($e$)	52
BGET#i	149	HIMEM	176	PAGE	176	STRING$($i,s$)	50
CHR$($i$)	48	INKEY(i)	101	PI π	38	TAB(i{$,i$})	92
COS(e)	38	INKEY$($i$)	101	POINT(i,i)	114	TAN(e)	38
COUNT	93	INSTR(s,i{$,i$})	50	POS	93	TIME	97
DEG(e)	38	INT(e)	37	PTR#i	148	TRUE ←−1	42
EOF#i	143	LEFT$($s,i$)	50	RAD(e)	38	VAL(s)	52
ERL	157	LEN(s)	50	RIGHT$($s,i$)	50	VPOS	93
ERR	157					@%	94

STATEMENTS AND COMMANDS

The statements and commands of BBC-BASIC are summarized overleaf.

STATEMENTS AND COMMANDS *marks those usable only as commands

Abbreviations: e = *expression*; c = *expression used as a condition*⤝ zero represents *false*, non-zero represents *true*; i = *expression truncated if non-integral*; s = *string* (e.g. "AB" or X$); q = *quotation* (e.g. "AB" but not X$); l = *line number* (integer 0 to 32767); inc = increment for l ; n = name

★ AUTO { [l / , inc / l, inc] }   153

BPUT # i, byte (byte is: 0 ≤ i ≤ 255)   149

CHAIN   154

CLEAR   154

CLG   110

CLOSE # i   143

CLS   105

COLOUR i (i = 0, 1, 2, ... 128, 129, ...)   105

DATA [constant / q / characters] (q needs no quotes in a DATA list e.g. DATA 6, ABC, **)   103

DEF FN name { ([n / n% / n$]) } { = [e / s] }   79
{ statements } = [e / s]   (one liners) (multi-liners)

DEF PROC name { ([n / n% / n$]) }   82
statements
ENDPROC   (n names a dummy argument)

★ DELETE l, l   153

DIM [n / n% / n$] ([e])   (n names an array)   69

DRAW x, y (x & y are: 0 ≤ i ≤ 2^16)   113

ELSE   see IF

END   57

ENDPROC   see DEF PROC

ENVELOPE [e_j] (j = 1 ~ 14)   134

ERROR   see ON

FN   see DEF FN

FOR [n / n%] = e TO e { STEP e } ... NEXT [n / n%] (n names a variable)   60

*FX [byte]   (byte is: 0 ≤ i ≤ 255)   171

GCOL operation, colour   (operation is: 0 ≤ i ≤ 4 / colour is: 0 ≤ i ≤ 15)   110

GOSUB l ... RETURN   64

GOTO l   56-7, 154

IF c [{THEN} [st'mt] { ELSE [st'mt] } / THEN l]   59

INPUT LINE { q { [' / ,] } } [string-identifier]   98

INPUT { q { [' / ,] } } [numerical-identifier / string-identifier]   98

*KEY integer [character]   175

{ LET } identifier = e   33

★ LIST { [l / l, / , l / l, l] }   153

✶ LISTO i (0 ≤ i ≤ 7)   152

✶ LOAD [s / ""]   (cassette only)   138

LOCAL [n / n% / n$]   79, 82

MODE i   (0 ≤ i ≤ 7)   154

MOVE x, y (x & y are: 0 ≤ i ≤ 2^16)   113

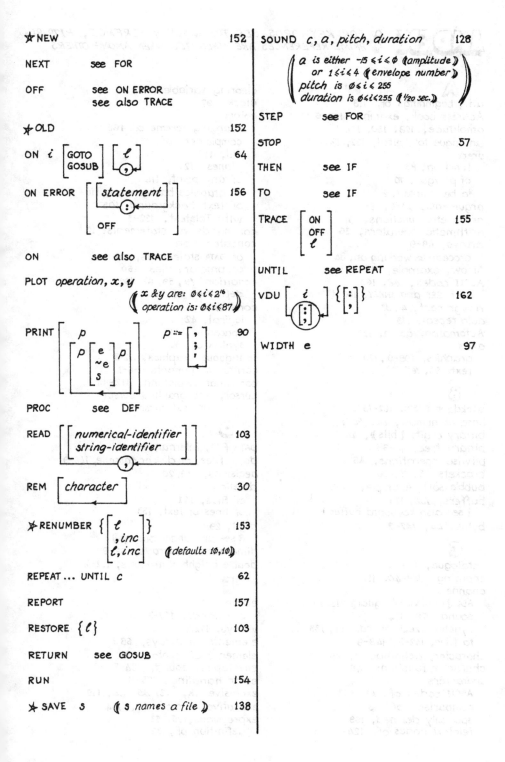

P

pitch, of sound, 128, 134
pixels, 108
planes, of colour, 121
plotting, 112-14
pointers
  to arrays, 72-3, 75-6, 84-5, 86-7
  to data file, 148
precedence, 5, *15*, 43
prefix operators, 29
printer
  enable and disable, 165
  output to, 172
procedures, 24
  definition of (PROC), 78, *82-7*
program files, 138-9
prompts, 16, *98-9*
punctuating PRINT list, 16, *90*

Q

Quicksort, example, 86-7
quotation, 32, 98, 103

R

random numbers, 40-1
Rate of interest, example, 63
Reactions, example, 104
recursion, 85-7
remarks, 30
renumbering, 8
Repayments, example, 17
round, musical, 131
running a program, 8, *154*

S

saving programs, 9, *138-9*
screen clear, 10, *105*
separated graphics, 122-3
Sexism, example, 51
Shapes, examples, 20, 65
sorting techniques
  bubble, 72-3, 85
  monkey puzzle, 74-6
  Quicksort, 86-7
sound statement, 128
spacing, 31
  in PRINT list, 90-3
specially defined characters (Я), 169
statements, 4, 12, *34*

strings, 4, *18*
  comparison of, 49
  definition of, 32
  expressions as, 53
  functions for, 48, 50, 52
  in PRINT list, 90-3
  length of, 18, 50
  logical operators with, 49
  misuse of, 98, 103
  null, 49-50, 69, 81, 101
structures, programming, 56-7
subscripts of arrays, 69
symbols, definition of, 29
synchronization, 133
syntax, notation for, 28-34

T

tabulation, neat, 96
tape and disk systems, 171
Teletext graphics, 48, 122-5
text cursor, 7, 93, 104, 166
text window, 152, *167*
time, on clock, 97
tracing errors, 155-7
tree, binary, 74-6
Triangle, example, 39
true, 42
truncation
  of subscripts, 69
  on assignment, 33
  on input, 98
types, 14, 68
typing on keyboard, 6
Typing skill, game, 102

V

variables, 13, 68
vectors, 73, 75

W

waiting time, 101
width of screen, 93, *97*
window
  graphics, 109, *170*
  text, 152, *167*